A HOUSE IN BALI

A
HOUSE
IN
BALI

COLIN McPHEE

With an Introduction by
JAMES MURDOCH

TUTTLE Publishing
Tokyo | Rutland, Vermont | Singapore

"Books To Span The East And West"

Tuttle Publishing was founded in 1832 in the small New England town of Rutland, Vermont [USA]. Our core values remain as strong today as they were then—to publish best-in-class books which bring people together one page at a time. In 1948, we established a publishing office in Japan—and Tuttle is now a leader in publishing English-language books about the arts, languages and cultures of Asia. The world has become a much smaller place today and Asia's economic and cultural influence has grown. Yet the need for meaningful dialogue and information about this diverse region has never been greater. Over the past seven decades, Tuttle has published thousands of books on subjects ranging from martial arts and paper crafts to language learning and literature—and our talented authors, illustrators, designers and photographers have won many prestigious awards. We welcome you to explore the wealth of information available on Asia at **www.tuttlepublishing.com**.

Paperback edition published with the permission of the Colin McPhee Estate by Periplus Editions (HK) Ltd, 2000

www.periplus.com

Copyright © Colin McPhee 1944, 1945, 1947
Introduction © James Murdoch, 2002
All rights reserved, including the right of reproduction in whole or in part in any form.

First published in 1947 by Victor Gollancz Ltd., London, 1947
First Periplus edition, 2000
Second printing, with an Introduction, 2002

ISBN 978-0-8048-5371-2
(Previously published as
ISBN 978-962-593-629-1)

Distributed by:

North America, Latin America & Europe
Tuttle Publishing
364 Innovation Drive
North Clarendon, VT 05759-9436 U.S.A.
Tel: 1 (802) 773-8930
Fax: 1 (802) 773-6993
info@tuttlepublishing.com
www.tuttlepublishing.com

Japan
Tuttle Publishing
Yaekari Building, 3rd Floor
5-4-12 Osaki, Shinagawa-ku
Tokyo 141-0032
Tel: (81) 3 5437-0171
Fax: (81) 3 5437-0755
sales@tuttle.co.jp
www.tuttle.co.jp

Asia Pacific
Berkeley Books Pte. Ltd.
3 Kallang Sector
#04-01, Singapore 349278
Tel: (65) 6741-2178
Fax: (65) 6741-2179
inquiries@periplus.com.sg
www.tuttlepublishing.com

Indonesia
PT Java Books Indonesia
Kawasan Industri Pulogadung
Jl. Rawa Gelam IV No. 9
Jakarta 13930
Tel: (62) 21 4682-1088
Fax: (62) 21 461-0206
crm@periplus.co.id
www.periplus.co.id

25 24 23 22   5 4 3 2 1
Printed in Singapore   2204TP

TUTTLE PUBLISHING® is a registered trademark of Tuttle Publishing, a division of Periplus Editions (HK) Ltd.

CONTENTS

Part One

Part Two

Part Three

INTRODUCTION

MMUSICALLY SPEAKING, Colin McPhee is Bali's bridge to the West. Although his reputation as a composer and writer is based on a comparatively small body of work—essentially three significant books about Bali and its music, four major musical works, and about forty transcriptions of Balinese music—McPhee's influence on world music, and in particular in enlightening the world on the sacred gamelan of Bali, has been major. Without his pioneering voyage of discovery into the music of Bali, which resulted in years of intensive investigation and writing, Western music would have had no well-documented model for the sweeping new style of music, known as "Minimalism", that appeared at the end of the twentieth century. McPhee provided that essential key.

During the twentieth century, most composers had faced the dilemma of following one of two styles of composition: the dense and complex "twelve-note" music, or the accessible neo-classical style. McPhee led the way to a new path—a middle way. *A House in Bali* is the story of his voyage of discovery, a story which he tells in a charming and subtle way. Into this book McPhee has poured not only his love of Bali and the Balinese and their musics, but in the process also informs us, without any hint of lecture, about a culture that has survived not only centuries of continuous living, but also the onslaught of the twentieth-century tourist invasion. In his sensitive prose, he rarely explains anything, but gives the context, and leaves it to the reader to make deductions.

Although the Dutch had occupied Indonesia for 400 years, the island of Bali itself was not successfully invaded until nearly a hundred years ago, in 1906. McPhee observed and recorded Balinese music a mere thirty years after this event, in the 1930s. He was thus able to capture a unique society in transition, almost in crisis, one could say. He does it with love, tenderness and laughter, and in the most graceful prose, all tinged with nostalgia and regret at a changing culture. His record of this change, beautifully chronicled in *A House in Bali*, is therefore of as great an importance to the Balinese heritage as it is to the West's perception of the value of other cultures.

Born in Montreal, Canada, in 1900, of Canadian and Scottish parents, McPhee was raised in Toronto, where he had an early and standard music education. Here he studied under a pupil of the famous composer Franz Liszt. He became a virtuoso pianist and performed, to much acclaim, concerti with the Toronto Symphony Orchestra. He then moved to New York where he immersed himself in the "New Music" scene and began to compose seriously. He had a special interest in jazz, and learned to play it well enough to perform in New York nightclubs. He regularly visited Harlem to listen to its music and its singers, among them Billy Holiday. At this time, Latin American and Cuban music, in addition to jazz, were all having a major impact on Western music in Europe as well as in America. It was during this period that McPhee adopted American citizenship.

In late 1926, McPhee went to Paris to further study composition, as did so many American composers in the 1920s. Back in New York, in 1929, he, together with the budding anthropologist Jane Belo, was introduced to gamelan by way of early gramophone recordings at an exotic dinner party on Manhattan's East Side. In them, McPhee recognized the music sounds of his dreams. These were rare recordings (now available on CD, largely due to the discovery of McPhee's personal collection) made by the European companies Odeon and Beka in 1928. Although about 48 double-sided disks had been issued, of which McPhee heard perhaps nine or ten, in those days they were made on fragile shellac, at 78 rpm. That meant about 27 minutes of music. It was enough, however, to rivet his attention. Here was a music that was complex, as energized as jazz, and with a fascinating rhythm.

In Paris again, in 1930, McPhee met the Mexican artist and traveler Miguel Covarrubius, and his wife Rose, who had just arrived from Bali. They further fueled his interest in Bali. Here, too, McPhee heard Balinese gamelan live, for the first time, performed at the Colonial Exhibition by a group of Balinese dancers and musicians from the village of Peliatan, led by the great Balinese musician Anak Agung Gedé Ngurah Mandera. It was to change his life forever. The gamelan music of Bali became an obsessive passion for McPhee, totally permeating his musical life.

Within months of meeting the wealthy Jane Belo, she and McPhee married, and together, in 1931, they enthusiastically set out for Bali. With the aid of the extraordinarily talented painter/musician Walter Spies, who had been resident on the island for some years, they soon built a working kampong—a collection of wooden structures—in the adjacent village of Sayan. McPhee's music pavilion was built on a ridge with a spectacular view down to the river Ayung.

McPhee and his wife lived in Sayan on and off until the approach of the Second World War. In his music pavilion, McPhee proceeded to make an intense study of the complex music of the Balinese gamelan, so different from that of Java. He developed an intimate knowledge of all the musical genres of Bali, documenting them in Western notation, one of the first composer musicians to do this. Together with I Made Lebah (1903-98)—musician, drummer, driver and friend—McPhee scoured the island's palaces, temples and remote villages, listening to and studying the various musics still to be found there, and documenting them on paper, in notes and notation, and in photographs and film (tape recorders not yet being invented and available until after the war!). McPhee, sometimes with his wife and sometimes without, also traveled widely in Java, and then further afield, to Cambodia, Thailand, Vietnam, China and Japan, experiencing at first hand the complex as well as the simple music of non-Western cultures.

Henry Cowell, his friend and mentor, and one of the generation of talented young composers working in New York at this time, noted that while he himself stayed at home and listened to recordings, Colin McPhee actually went to hear these musics at first hand. His wife Jane also undertook various projects in Bali, in particular a study of trance. She was to publish articles and books on her research. McPhee never alluded to his wife in his books as he believed that the introduction of a domestic situation would cloud the impact of his story.

Fortunately for Belo, and for McPhee, the young American anthropologist Margaret Mead and her British husband Gregory Bateson arrived in Bali at this time, where they began a long and painstaking research into the lives of Balinese hill people. Their friendship and professional expertise assisted each other. Mead went on to become a famous international figure, and was to encourage McPhee's interest in Balinese music all his life.

Both McPhee and Spies feared that the intense culture and the arts of Bali were headed for decline because of a lack of sponsorship. Previously, the custodianship of the arts and culture of Bali had rested in the hands of the provincial aristocracy, in the massive palaces and, of course, in the thousands of Hindu Dharma temples present in every village. Neither McPhee nor Spies would have foreseen the overwhelming effect of mass tourism that began in the 1970s and 1980s. Tourism became the next great wave of sponsorship. However, it came at a great price. That price included a startlingly reduced repertoire, which now, at the beginning of the twenty-first century, consists mostly of a small collection of the most popular works, truncated for the limited attention span—and available time—of international tourists.

Dance is inseparable from music in Bali. McPhee saw this, and took a great interest in the symbiosis of dance. He discovered a huge talent in one of his small houseboys, Sampih, who was part of a noisy group of brown dolphin children who liked to swim in the river below McPhee's house. One day Sampih saved McPhee from almost certain drowning during a flash flood which coursed down the river Ayung from the mountains beyond, snaking under McPhee's house. McPhee had been caught unawares, but Sampih knew all the river's boulders and snags and was able to guide him back to safety. Seeing the great Tuan safely on shore, Sampih vanished in a flash of shyness and was not seen for a week.

McPhee brought in some of the best dance teachers for Sampih and soon he became a star in his own right, eventually touring in America and in Europe in 1952 with the top gamelan group from Peliatan, the neighboring village to Ubud, which was rapidly becoming the center of the arts in Bali. When Sampih was murdered in Bali in 1954, McPhee was devastated.

At the end of 1935, McPhee took a break from Bali, traveling to Mexico where he finished composing a work based on Balinese music. Written for a standard Western symphony orchestra, but with the addition of an enlarged percussion section, it was commissioned and conducted by Carlos Chavez and played by the Mexico Symphony Orchestra. Years later it was repeated in New York, conducted by Leopold Stokowski. Called Tabuh Tabuhan, the work is available in several performances on CD.

McPhee returned to Bali at the end of 1936, and renewed his studies on Balinese music, sensing that time was running out for him. By the end of 1938, with the threat of war looming, the expatriate community of artists began to evacuate, and on Christmas Day 1938, McPhee left Bali for America, never to return. His wife, from whom he was recently divorced, had left Bali many months before. His major work had been done. His documentation and comprehensive notes, photographs, film, notations of music, all were in his trunks on the ship that took him back to New York via the Cape of Good Hope.

To produce a book from his field work was to take another twenty-five years of labor. He became obsessed with it, finding it hard to relinquish to a publisher. A perfectionist, he drove his editor to despair. The outcome, a musicological masterpiece called *Music in Bali,* was eventually published posthumously by Yale University Press in 1966. Although it is long out of print, *Music in Bali* remains the classic work on Balinese music, and is the leading reference work for Balinese musicians, composers, dancers and choreographers. Western composers such as Benjamin Britten, Philip Glass, Steve Reich and Peter Sculthorpe, are all deeply indebted to McPhee's love for, and scholarship on, Balinese music.

What happened to Colin McPhee after he returned to New York? There is where *A House in Bali* ends. When McPhee left Bali, Walter Spies looked after the house and its gamelan instruments until he was imprisoned by the Dutch authorities as a German citizen. He subsequently lost his life on a prisoner-of-war ship traveling from Sumatra to Ceylon when it was bombed by a Japanese warplane. Everyone on it perished. Theo Meier, the Belgian painter and another long-time resident in Bali, then stayed in the McPhee house after war was declared in Europe.

The next occupant was the legendary Hungarian pianist Lili Kraus. On a world concert tour, and stranded in Jakarta by the war, she fled to Bali, and through her network of artist friends soon came to live in the village of Sayan, in McPhee's house. Amazingly, McPhee's concert grand Steinway piano, which his wife had bought for him for his music pavilion, was still there. In Bali, Lili Kraus would present to local expatriates a weekly recital of Mozart and Schubert, before she, in turn, was incarcerated in a prisoner-of-war camp. When she was finally released, she resumed her world concert tour, many claimed as an even greater performer of the world's great Western classics.

In New York in the climate of a world war, few were interested in the exotic music of Bali. Nonetheless, McPhee set to and wrote his few articles about Bali, and worked on his ground-breaking books. First of all, there was *A House in Bali*, first published in 1947, although copyrighted by the author in 1944. It received excellent reviews but sold limited copies. Next came the charming children's book, *A Club of Small Men* (1948), . . . "this innocent tale . . .", as he wrote in his dedication to Peggy Glanville-Hicks, his friend and kind of amanuensis. His monumental tome, *Music if Bali,* as noted above, was finally published in 1966. Besides his musical talents, McPhee was an excellent photographer, as seen in *A House in Bali.* His collection of photographs, field notes, papers and correspondence, and recordings of Balinese music, are lodged at the UCLA Ethnomusicology Archive.

McPhee became tangential to mainstream music in America. He led a frugal life, and was subject to bouts of self-destructive depression and alcoholism. He desperately missed Bali, its way of life, his strong friendships with his group of Balinese musicians, and the daily experience of a music, the mysteries of which he had so painstakingly unraveled for himself and, through his books, the world. His precarious existence did not change until the doyen of American ethnomusicologists, Mantle Hood, offered him a salaried position in 1960 at the recently created Music Department at UCLA. By this time, he had been commissioned for the first time and had composed his Symphony No. 2 (1957) and a work called Nocturne (1958), now both recorded, and both expressing the quintessence of nostalgia for Bali, his dream country. He died in California in 1964 of cirrhosis of the liver.

During the 1990s, McPhee's musical achievements began to be acknowledged, and today his position in world music is assured. In America and Europe, there are now many hundreds of Balinese gamelans being studied and performed on by non-Balinese musicians. Many composers have written for the gamelan or used a knowledge of gamelan to inform their work for Western instruments. Of McPhee's house in the kampong in Sayan, the setting for *A House in Bali*, nothing remains except the remnants of the original foundations and his music studio, which has long been renovated. Still extant are some of the original instruments of *The Club if Small Men,* and indeed, several of the small men themselves, now great-grandfathers in their seventies.

JAMES MURDOCH
Ubud, Bali
January 2002

PART ONE
THE PORT

THE SHIP HAD SAILED from Surabaya for Bali in the late afternoon.

The boy stumbled down the stairs with my bags to the cabins that ran along either side of the dark saloon, and carried them to the state-room that lay directly over the propeller. I opened the door to finda portly Chinese merchant very much at home on the lower berth. He had removed the top to his white silk pyjamas, and he lay there, relaxed as a reclining Buddha, smoking a pipe of opium in great tranquillity. On the upper berth he had neatly arranged his considerable luggage, which included a cage containing a restless starling. The porthole was clamped down so that no breath of air might trouble this cosy paradise. I had not the heart to disturb him, and after the boy had set down my bags I closed the door and went upstairs.

I spent the night on deck, leaning over the rail and looking into the darkness for some thin beam of light to signal the presence of land. The ship made a gentle commotion in the water, churning it into foam that dissolved with a faint hiss. The engines moaned in their sleep, and from time to time some inner vibration of the ship caused the little coffee cups, left on the tables by the deck boy, to ring softly in their saucers.

Even if l had had the cabin to myself could not have slept, for I was filled with an inner excitement that kept me wide awake. I had come all this way on a quest of music—to listen to the *gamelans* the strange and lovely-sounding orchestras of gongs that still made music, it seemed, in the courts of Java and the villages and temples of Bali, and as I looked out into the night I could hardly believe that this musical adventure was actually about to begin.

I was a young composer, recently back in New York after student days in Paris, and the past two years had been filled with composing and the business of getting performances. It was quite by accident that I had heard the few gramophone records that were to change my life completely, bringing me out here in search of something quite indefinable—music or experience, I could not at this moment say. The records had been made in Bali, and the clear, metallic sounds of the music were like the stirring of a thousand bells, delicate, confused, with a sensuous charm, a mystery that was quite overpowering. I begged to keep the records for a few days, and as I played them over and over I became more and more enchanted with the sound. Who were the musicians? I wondered. How had this music come about? Above all, how was it possible, in this late day, for such a music to have been able to survive?

I returned the records, but I could not forget them. At the time I knew little about the music of the East. I still believed that an artist must keep his mind on his own immediate world. But the effect of the music was deeper than I suspected, for after I had read in the early books of Crawfurd and Raffles the quite fabulous accounts of these ancient and ceremonial orchestras, my imagination took fire, and the day came when I determined to make a trip to the East to see them for myself.

I leaned against the ship rail recalling all this and watching the phosphorescent wake fade into the blackness. I could not get used to the changed appearance of the sky; constellations that once had been flat designs now took on new dimensions, disclosing planes that extended far into space. Suddenly the night was luminous, and the silhouette of mountains, surprisingly near, stood up against the sky.

As the sun rose the mountains grew streaked with descending ridges and shadows, and along the foothills the palms glistened in the early humid light. But with the day the mountains flattened once more into cones, and within an hour, as we landed, the sun was throwing light and heat in all directions.

The little port town of Buleleng lay white along the edge of the sea. On either side of the main street, beneath the shade of enormous overhanging trees, were the shops, half hidden within a long arcade. Here thermos bottles, flashlights and celluloid dolls were sold by the Japanese, batiks and Manchester *sarongs* by Bombay men. The Chinese shops were crammed with everything under the sun, ironware, porcelain, hams, lacquer, smoked duck, silks and firecrackers. Arabs, Chinese, and Balinese in gay flowered batik strolled through the arcades. They sat peacefully in tiny restaurants, smoking, drinking synthetic pear juice coloured that seductive pink which is the symbol of sweetness in Mexico and Harlem, Naples, Kong and Batavia. The town gave forth the faint, voluptuous scent of all eastern cities, of nutmeg and aromatic cigarettes, coconut oil, gardenias and drying fish. From somewhere came the sound of sweet crystal music; of a gong, and above it thin chimelike melody, commencing, stopping, commencing once again.

A car was waiting to take me over the mountains to the south shore, but I was in no hurry to leave. I turned off the main street and wandered down a maze of lanes. Here the shops were simple boxes with one end knocked away, their contents spilling into the street. Copra and coffee merchants, photographers and dentists crowded side by side. The dentists were Japanese, and their offices held no secrets from the passer-by. In the centre of each a plush chair balanced on uncertain machinery; the walls were covered with terrifying charts, while glass cases exhibited pearly molars and sets of golden teeth.

The music had stopped, but suddenly it began once more, louder, very near. At the end of the street stood a small Chinese temple, and the music came from inside the open door. Now that I was near it was no longer a single voice suspended in the air; instead, it had become strong and definite, composed of many different kinds of sounds. It clashed, rang and echoed, and beneath it all was the persistent beat of drums that rose at one moment to a fury, fell the next to an almost inaudible throb.

Inside the temple it was cool and dark. Incense burned on the altar; along the walls were empty gambling-tables, and on the cement floor beside them lay a few sleeping Chinese, dead to this world. Near the door mats had been spread and on them, in the midst of a confusion of gongs and instruments with great metal keys, sat a score of Balinese musicians. In the shadow you could barely make out the enormous gongs that hung in the back of the orchestra, but the light from the door reflected on the small gongs in front that were set out in horizontal rows. With serene and unified gestures the men struck the gongs and keys with little hammers and mallets; those beside the great gongs at the back held sticks with thickly padded knobs. Only once in a long time did they seem to come to life, raise their hands to strike, with infinite gentleness, the knob of the gong that hung beside them.

The melody unrolled like some ancient chant, grave and metallic, while around it there wove an endless counterpoint of tones from the little gongs in front. From time to time, above the drums there floated the soft, reverberating tone of a great gong, deep, penetrating, seeming to fill the temple with faintly echoing sound.

The music came to an end and the men laid down their mallets. They started, but their gaze was not unfriendly. A young Chinese came up to speak a few polite words in English, and I began to question him. It seemed that the players had been engaged for the temple ceremonies as there were no Chinese musicians in Buleléng. The name of the piece just played? He consulted the drummer. The Sea of Honey.

Once more the men took up their mallets, to begin the more animated Snapping Crocodile. I stood there utterly fascinated. It was even more incredible than I had imagined. But this time when the musicians came to the end they did not begin again. Some rose and went out. I waited for a while, hoping they would return, but as I looked at my watch I saw it was time to leave if I wanted to reach Den Pasar on the south shore of the Island by sundown. I went out reluctantly and walked back through the narrow streets in the direction from where I came.

The driver kicked off his sandals, curled his toes over the clutch and started the car. Before we had left town the road began to climb, past the trim colonial bungalows, past the house of the Resident, a baroque pile of white columns and cast iron, up and out into the ricefields that rose in everdiminishing terraces as the road grew steeper. Below us the sea flattened out into a wide expanse of blue, separated from the sky by a sharp black line. The ship, already headed for Celebes, was a tiny object that crawled across the surface of the ocean with the determination of a snail.

The car ran slower and slower as it climbed the mountain, panting in the heat of the sun. As we left the fields and entered the forest there was the sound of a minor explosion and a jet of steam burst from the water cap. The driver stopped the car and got out with a sigh.

I wandered up the road. The forest was flooded with a soft golden light that glanced off the surface of huge thick leaves, turned others transparent, and penetrated caves that lay between tense, clutching roots. Not a flower to brighten this secret world; nor a sound, except the sudden brief note of some bird that rang for a moment like a tuning-fork. I returned to find the driver at work on the radiator. It had boiled dry, and the heat had melted the solder in seams that had obviously opened often. The driver resourcefully packed moss into the spaces, stuffing it in with a match. Then he plugged the hole with a wedge of wood. From the car he produced a tin marked Best Australian Butter and filled it with water from a brook by the road. He poured it in and banged down the cap. Then he smiled, said something I did not understand, and got back in the car.

The forest thinned; we were on the bare summit of the mountain, and the road now ran along the rim of a giant crater. The inner wall was covered with jungle, and far below shone a lake. Within this bowl rose a cone, its slopes streaked with lava that had once run down far into the valley, and from its side came intermittent gusts of steam that slowly dissolved in the air.

Now the road began its long descent to the sea, disappearing ahead of us in the zone where the trees began. Soon there were fields of corn, huts, and at last a village, hidden beneath a grove of trees. All at once the road was filled with people and animals. Scenes flashed by; harvesters deep in yellow rice, a ring of noisy children around two copulating horses, a file of chanting women with offerings on their heads, a long procession with golden parasols that marched to the sound of gongs and wildly beating drums. The driver slowed up for pigs and ducks, but cut through chickens and dogs with indifference. Grey, starved and tottering, on walls, in doorways, the dogs infested the villages. They were so anæmic they could hardly drag themselves off the road. We drove along, knocking them to one side with a thud.

All at once we were by the sea, now purple in the late afternoon. Towering pink clouds hung motionless in the sky, making soft glowing patches on the surface of the water. The road ran past unloading fishing *praus*, past nets already spread on poles to dry. White plaster houses with tiled roofs appeared; in a moment we were in Den Pasar and had turned in the driveway of the hotel.

I was exhausted and could hardly wait to get out of the car. The hotel was a large cool bungalow, and I was shown to a room that opened on to a deep veranda one step above the lawn. Between the palms one could see people and little carriages forever passing along the road. I rang for a drink, and sank into the low, cushioned chair.

As I waited a new sound rose in the sky, high up, shrill and tremulous, sweeter than anything I had heard that day. I looked out. A flock of pigeons circled in the last rays of the sun. The sound seemed to follow them, and I could not think what it was. I called the boy, who said that the owner of the birds had hung little bells to their feet and attached bamboo whistles to their tail feathers. Round and round they flew, trailing across the sky wide hoops of sound. And then they vanished, the bells dying suddenly into nothing.

DEN PASAR

DEN PASAR WAS A rambling town of white Government buildings, a dozen European houses, and a street or so of shops, surrounded by an outer layer of huts crowded beneath a tangle of trees and palms. There was peace and order in the large square around which the European houses were set. Here in the late afternoon the doctor, the Shell agent, the school inspector and the hospital nurse played tennis; in another part of the field a desultory game of football took place among the Balinese. They wore striped jerseys and shorts, striped stockings, and boots that were too heavy, so that when they ran and kicked you thought of motions performed under water.

The shops were a repeat of Buleléng—a line of Chinese grocers and goldsmiths, Chinese druggists, photographers and bicycle agents. There was also a single Japanese photographer (as there seemed to be in almost every small town in the Indies) who did little business, but whose shop was strategically placed at the main crossroad where you could see the European offices and houses as well as the Chinese shops. On a side-street Arabs sold textiles and cheap suitcases. In the Javanese ice-cream parlour you could buy hilariously coloured ices when the electric equipment was in order. There was no church, but the Arab quarters contained a mosque; a small cinema ran Wild West pictures twice a week. At one end of the main street lay the market, where people picked their way through a confusion of pigs and pottery, batiks, fruit, brassware and mats.

During the day there was the incessant clang of bells from the pony carts that filled the streets, and the asthmatic honk of buses and cars forever driving in and out of town. The crowing of a thousand cocks, the barking of a thousand dogs formed a rich, sonorous background against which the melancholy call of a passing food vendor stood out like an oboe in a symphony.

But at night, when the shops had closed and half the town was already asleep, the sounds died so completely that you could hear every leaf that stirred, every palm frond that dryly rustled. From all directions there now floated soft, mysterious music, humming, vibrating above the gentle, hollow sound of drums. The sounds came from different distances and gave infinite perspective to the night. As it grew late the music stopped. Now the silence was complete, only at long intervals pierced by a solitary voice, high, nasal, nostalgic, singing an endless tune; or else broken by the sudden hysteria of the dogs that began in a thin, single wail, rose quickly to a clamour of tormented voices and died once more into silence.

The hotel with its cool lobbies and tiled floors was an oasis after a few hours in the glare and heat that I loved, but which drained me of the last drop of energy. I could not believe the thermometer when it registered only 85. After a walk through the town I would collapse on the bed, which, like all beds in the Indies, had no springs. I broke into a rash which the hotel manager recognized at once as red dog, and only the chance discovery in my dictionary that *roode hond* meant prickly heat in Dutch kept me from rushing to the doctor.

I was not trying to learn Dutch, however, but Malay.

Malay is a language that seems childish and simple so far as expressing daily wants is concerned, and turns out to be elaborate and ambiguous when it comes to conveying a complex thought. It is the Esperanto of Malaya and the Indies, and you can even hear it in Colombo and Hong Kong. The vocabulary contains much Arabic, a little Sanskrit, Portuguese and Javanese, a little Dutch and English, and a few lovely-sounding primitive words for such common objects as man, fish and co-conut, that are known from Madagascar to Easter Island. I had begun to study when on board ship, but up to now I had not ventured much past asking for hot shaving water, more coffee, and ice water.

It was only after I met Sarda that I felt the need for a great-er vocabulary. When I wanted a car I phoned the Chinese ga-rage, and they had got in the habit of sending me a certain an-cient though well-preserved Buick. Sarda was the name of the self-possessed and handsome youth who drove it with an air of utter scorn.

He dressed with elegance. His batik *sarong* was crisp and new, covered with a design of flowers and tennis rackets. He wore a silk sport shirt, and over it a white jacket, elegantly tai-lored American style. In the breast pocket were an Ever-sharp, a fountain pen and a comb. On his feet were sandals and on his head a batik headcloth, in the folds of which he had fastened a rose.

At first I sat in the back seat of the car, alone with my camer-as, thermos and sandwiches, but I soon grew weary of this iso-lation and moved to the front, where I could talk to Sarda as we drove. The hotel manager strongly disapproved. For in this little gesture anything apparently was to be read, possible friendli-ness and intimacy, and even worse, equality, so abhorrent from the colonial point of view. You must keep your *distance*, said the manager; the correct place for a white man is in the back seat. In the old days, he continued, Hollanders married natives; to-day it is different. Take them to bed if you like, but see they come in at the back door.

He spoke in heavy earnestness, but without hatred. He was a red-faced man, forever dripping sweat. He bullied his boys, sometimes in roaring fury, sometimes in tired routine. Yet he must have got on with them, nevertheless, for the service was excellent.

Ahmat! he shouted, as we sat in the lobby. Ahmat! he bellowed, and I thought his voice would shatter the glass over the huge picture of the Queen of the Netherlands that hung above us.

A slim figure approached.

Bring two gin-bitters, and hurry!

He blotted his forehead with a damp handkerchief.

Lazy! he complained. You can teach them nothing. Ten years I've been here, he moaned. If it weren't for the girls. . . . Did you notice the little one by the door selling rings?

We finished our drinks and I got up. He had a final word for me.

I don't like to see you there in the front seat. The white man must never forget to maintain the dignity of the white race.

He gave a gentle belch.

Then as an afterthought he added, If you really must sit in front, drive the car yourself and let the chauffeur sit behind.

But I continued to sit the way I pleased. We drove with the top down, the hot sun beating on our heads. It was only when we passed the tennis court or entered the hotel driveway that I felt self-conscious, ostentatious and subversive.

At the hotel itineraries were posted for those who had only a few days on the island. Each day was crammed from dawn till sundown. "Thurs. a.m.: sacred pool; tombs of the kings; palace at Karangasem; lunch at resthouse. Afternoon: bats' cave; sacred forest; giant banyan; hot springs. Dance performance at hotel, 9 p.m."

I preferred to drive at random through the island, getting lost in the network of back roads that ran up into the hills where, as you looked down towards the sea, the flooded rice-fields lay shining in the sunlight like a broken mirror. The sound of music seemed forever in the air. People sang in the fields or in the streams as they bathed. From behind village walls rose the sound of flutes and cymbals as invisible musicians rehearsed at all hours of the day and night. Temples in a state of celebration shook with the heavy beat of drums, the throb of enormous gongs, and as we drove home at night we passed through village after village where, by the roadside, amid a blaze of little lamps, people had gathered to sit and watch the puppets of the shadow-play.

As the car ascended from the sea into the mountains, the style and mood of the music seemed to change. In the lowlands, musicians played with a bright vivacity, while music shimmered with ornamentation, rich and complicated as the ornamented temples themselves. But in the hills, as you travelled higher and higher, among villages that lay farther and farther apart, the music, like the architecture of the temples, grew more austere, took on an air of increasing antiquity and severity. Here, in the mists and clouds, where temple walls were green with moss and roofs overgrow with ferns, only rarely was the quiet broken by the grave sound of ancient ritual music at some village feast.

Although Sarda was clearly bored by these excursions into the hills (Mountain style! he would remark loftily while we watched some slow-moving dance) he soon grew resigned to stopping the car at the sound of music. I would get out, and make my way through the crowd to where the musicians were gathered. No one seemed to mind this intrusion in the least, and as I sat there, listening, and watching the confused events of a temple feast, the women with their towers of offerings, the ceremonial dancing before the altars, the processions and the bursting firecrackers, all sense of time had vanished completely.

Sometimes, after a long morning of casual exploration, Sarda would stop at the market-place of some village, where we would sit at the little coffee-stall for a glass of tea or tepid beer. Above the murmur of the market there drifted from the open door of the tiny Government school the sound of children's voices, sleepily chanting the multiplication table to the rap of a ruler. The presence of the car was not long in attracting a group of boys. Comments began.

Essex.

No, Buick 1927. An old model.

An old man would ask: How can it be? A chariot going like that, along, without horse or cow.

Unsympathetic laughter banished him to the dark ages.

Wake up, grandfather, think! You push in the foot, pull the handle and it goes.

Sarda listened in scornful silence. He would turn to me.

The talk of mountain people! He would start the car with a flourish, and we departed with magnificent suddenness, like gods.

In the early morning the island had a golden freshness, dripped and shone with moisture like a garden in a florist's window. By noon it had become hard and matter-of-fact. But in the late afternoon the island was transformed once more; it grew unreal, lavish and theatrical like old-fashioned opera scenery. As the sun neared the horizon men and women turned the colour of new copper,. while shadows grew purple, the grass blue, and everything white reflected a deep rose.

One evening, as we drove along, the full moon rose above the fields, scarlet, enormous, distorted beyond belief in the invisible haze. I told Sarda to stop the car, and sat looking in silence. A tone of romantic enthusiasm in my voice, possibly, had set Sarda thinking, for suddenly he asked,

In America you have no moon, perhaps?

He spoke so simply I could not tell if irony were intended or not. I told him we had, and at this he started the car, saying I would be late for dinner at the hotel.

It was during this first week that, one late afternoon, we came to a village bright with banners and streamers. In front of the temple a crowd was gathered, and the sound of swift, complicated music filled the air. I pushed through the wall of people to a clearing, where at one end sat the musicians among their instruments. At the other end a pair of curtains stretched on a wire marked a stage entrance.

The music rose and fell with almost feverish intensity. Before the orchestra two drummers leaned forward over their drums, their hands beating against the drum-ends like moth wings against a lamp. Suddenly the music came to a halt. There was a pause, while the players rested. But soon they came to attention once more. They picked up their little hammers and mallets; there was a signal-accent from the first drummer, and once more the music broke on the air like a shower.

The curtains parted, and through them appeared a child (could she be nine?) clad apparently in gold. The setting sun cast a spotlight through the trees, and she glittered like an insect as she moved. Soon she was followed by two others; the folds in their skirts were stiff and metallic, and in each headdress golden flowers nodded from the ends of wires and trembled with each motion of the body. Dance and music were like a single impulse. The children darted like humming-birds. Their gestures had infinite elegance, and they seemed like little statues, intricate and delicate, that had come to life—not with suppleness, but, like the sequence of images in a film, in a series of poses that lasted the mere fraction of a second. You felt they were conscious of every sixteenth-note in the music.

At first the dance was formal and abstract. The story had not yet begun, said Sarda. But soon it grew clear that a drama was unfolding. There was a scene of tenderness, followed by a march around the stage. The first child took up a pair of golden wings and became a bird. The second waved a *kris* to ward it off. There was another march, a battle. The dancers went rapidly from role to role.

Now the King of Lasem takes leave of the Princess Lang-kasa-ri, whom he has carried off, said Sarda. He goes to fight her brother. A raven flies before him. He stumbles over a stone. He will be killed. . . .

At last the music came to an end, and the children, their foreheads damp with sweat, sat down by the musicians, drooping like wilted flowers. There was something poignantly troubling in the cool, pre-adolescent grace, the serenity of the faces that were neither innocent nor corrupt.

Over and over the hypnotic music seemed to ring in my ears above the motor of the car as we drove home in the night.

Those are the *légong* dancers of the Prince of Saba, Sarda remarked. They say he is madly in love with the first, but he cannot marry her yet. He must wait her first menses. His second wife is sick with jealousy.

What does the little girl think about it?

Probably nothing. She wouldn't dare. She is only a peasant. You would think he would prefer one of the others. They are prettier, and one is a princess, the other a Brahman.

They seem very young.

But who desires an opened flower? And besides, if you want virginity . . .

And he, what is he like?

A great gambler, a great lover of dancing. His musicians are famous. He was playing the drum just now.

I remembered the dramatic-looking young man who drummed so feverishly, his eyes fixed on the dancers as they moved across the stage. His energy seemed to flow into every accent of the music, every motion of the dancers, through their bodies and out into the fragile hands that were forever forming new and beautiful designs.

And who trains the dancers?

He trains them himself, they say.

We rode on in silence. It was too late for dinner at the hotel, and I went to the Chinese restaurant on the main street. It was almost closing time, and I sat alone with Sarda while the sleepy cook took down a pan and fanned the dying fire. From somewhere in the back came the sound of a flute above a faintly twanging zither.

We drove down to the sea. The moon was high, and the beach was flooded with silver light. Around the bay in the distance the mountains were small and transparent.

I feel like swimming, I said. Is it safe?

Yes; here there are no sharks.

Will you come along?

Sarda put the key of the car in his pocket and got out.

We undressed, hanging our clothes over the side of a dugout that lay drawn up on the beach. We walked slowly into the water. Far out you could hear the surf on the reefs; far out the little lamps of the fishing *praus* shone and bobbed up and down.

When we came out we sat on the rocks to let the faint breeze blow us dry. I did not want to return to the hotel. For a long time I lay on the sand, listening to the sea breaking on the reefs, letting the sand flow through my fingers.

Tuan seems very happy here, remarked Sarda a few days later.

Very happy indeed, Sarda.

Why remain at the hotel? I know of a small house for rent in a village not far from Den Pasar. It is not dear.

In my mind I saw a thatched hut against a background of tree-ferns and bamboos. I suddenly realized how bored I was with the hotel, how imperative it was to live my own way, in my own house. I told Sarda we would go to the village the following morning. If the house had a roof I was determined to take it.

THE HOUSE IN KEDATON

THE HOUSE WAS SMALL and square, with a roof of corrugated tin and walls covered inside and out with damp white plaster. It had four rooms of exactly the same size, with a shuttered window to each, and the floors were cement that threw back a ringing echo at the least noise. In the back was a still smaller building which contained kitchen, bath and a place for a servant to unroll his sleeping-mat.

The house stood on a small rectangle of ground surrounded by an almost empty moat, overgrown with moss and ferns, from which a frog croaked dismally from time to time. Once this moat had been filled to the brim; for the house, it seemed, had been built as a "pleasure retreat" for a Brahman priest of the village, and was still known to all as the *Gunung Sari*, Mountain of Flowers. But the priest had long since given it up, and now rented it from time to time to a passing white man who wished to live native style.

The doors creaked; the rooms were musty; the place had been shut a year. But from the deep veranda in front you looked out through the palms over gleaming ricefields and caught a glimpse of the sea beyond. Arrangements were conducted through the businesslike young grandson of the old priest, who said that the rent would be forty guilders a month and that I could move in when I wished. He promised there would be the necessary furniture when I arrived.

The disapproval of the hotel manager when I told him my change in plans was real if not eloquent. But when he saw I would not listen he suddenly became surprisingly human, and offered to lend me linen, silver and comfortable chairs. I thought I even detected the slightest inflection of envy in his voice as he now gave advice about white ants and warned about the water. He said I would need a cook and a houseboy, and that my room boy could easily find them for me.

That evening an exceedingly languid youth in white jacket and trousers approached my veranda at the hotel, sat down on the floor and bowed politely, hands clasped below his chin. He did not look very efficient, but the room boy said he had recently worked in the hotel. He said also that he had found me a cook, and the next morning as I went out in my pyjamas for the early cup of coffee she was already waiting for me, standing patiently in the wet grass. She was a short, plump Madurese with a round face that had the expression of a sulky child. She was barefoot, and wore a white *sarong* covered with red peacocks; a short white jacket parted at the seams under her arms in order to meet across her breasts, exposing a triangle of midriff.

This is the *koki*, said the houseboy. She can cook Dutch,

Good day, *koki*, I said.

Tabé tuan; tuan chari koki?

She spoke in the strange, childish singsong of the Indonesian servant, colourless and remote. I gave her some money, told her to buy pots and pans, and said I would have lunch at the house two days later.

Two days later the house had become warm and alive. I found the priest's son and two other boys waiting to welcome me. They had swept the house clean and arranged the furniture in careful order. The *koki* and the houseboy were already there; the shutters were wide open, and about the place there was an air of expectation.

Two of the rooms had been furnished exactly alike. Each contained a loose, musical iron bed, draped like a girl at her first communion in limp white netting. In the bed were two pillows, and down the centre ran the dutch wife, a long bolster, plump as a sausage. Against a wall in each room was a table with an enamel jug and basin, and above it a small mirror. In the corner stood a chair. The third room contained a bare dining-table and four chairs symmetrically placed. The fourth room contained nothing at all. On the open window sills the boys had placed drinking glasses with bright flowers that shone transparently in the morning sun.

The *koki* was already at home. She sat on the kitchen floor, fanning the fires of three small braziers and stirring the contents of the pans on top. Around her were bowls of grated coconut, fried onions and ingredients I could not identify. On the mat beside her lay little mounds of red peppers, garlic and nuts. There was a litter of bananas, duck eggs and crabs, some Australian butter in a large tin, and a stupefied chicken, tied by the leg to a nail in the wall. Her cigarettes and betel were within easy reach. An emaciated dog had already adopted the place and sniffed in the corners of the room.

In the air was a powerful, complex smell, acrid and pungent, of burnt feathers, fish and frying coconut oil. I was to find this a daily smell, punctual and inevitable as the morning smell of coffee at home. It came chiefly from *sra*, a paste of shrimps that had once been ground, dried, mixed with sea-water, then buried for months to ferment. It was used in almost everything, fried first to develop the aroma. It was unbelievably putrid. An amount the size of a pea was more than enough to flavour a dish. It gave a racy, briny tang to the food, and I soon found myself craving it as an animal craves salt.

Each night I gave the *koki* a guilder, at that time about forty cents, which she converted into Chinese coins when she went to the market at dawn. She bought a pair of chickens or a beautiful fish, vegetables, fruit, eggs, rice, beancurd, a handful of dried fish for herself and the boy, and had something left over to treat herself to cigarettes and betel.

Each morning she appeared around seven with a large washbasin balanced on her head. It had become a fantastic hat trimmed with pineapples, leeks, cabbages and bananas, from out of which peered a numb-looking chicken or duck.

Tabé tuan.

Tabé koki. How goes it?

Yes, *tuan*.

She was too remote, too indifferent to fill in the correct reply. She trudged silently to the back of the house. But it would not be long before her voice took on another tone. She was a woman with a little, shrewish temper, and she refused to get along with the houseboy. She was a Madurese and a Mohammedan, while he was a heathen Balinese, and a pork-eater into the bargain. Her scolding would burst forth in a sharp chatter that rose to a squeak and disappeared in the higher overtones of final exasperation.

For lunch she cooked Javanese style, which meant rice, accompanied by a dozen different dishes that were enough for six people. The table was crowded with bowls in which fish and fowl swam in sauces of green, yellow or scarlet. Some dishes tasted somewhat like curry, though infinitely fresher in flavour; some were so hot with spice they brought tears to the eyes and sweat to the forehead.

The preparation of these dishes was involved, and took hours of patient labour. The idea, it seemed, was variety to please a gourmet's palate, for a chicken was never cooked in one way only, but divided into parts, to be fried, broiled, stewed, shredded, and seasoned with great care for contrast. A fish she cooked in the same way. This, however, was not enough, for there were endless little side-dishes of strange delicacies—stewed acacia blossoms, preserved duck eggs, tiny octopus fried crisp and looking like a dish of spiders.

Her sweets were even stranger. For lunch would end perhaps with corn and grated coconut mixed with a syrup of palm sugar, soggy little balls of rice paste treacherously filled with more syrup, or a sliced pineapple to be eaten with salt, red pepper and garlic.

But at night the *koki* "cooked Dutch." Then she would send in a meat loaf, or duck in a black and curious sauce. Pancakes and blancmange alternated for dessert.

The houseboy was strangely limp and colourless. He had said, Call me Gusti (prince) though it seemed he had no right to the title. *He a gusti?* exclaimed the koki to me privately. She laughed derisively. In the early morning Gusti brought me luke-warm coffee while he was still half asleep. He dragged the mattress into the sun, moved chairs and dusted as though it took his last ounce of strength. He managed to wash a shirt or two each morning, and spent the afternoon in a delicious dream-world of cigarette smoke and slow, thoughtful ironing. First he did my shirts, then a pair of trousers. After this he rested. Then he pressed his own shirt and jacket, or spent an hour ironing fancy pleats into his *sarong*. This he wore when not in the mood for trousers, wrapped neatly around his waist and falling down the front in folds, which lay in flat accordion pleats that opened out when he walked, reminding you of Egyptian reliefs.

Soon the house was running of its own accord. I grew deaf to the *koki's* voice; as I learnt to understand what she was saying it became clear that she scolded much of the time simply to keep in practice; these outbursts were her daily vocal exercises, necessary to keep her voice flexible in the long complaint of woman against man.

The village was laid out square as a chessboard. Like all villages on the island, it was a network of roads and lanes that ran north and south, east and west. It gave the impression of lying in the heart of a lovely forest; the houses were hidden behind walls in a jungle of breadfruit-trees and palms, whose long fronds drooped like plumes and reflected the morning sunlight at a thousand angles.

The house lay just off the main road at one end of the village. Across the way stood the Temple of Origins. You walked down the road past the Temple of the Village Elders to the market and the men's clubhouse. Then you came to the Temple of the Earth's Axis. Out in the fields stood the little temple for Sri, the rice goddess. Still farther away you could see from the house a group of shrines for Saraswati, goddess of learning. Beyond the graveyard at the south edge of the village stood the Temple of the Dead. Silent, deserted, each temple waited for its feast day, when the courts would fill with people and the walls echo with music.

At the market-place in the centre of the village all was life and movement from dawn till late at night. Here people came to meet and gossip, and buy a handful of dried fish or a measure of rice. Once in three days, on market-day, you could buy pigs and ducks, mats, Japanese textiles, hardware from China and Java. Here too, in the shade of the great banyan that covered the entire market, men gathered each day to talk idly, or sit and think about nothing at all. They brought their fighting cocks, and sat for hours absent-mindedly massaging the firm, tense legs, or running the long silky necks through their fingers.

At night the men's clubhouse became the social centre. It was a long hut of bamboo and palm-thatch, with a raised floor of earth that had dried hard as a rock. Here the *gamelan* that belonged to the music club of the younger men in the village was kept. In the daytime you seldom passed without hearing from within a soft chime of gongs or metal keys as some child, sitting in the cool darkness of the empty hut, improvised and learnt for himself how to play. But after dark the hut was a luminous centre surrounded by a blaze of little, lamps. Outside the saleswomen had set down their tables of sweets and betel, while the members of the club gathered inside to practise. Now was the time to go through the music they already knew, for the sheer pleasure of it, or work over the difficult parts of some new composition they were just learning. They used no notes (indeed there were none, it seemed); each phrase of the melody, each intricate detail of accompaniment they had learned by ear, listening carefully and with infinite patience to the teacher who had, perhaps, been called from some other village. Late into the night they played. From the house I could hear them going over phrase after phrase, correcting, improving, until the music began to flow of its own accord. I fell asleep with the sounds ringing in my ears, and. as I slept I still heard them, saw them rather, for now they seemed transformed into a shining rain of silver.

NYOMAN KALÉR

A BALINESE VILLAGE IS divided into wards or *banjars*. Each has its headman, its priest, its separate community life. Sometimes the village is a peaceful one, with a harmonious relationship between all *banjars,* but often (I was to find out) there is bitterness and rivalry between adjacent wards, especially among the youths and younger men. One evening shortly after I had come to the village I received a call from the head of my own *banjar.*

It was dusk, and I was sitting on the veranda talking with Sarda when I heard the sound of steps on the gravel. I looked out, to see three figures approaching single file through the trees. The leader walked in a curious way. He seemed to drift in, for although he advanced in a straight line his body slanted sideways to the right, while his head tilted slightly to the left. He gave the impression of being on the point of going off in any direction.

But there was authority, I could see, in the way he came up the two steps of the veranda and sat down on the floor a little distance from my chair. His two young followers sat respectfully on the lower step.

Sarda introduced him.

This is Nyoman Kalér, head of the *banjar* and teacher of the *légong* dancers.

He wore a tight white coat, cut in the old colonial style, with brass buttons that ran up to the neck; a worn *sarong* and a tightly knotted headcloth completed his attire. He bowed politely before speaking.

Tuan has just arrived? They say *tuan* is from America.

He spoke in a gentle, friendly voice. He was a slight man, perhaps thirty, with intelligent eyes and a smiling, well-shaped mouth that was both sensual and vaguely sarcastic. There was also something a little pedantic about him, something birdlike in the way he inclined his head first one way then another as he talked.

The boys sat very still and silent, their hands folded in their laps. The older one had the features of Nyoman Kalér, but in his face there was only serenity. A small white flower bud hung down the centre of his forehead, its stem fastened in a hair.

Tuan has come to paint pictures perhaps?

My visitor came directly to the point.

I explained that I was a musician, that I composed music, and had come here simply to listen to Balinese music. I told him I expected to remain several months. I said I was happy to know he was a musician like myself, and I hoped he would come often to the house.

Yes, he replied, willingly! And if he could be of service I had only to ask.

After a short time he politely asked permission to depart. All three bowed, rose and walked out into the dark.

He is a clever man, remarked Sarda after they had left. He knows a lot besides music and dancing.

Gusti's comment was less enthusiastic.

They say he can become a *léyak*.

What do you mean?

He hesitated, lowered his voice.

He knows how to turn himself into a monkey or a ball of fire.

The boy with the flower, who was he?

His nephew, Madé Tantra.

Two days later Nyoman Kalér made a second appearance. He came alone, in the middle of the morning, and the time passed in the most agreeable of conversations. As we sat there, smoking and drinking coffee, I began to question him about music in the village.

It turned out that in our *banjar* there were three separate *gamelans,* and he was the head of all three. One belonged to the *légong* club. There was also the *gandrung* club.

What is *gandrung?* I asked.

The dance is something like *légong,* but the dancer is a boy in girl's clothes. He dances in the streets for a few pennies, going from door to door. There is another *gandrung* in the next *banjar,* but ours is better. When he dances there are always many who step out to dance with him. They can hardly wait their turn. . . .

There was a look of satisfaction in Nyoman's face. He took a heart-shaped betel leaf from a little pouch, folded it and put it in his mouth.

The third *gamelan* was seldom seen. It was kept locked in the Temple of the Sea and taken out only on feast-days, to play the stately ceremonial music without which no celebration would be complete.

And the *gamelan* that practises each night in the clubhouse by the market? I asked.

His voice was suddenly thin as he answered, It is the music club of the *banjar* to the south; and though he smiled there was a curious withdrawal in his eyes. He sat for a while, preoccupied and no longer communicative, and soon he rose and took a ceremonious departure.

Sarda explained. Hot rivalry burned between Nyoman's *légong gamelan* and the club of the other *banjar.* Members did not speak. Moreover, in the past month the other club had been called twice to Den Pasar to appear at the hotel. Nyoman's club had gone there only once. . . .

Late that afternoon I heard the animated sound of gongs, cymbals and drums passing along the road, and as I looked through the trees I could see the rival club, wearing their brightest clothes, marching in procession towards Den Pasar.

They are going to meet the bus from West Bali, said Sarda. Gusti Bagus, who is head of their *banjar,* emerges to-day from jail, and they are going to greet him.

He had sold some ricefields, it seemed, that belonged to his brother. He had been away six months.

Nyoman Kalér had been a dancer as a boy. He was brought up at the old court of the Prince of Blahbatu. His father was one of the *parakans,* feudal retainers, of the Prince, and had been, among other things, a member of the palace *gamelan.* Nyoman Kalér (lithe and attractive, as a child, I imagined) had been trained as a court dancer.

What kind of dance? I asked him one time.

Nandir; it is no longer danced. It was the same as *légong.* Boys took the part of girls then more often than to-day.

Why did you stop?

I grew up and my suppleness was lost.

He had turned to music. He could, of course, have become an actor as he grew older, for in the ancient theatre of the court, so formal and highly stylized, it was very hard to say where dancing ended and acting began. But he had no voice, he said. He was, moreover, too slightly built for the heroic *baris* or warrior's dance; or the equally heroic *topeng,* the honoured mask-plays that had to do with the ancient kings of Bali. With the death of the old Anak Agung the court had fallen into a decline. Nyoman had left, to come to Kedaton, where his family owned ricefields. When the *légong* club was formed he had trained both dancers and musicians. The little dancers had been a great success; soon he was in demand in other villages, and to-day he was well-established. He belonged to the peasant class, and the other men in his household worked the ricefields. I thought, however, he had chosen well, for I could not possibly imagine him behind a plough, or bending over to set out, one by one, the young rice plants in the flooded fields.

In these early conversations with Nyoman I caught glimpses

of ancient and brilliant courts, of palaces forever ringing with music and crowded with actors and dancers. For at one time the princes of Bali had been great patrons of the arts. Many of them had come from Java to escape the wave of Islamic culture that had begun to spread through the land. With their wives and concubines, their soldiers, craftsmen, actors and musicians, they continued in Bali to live in a splendour half barbarous, half provincial, patterned on the great and luxurious courts of the Javanese rajahs.

But now a glittering court life was almost a thing of the past. Government pawnshops overflowed with treasures from the palace. Gongs and jewelled *krises,* golden rings and head-dresses filled shelves and glass cases, while the palaces decayed and grew cluttered with rocking chairs and mirrors, umbrel-la stands, *jardinières* and telephones. As they passed along the road, the six rajahs now glared at each other from closed Pack-ards. You could tell their cars at once by the tiny golden parasols above the radiator caps, and by the swift, efficient driving of the chauffeurs. The princes rumbled by in open Fords which they were forever repairing by the roadside. Now and then they passed on motor cycle.

At the court of Blahbatu, said Nyoman, recalling twenty years before, there were two great orchestras. In the outer pal-ace stood the massive *Gamelan* with the Great Gongs, to play for ceremonies and welcome the arrival of guests. In the in-ner palace an assembly of little gongs and keyed instruments more delicately formed, sweeter and softer in tone, played a far more romantic music. This was the *gamelan Semar-pagulingan,* the *Gamelan* of Semara, God of Love, God of the Pillowed Bed. The music, said Nyoman, soothed and rejoiced the heart with its sweetness. Every evening it began; off and on the musicians played, late into the night. . . .

Where is the *gamelan* now? I asked.

It had been pawned long ago, said Nyoman, and later bought

by the men of Sukawati, and transformed into a *gamelan* for *légong*.

But the *gamelan* of state remained, he thought, and one day we drove to Blahbatu to see the instruments, for they were, it seemed, unusually large and handsome. (The gongs you could hear for miles, said Nyoman.) The keys had been dismounted and stored away, and now only the carved wooden stands were to be seen, crowded in a shed and covered with dust.

But if the courts of Bali to-day grew increasingly silent, in the villages music rang more loudly than ever. No temple feast could conceivably begin before the arrival of the *Gamelan* with the Great Gongs, whose stately ceremonial music, mingling with the prayers of priest and the chant of worshippers, was considered as necessary for the pleasure of the gods as incense, flowers and offerings. For the further entertainment of the gods (and mortals by happy coincidence) a variety of dances and masques were rehearsed to the more delicate *Légong Gamelan*—democratically adapted from the princely *Gamelan* of the Love God. Processions marched to the lively beat of the *Gamelan* of the Little Gongs or the more primitive *Gamelan* of the Bamboo Rattles. Anonymous, unwritten, the music on these occasions was ancient as the rites themselves, unchanged, apparently, for centuries.

For the boys and young men of the village, however, music had become something more intense than the mere accompaniment for ritual or ancient dance. A new wave of musical enthusiasm had recently swept the island, and clubs formed overnight as young musicians organized to learn *kebyar*, the new, the deliciously exciting music that had first been heard around Buleléng, and was now taking the island by storm. Night after night villages shook with the crash of cymbals and the brassy clang of little gongs as the clubs furiously rehearsed for an approaching competition. Then was the time for outstanding clubs to meet and tirelessly play against each other all day and all night. The verdict of the judges sowed seeds of bitterness, and the kindest word was *Sape*—a tie! Otherwise the losers brooded for months, while the winners were insufferable.

But in the shade of this emotional florescence, so torrid, in so high a key, the more conservative clubs continued to produce their classical plays and dances. These remained dear to the hearts of all. Night after night people gathered to watch as some youthful group of actors rehearsed beneath the trees. They sat entranced before the lighted screen of the shadow-play, never tiring of the ancient legends of Prince Rama, or the endless wars of the Pandawas. Drama both entertained and edified; the exemplary restraint of the legendary heroes and the nobility of their words presented an ancient ideal of conduct and manners.

As for *kebyar* (commented Nyoman), it was like an explosion; once the sound had died nothing remained.

THE MASKS

O NE MORNING AN OLD WOMAN came in with a covered basket and sat down on the lower step of the veranda. She had some "ancient objects" to sell. Did I wish to see them?

She uncovered the basket and took out a pile of brocades, a *kris*, a silver dish. At the bottom of the basket were several masks, and these she now arranged in a row along the floor. They were worn with age, but two seemed to me very beautiful. I bought them and hung them on the wall.

The two masks differed as night from day. The one, dark-coloured, devoured with fury, was the complete negation of the other that hung beside it, a fragile, chalk-white shell, serene and shadowless. It grew in mystery the more I looked at it. It had the same sexless calm that I had found so haunting and enigmatic in the faces of the little *légong* dancers I had seen at Saba. I had caught the expression again in the face of Made Tantra as he sat on the veranda the night of Nyoman Kalér's first appearance. The next time Nyoman came to the house I questioned him.

Those masks on the wall, whose masks are they?

He did not answer immediately. That depends, he said. It is hard to say. They would follow the story. The small one is that of a prince—perhaps Rama. It was the gentle type, the "sweetly brave," the restrained, the *manis*. He got up from the chair, went to the end of the veranda and turned around.

He had taken a dramatic pose that was both sculpturesque and fluid. At first it was purely two-dimensional, as though he were part of some temple relief. His thighs were turned outwards, his knees bent, while he slowly raised his arms, closing his hands in formal designs. He narrowed his eyes, seemed to gaze far away, while the shadow of a smile now played about his mouth. He began to move forward into a third dimension. He gently shifted his weight from foot to foot with lovely control, while head slanted, hands turned, in perfect harmony with his movements. It was strange and dreamlike, like swimming seen in a slow-motion film.

He spoke some lines; his voice rose in stylized falsetto, sweetly harsh, indolently rising and falling in formal declamation. He created an atmosphere of remoteness and utter unreality, created a character that seemed both feminine and tense with hidden force. He paused, returned to this world.

Like that, he said. So Prince Panji would enter in the *gambuh* play. But a *keras* character, violent and unrestrained, is very different, he continued. When the King of Lasem appears, he moves like this. . . .

He drew himself up proudly. His gestures lost all suavity. His face was transformed; his eyes stared, his mouth was tense, drawn down at the corners. He advanced menacingly, and as he spoke his voice was loud and rasping. He stopped.

It was only a brief impression, a mere indication that he had given, but with it the masks on the wall seemed to take on depth and meaning.

But the masks, I said. When would they be used?

There were three different theatres, he explained, three different kinds of actors. In one theatre you see the actors as ordinary men; in the second they are masked. In the third the actors are simply shadows thrown upon a screen, the shadows of little puppets, operated by a single man who recites and improvises around the ancient tales.

I had read about this mysterious little theatre perhaps the most ancient of all, claimed by some to have its origin in rites in which the shades of the departed were called back to this world. Even to-day much of the magic atmosphere, it seemed, remained, for Nyoman talked of the great care taken of the puppets and the offerings which must be made for them before a play could be given.

I must see a shadow-play, I said. I've been in Kedaton two weeks and not yet seen one.

It is not often the village is so quiet, he said. We sat there talking. From the kitchen came the sound of a broken glass, followed by the familiar outburst of scolding.

I was hoping Madé Tantra would come again, I said. As yet I have no friends here in Kedaton.

I will tell him, said Nyoman. He rose, and after saying good-bye walked down the path beneath the trees to the roadway.

A SHADOW-PLAY

ONE MORNING AS I RETURNED home from a walk in the ricefields, I entered the gate of the Temple of the Dead which lay at the edge of the graveyard beyond the village. A wall ran round a small group of pavilions and shrines set out in order along the sides of the courtyard. The stone bases were carved, and inlaid with Chinese porcelain plates. Between the altars grew flowering shrubs, and in a corner a twisted frangipani leaned forward, its naked branches bursting with starry blossoms. The courtyard was swept clean, immaculate except for the newly fallen flowers that shone like bits of paper on the black earth. There was an atmosphere of peace, silence and decay, of neglect and loving care. Gold and lacquer had tarnished, thatch had worn, while moss and mould crept over the vines and leaves that sculptors had once cut into the stones.

In the walls reliefs were filled with little figures—animals, fishes, humans, birds. In a baroque jungle of plants and scrolls heroes made war against demons, made love to maidens. Elegant and archaic, mystic and sensual, they moved in a shallow world which, however, was given infinite perspective by the ever-changing shadows cast by the sun. Between heroic episodes were scenes from daily life. Here the artist had turned from mythology to the joys of reporting. Men slew pigs, played flutes and gongs, fished and made exuberant love. Their activities had been recorded with an observant eye and an obvious love for detail, detail that seemed miraculous when I touched the stone that had been cut. Nets had mesh; flowers, stamens; vine trendrils stood out in actual spirals. I felt that if an earthquake should destroy them, these walls would quickly be built once more, carved with the same antlike patience.

As I passed the market I met Nyoman and Made Tantra. We sat for a while at the counter of the Javanese coffee-stall, piled with fruit and gaudy cakes, while Nyoman told me there would be a shadow-play that night in Kuta, a half-hour's drive away.

Will you go, Nyoman?

No, I must teach.

Perhaps Madé Tantra would like to come with me?

Madé Tantra spoke at last: Yes, I should like to.

I said that Sarda would call for him in the car on his way to the house that evening. We finished our coffee and left.

It was late in the evening when we arrived, and the performance was about to begin. Around the clearing in front of the men's clubhouse a hundred oil-lamps glowed on a hundred little tables. Some of these were for gambling, and the men sat around them noisily betting and banging down coins. Behind others sat the saleswomen with their sweets and bottles of *arac*. The air was filled with the scent of flowers that lay spread among the wares, to be sold to those seized with the sudden desire to make themselves attractive.

In a booth to one side was a lighted screen, and on the ground in front the people sat, waiting for the play to begin. From behind the screen came the sound of soft, swift music. I went to the back, to find a small crowd collected to watch the *dalang* (the operator) set up the puppets.

Half in trance he sat there cross-legged, close to the screen, beneath the light of a flaring oil-lamp that swung above his head. With careful deliberation he took a figure from the box, studied it, lovingly arranged its arms. At last he handed it to an assistant, to search for another in the box that was packed with figures.

The little puppets reminded me of the carvings I had seen that morning in the temple walls. They had the same delicacy, the same two-dimensional style; but instead of being cut in stone they had been chiselled out of thin leather and the details of their costumes stamped in tiny holes and slashes. They were not flexible, for only the arms moved, jointed at the shoulder and elbow. They were controlled by thin sticks attached to the hands; another stick ran down the centre of the body to brace it, and stuck out to act as handle. The puppets were so pierced with holes that when held against the light they were like lace. They were painted in gold and bright colours, and when the light fell on them they sparkled iridescently.

One by one the assistants took them—gods and demons, mortals, animals and little properties—and set them in their correct place to the right or left of the screen. This was significant. Gods went to the right, demons to the left, mortals to either side, according to their character. At last only a small space remained in the centre of the screen for the dramatic action. The puppets stood huddled at the sides, and from the outside the screen seemed framed in a tangled forest of shadows. In the centre the lamp glowed dimly through the screen, a mystic flame, disembodied.

At last the *dalang* was ready. He folded his hands, closed his eyes, and his lips moved silently. He was pronouncing to himself certain magic formulas, so that (*a*) his voice might be sweet, (*b*) his jokes meet with success, and (*c*) his performance be pleasing to all—to the gods and to mortals, male, female and hermaphrodite.

He stopped. Between the toes of one foot he held a small block of wood, which he struck against the puppet box several times as signal that the play would begin. I went outside to sit among the crowd and see the play in black and white.

From behind the screen came the voice of the *dalang* as he changed in old Javanese the introduction; the phrases rose like an incantation, as though he were summoning the shadows from another world. At last his voice grew still, the music stopped; the screen was a luminous rectangle in the dark, and behind it the little shadow-figures now began to appear. They came and went like moths flying across a beam of light.

At first there was little action. The exposition was an endless dialogue between two rival princes. (The play was from the wars of the Pandawas, said Tantra. He couldn't say what part.) They stood there, facing each other, punctuating their speeches with a slight movement of their long, outstretched arms. Their voices gently rose and fell like the breathing of a sleeper, but suddenly they would grow sharp, stridently falsetto, frigid and vicious with hate. The arms rose with sinister restraint, denouncing with swift, menacing gestures.

But now the clowns appeared. There were two pairs, each pair devoted attendants to a prince. From behind their heroes they threatened each other grotesquely. Their voices were insinuatingly intimate and oily. When an attendant spoke to his prince he raised his arms in a *sembah* of respect. And yet his voice seemed to be slyly mocking, for when he spoke the audience laughed loudly at his lines.

The scene changed. A tender dialogue took place between prince and princess. Back and forth the shadows swam, eclipsing each other, becoming one in a brief embrace. The *dalang's* voice was now honey-sweet, incredibly feline and erotic. But again the clowns appeared, this time male and female attendants. Their love-making was scandalous, and the climax held a great surprise. The figure of the male servant was jointed at more places than the arms, for suddenly an enormous phallus sprang out. In the uproarious laughter of the crowd there rose falsetto catcalls from the boys and high nasal cries from the women, exaggerated and sardonic.

At other times they listened attentively, as though they couldn't bear to miss a word. They cheered the defeat of the foe, and when the favourite clown dealt death to hundreds by unhooking his proud emblem of virility and using it as a club the children yelled with glee.

Sarda slept in the car. Made Tantra sat beside me, lost in the play. Once he got up to bring me a banana-leaf of rice and turtle meat. Then he brought a glass of *arac*. We sat there long after the moon had disappeared behind the palms. The sky grew pale; on the screen action had died and the lamp grew dim. In the distance you could hear the surf on the rocks. As they waited for the *dénouement* people dozed, while piled against each other the children slept, relaxed as kittens.

Suddenly, as though to synchronize with the approach of day, the play broke into life. Music burst out; warriors appeared; arrows flew; demons were slain, princess rescued. Within five minutes the play was over; the audience rose to its feet and slowly evaporated.

As we walked back to the car a man came up and spoke to Madé Tantra.

Tantra! How did you get here?

I came with the *tuan*.

They talked for a moment; I got into the back of the car and opened the thermos of coffee. I was frightfully sleepy.

Who was that? I asked Made Tantra as he got in beside me.

Lotring, a friend of Nyoman's. He taught the musicians who played to-night. He is *very* clever. . . .

I thought of the delicate music I had been listening to all evening. It had a strangely rushing sound, an indefinable, nervous energy, a laciness that seemed to translate magically into sound the movements of the mysterious little shadows. Four musicians sat facing one another, and as hands moved with incredible rapidity up and down above the keys, I could only think of four perfectly co-ordinated little pianos. Sometimes the music rang out harsh and clanging as a furious battle between the puppets took place; grew languid for a love scene; died to almost nothing as the "sweetly gentle" prince lamented. As usual, the sounds kept ringing in my ears long after the music had stopped.

It's almost day, I said to Made Tantra.

But he was sound asleep, his head falling against my shoulder as we turned a curve. In the early morning light people had begun to stir. Smoke rose from the little offerings that burned before the doorways in every village. In the mist men followed their water buffaloes out into the ricefields. Once home I fell on the bed and slept till noon.

At the time of full moon these shadow-plays seemed to be taking place all over the island. I would count a dozen in one evening as I drove along at night. What was the occasion? I would ask Sarda.

A marriage ceremony, a tooth-filing. The dedication of a new temple or clubhouse. A cremation. . . .

How many *dalangs* do you suppose there are in Bali?

He thought. He could not say. Perhaps a thousand. There were ten within a mile of my own village.

I went with Nyoman Kalér one evening to see the *dalang* who lived at the other end of the village, a Brahman by the name of Ida Bagus Anom. He was a great scholar, said Nyoman, well read in the classics. His father had been a priest. . . .

He was a grave man, with large, heavy-lashed eyes that were both intelligent and mystic. He was not surprised to see me, for Nyoman had announced my visit the day before. We sat talking while a boy dragged out the heavy puppet box and opened it. One by one the *dalang* took out the puppets and passed them to me, pronouncing their names. Some were so fragile, so pierced with patterns that the leather barely held together, and when you held them in the light they seemed completely transparent. Others were dark and squat, clumsy and absurd. Some carried spears, others gongs and drums. There were elephants, tigers, amorphous sea beasts, horses with fine chariots.

One puppet I looked at several minutes. It had an air of delicate nobility, with eyes long and narrow, lips curved in smile, a slender torso in gold that disappeared in a cloud of filmy *sarong*.

Arjuna, said the *dalang*. One of the Pandawa princes. They belong to the right.

The right?

The side of the gods.

As I looked at it he began to recite.

Such is the nature of his smile, that it discloses not his heart. An air of serenity conceals his trouble. Still undetermined, he cares not to reveal his thoughts. His intentions he will not quickly tell. . . .

These lines, said Nyoman, introduced Arjuna to the audience.

I picked up another puppet. It was the figure of a demon-woman, with staring eyes, a fanged mouth, great pendulous breasts.

Durga, goddess of death, said the *dalang*. A puppet of the left.

A third figure seemed to have Arjuna's face, but on the head was a towering crown, and the body was coloured green. This was the god Indra. Siva the Protector was almost identical, except for his colour and his four arms. But Siva the Destroyer had a dozen demons' heads, was surrounded with flames, had clawed hands and feet.

One more puppet held my attention. It was fat and grotesque, clad only in a breech clout. The lined face was filled with craft and genial sensuality; the eyes were wise and weary. It was Tualén, the faithful attendant of the hero. This was the beloved clown, whose impudence delighted the crowd, the Falstaff, the Sancho Panza who deflated high-flown motives and sentiment, criticizing even the gods. He it was whose jokes were both cynical and obscene, who parodied so outrageously the poetic love scenes, who could be counted on to think of ways to outwit the enemy at the last moment, and always dealt the last triumphant blow in battle.

Tualén! said the *dalang,* looking at the puppet with affection. He is older than them all. . . .

He put the puppets back, arranging them with care. Each had its proper place in the pile. Tualén must go last, on top. He put the arms in order, set the figure gently down, and closed the lid.

The lamp of the shadow theatre is the sun, said Ida Bagus Anom as we sat there in the dark pavilion; the screen is the sky. The god of the shadow-play is Iswara. He paused, went on.

The lamp lies in the eye of the *dalang.* The fire lies in the liver, the smoke in the voice. The oil is the fat, the wick the marrow, the puppet-sticks the sinews. . . .

As we walked home I thought how all the puppets in this Lilliputian drama were matched against each other as in a game of chess. (I was to find this so in all the plays.) The plot resolved itself to a simple tug-of-war between the forces of right and left. A character belonged once and for all to one side or the other, and stood or fell accordingly. The cards, it seemed, had long ago been stacked against the demons, for things *must* come out right in the end, as surely as dissonance dissolves in concord. Since the outcome was known in advance, the play lacked tension, and scenes could be cut or extended at will without affecting in any way the plot. Puppets or men, the play could be brought at any moment to a satisfactory conclusion, could be folded up like a telescope should an unexpected shower of rain make this necessary.

THE DESIGN IN THE MUSIC

S EVERAL NIGHTS IN THE WEEK the *légong* club of which Nyoman Kalér was the head met to practise in the Temple of Origins across the road. There were some thirty musicians in the club, and thirty more members to help carry the heavy instruments. Some of the boys and men worked in the fields, others did nothing at all. They gathered together in the early evening, after they had bathed in the stream that ran by the house. Sometimes they rehearsed with the little dancers, but more often it was for the sake of the music alone, and for hours the air would ring with swift, chiming sounds that rose and fell above the agitated throb of drums.

At first, as I listened from the house, the music was simply a delicious confusion, a strangely sensuous and quite unfathomable art, mysteriously aerial, aeolian, filled with joy and radiance. Each night as the music started up I experienced the same sensation of freedom and indescribable freshness. There was none of the perfume and sultriness of so much music in the East, for there is nothing purer than the bright, clean sound of metal, cool and ringing and dissolving in the air. Nor was it personal and romantic, in the manner of our own effusive music, but rather, sound broken up into beautiful patterns.

It was, however, more than this, as I was to find out. Already I began to have a feeling of form and elaborate architecture. Gradually, the music revealed itself as being composed, as it were, of different strata of sound. Over a slow and chantlike bass that hummed with curious penetration the melody moved in the middle register, fluid, free, appearing and vanishing in the incessant, shimmering arabesques that rang high in the treble as though beaten out on a thousand little anvils. Gongs of different sizes punctuated this stream of sound, divided and subdivided it into sections and inner sections, giving it metre and meaning. Through all this came the rapid and ever-changing beat of the drums, throbbing softly, or suddenly ringing out with sharp accents. They beat in perpetual cross-rhythm, negating the regular flow of the music, disturbing the balance, adding a tension and excitement which came to rest only with the cadence that marked the end of a section in the music.

Tiny cymbals pointed up the rhythm of the drums, emphasized it with their delicate clash, while the smallest of bells trembled as they were shaken, adding a final glitter, contributing shrill overtones that were practically inaudible.

Not long after I became acquainted with Nyoman Kalér, he had said I was welcome to come and listen as the men practised, and the friendly members of the club soon grew used to seeing me enter the courtyard after dark to sit beside them while they played. Their instruments were arranged in careful order, like an orchestra. The deep-voiced *jégogans*, with their heavy, trembling keys, were ranged at either side, while in the centre stood the soft-toned *g'ndérs* that played the melody. At the back were placed the little *gangsas*, on which the brilliant ornamental parts were performed. The drums, the leading instruments, were placed in front. At a short distance away the tones merged and blended so that the *gamelan* sounded like one great instrument.

I sat watching the concentration of the players. Boys of fourteen, men of twenty or sixty—all gave themselves up to the serious business of rehearsal. The music was rapid, the rhythms intricate. Yet without effort, with eyes closed, or staring out into the night, as though each player were in an isolated world of his own, the men performed their isolated parts with mysterious unity, fell upon the syncopated accents with hair's-breadth precision. I wondered at their natural ease, the almost casual way in which they played. This, I thought, is the way music was meant to be, blithe, transparent, rejoicing the soul with its eager rhythm and lovely sound. As I listened to the musicians, watched them, I could think only of a flock of birds wheeling in the sky, turning with one accord, now this way, now that, and finally descending to the trees.

What is the object of this club? I asked one night.

A little pleasure, a little profit, said Nyoman.

For the feasts and celebrations of Kedaton, their own village, they gave their services, as they were expected to do. In the temple they accompanied the ceremonial dances before the altars, played far into the night as they lulled priest and priestess to sleep with trance-music.

But when their *légong* dancers appeared in other villages, said Nyoman, the club expected to be paid. The money went into the treasury to be saved until the time of *galungan,* the week of feasts and holidays. Then was the time for joyous liquidation. The club bought pigs for a banquet and divided the remainder of the funds for holiday spending. But often it would be found that there was only a very small sum to share, for in the past six months the funds would have melted away on new costumes for the dancers, new gold leaf for the instruments, or a new set of headcloths for the members of the club.

For a club must sparkle, said Nyoman, when it appeared. Especially in another village. Otherwise they would be too *ashamed. . . .*

The iridescent music of Nyoman's *gamelan* had its roots in a distant past, could be traced to the courts of ancient Java, and from there to a still more ancient India and China. Here to-day it had blossomed miraculously into something new. Successive generations of musicians had recreated it, transformed it, quickening the rhythm and modifying the instruments so that they rang with greater brilliance. An elaborate technique of interplay among the different instruments had slowly evolved, a weaving of voices around and over the melody, enveloping it in a web of rich though delicate ornamentation. And yet no separate part was in itself too difficult; all united to form a shimmering, pulsating whole, held together by the discipline of long rehearsal. As for the composers themselves, who could say? Long since dead, they were, presumably, simple craftsmen. Their names were unknown.

But how was it possible, I asked, for men to remember through the years this music of the past? If there were no notes. . . . In my country, I said, we write down our music. I showed him a printed page. He looked at it with curiosity.

There are also written notes in Bali, he said. But few people can read them, few have ever seen them. A book is rare.

If you could find one for me. . . .

He thought his friend Lotring, a musician who lived in Kuta, owned one. He would go one day and see.

He came a week later saying, Here is the book.

It was a bundle of dried palm leaves, trimmed and neatly tied together. It was old and brittle, and crumbled as I opened it. Inside, three or four lines of Balinese script stretched across each strip of leaf.

That is the *pokok,* the stalk, the trunk of the music, he said.

It was nothing more than the meagre tones of the chant in the bass, the barest of outlines. Nothing to indicate rhythm, nothing to indicate melody or the elaborate interweaving of sounds. A scratch here and there marked the accent of a gong and that was all.

It was only a reminder, said Nyoman. The rest, he explained, existed in the mind of the teacher.

Balinese music is based on five tones. In the sacred writings of the priests these tones have cosmological significance, for they are linked with the gods of the five directions, north, east, south, west and centre, where in the middle of a lotus sits Batara Siva, Creator, Destroyer, Lord God of All. His mystic colour is white; his sacred syllable *hing*; and the tone for this syllable is *ding*.

The gods of the other directions have also their colours— red, yellow, blue, black; their syllables and tones—*dong, déng, doong, dang.* . . .

But he didn't think, said Nyoman when I asked him, that the boys and men of the clubs thought of this as they played.

Music is for pleasure, he said. It pleases both gods and men. In the writings of the priests there were long directions about the dances and *gamelans* "necessary" at a temple feast. It was to be regretted that to-day these directions were only half carried out. The gods felt slighted, complained more and more frequently, through the mouth of the priest or medium in trance. . . .

Thus music, I learned, had its "stem," its primary tones (which it was possible to preserve in writing) from which the melody expanded and developed as a plant grows out of a seed. The glittering ornamental parts which gave the music its shimmer, its sensuous charm, its movement—these were the "flower parts," the "blossoms," the *kantilan*. (Like a dancer, Nyoman explained in parenthesis, whose body is the trunk, whose arms and head are melody, and whose hands form the flowers, which are the "gilding" of the dance.)

It was in these flower parts, he said, that a teacher showed his inventiveness, a *gamelan* its ability. The style was always changing, although the stem-tones remained the same. When he was a child, at court, the music had been slower, simpler, softer. But to-day it had become very difficult. . . .

One evening Nyoman brought to the house a *g'ndér* from the *gamelan* and began playing the soft love-music from the *légong* dance. A row of thin metal keys hung suspended over a row of upright bamboo tubes, and trembled at the least touch. As he sat there on the floor, the keys came to his shoulders. He held a little mallet in each hand; his fingers were relaxed, and the mallets seemed to fall upon the keys rather than strike them. The tones were limpid, with a mysterious, prolonged echo from the tubes, and as he played he seemed to lose himself in the dreaminess of the sounds he was producing.

A *g'ndér* is delicately adjusted and easily goes off pitch. If the bamboo resonators are out of tune, the tone is dead, but when the instrument is perfectly in tune it has a haunting sound, prolonged and softly ringing. It is the presence of many of these instruments that gives a *gamelan* its floating, disembodied sound.

The *g'ndér* was followed by a drum, on which Nyoman began to explain the different drum strokes. He held it across his knees, drumming lightly with his fingers—you only used the sticks for the great ceremonial music or the heroic dances. He used the finger tips, the palm of the hand, the ball of the thumb, striking the drum sometimes near the middle of the parchment to give a deep, hollow sound, or near the rim, when it rang out tensely. The two hands fluttered in endless patterns—the soft, rapid throb for the love scenes, light tripping rhythms for more playful moments, tense, heavy drumming filled with sharp, excited accents for the battles, the abductions, the appearance of a god or demon.

Another day he brought a little *gangsa*, to show me how the flower parts were composed. Soon the house was filled with gongs, drums, cymbals and flutes, looking like a museum in disorder. But I wished for a piano, for I was beginning to feel out of practice. I was also eager to try out some of the melodies from the *légong gamelan* that I had begun to write down, to see how they would sound.

It was by chance that I heard of one that belonged to a resident on the island who was willing to let me have the use of it for a few months. It created a sensation in the village when it arrived, for nothing like it had ever been seen. It was a shrill upright; its tones echoed disagreeably against the walls and the cement floor, but it was surprisingly in tune. The afternoon of its arrival the house was filled with visitors who came to listen to the strange new music that was suddenly heard in the village. They pressed the keys, examined the pedals.

What a great voice! they exclaimed. What a number of "leaves" (the keys). What are the foot-brakes for?

I showed them the mechanism. I played a melody from the *légong* which I had written down, filling in the gongs with the left hand. Lost in admiration they left to spread the news in the village.

The *g'ndér* looked very fragile beside the piano. It was beautifully carved; little animals peered out from a forest of leaves, and its keys jangled softly as we moved it. The piano was a monument of cold efficiency. As a ruler is marked, it divided the octave into twelve precise degrees. The tuning of the *g'ndér* was more irregular. Only some of the tones agreed with the piano, while others were strange and unaccountable as certain tones in the voice of a Negro blues singer. Heard separately, each instrument sounded convincing. When I listened to one after the other I was deeply disturbed. The piano sounded harsh and out of tune after the softer intonation of the *g'ndér.*

Since the piano had twelve tones to the *g'ndér's* five, the music I played held no meaning for Nyoman. Tourists have brought back romantic tales of the Balinese taste for Bach, but this was quite impossible. Nyoman's reaction to Western music was typical. It was a complicated noise without order, tempestuous and baffling in its emotional climaxes, dragging on and on and leading nowhere.

Your music is like someone crying, he said. Up and down, up and down, for no reason at all.

A simple tune on the white keys might catch his interest, but the harmony of the left hand ruined it for him. His ears could not filter the sound made by so many notes so closely spaced.

His reaction to rhythm was just as negative. Balinese music is tense and syncopated like jazz, and when I played a waltz, or an adagio from some sonata, Nyoman would exclaim—Where is the beat?

Where is no beat! Like a bird with a broken wing!

Only my jazz records would he listen to at all. He found the singing curious, the trumpet of Louis Armstrong fantastic, but he felt the rhythm at once.

THE GODS DESCEND

IN TWO DAYS IT WOULD BE be full moon, when the feast of the Temple of the Ancestors would take place.

For a month the women of Nyoman Kalér's household had been busy, like the women of every other household in the village, in preparing the offerings, the endless cakes, fritters, sweets, and ceremonial objects made of palm leaf. In Nyoman's house confusion reigned, especially the last few days, for new costumes were being made for the three little *légong* dancers, and snips and scraps of bright-coloured cloth lay scattered about among the piles of cakes and fruits. Men cut and sewed; over a table three boys leaned, their faces flecked with gold leaf as they painted enormous flowers and birds in gold on the costumes of the dancers.

The morning mist was still in the air on the day of the feast as one by one the men came out of their doorways and walked towards the temple, to begin the festive cooking. It was not long before the courts were in a turmoil. Soon there was the sound of chopping as groups of men prepared the spice, the sound of soft scraping as they grated huge mounds of coconut. Above the laughter and conversation pigs shrieked as they were carried into the kitchens. Ducks gabbled, while about the court chickens fluttered, blood still dripping from their necks. From simmering caldrons the acrid steam of bitter *blimbing* leaves mingled with the bright aroma of frying pork. Cooks stirred, prodded, turned the spits, carefully lifted from pans wide coils of sausage, to set them out to cool above the reach of dogs that now flocked in the courts. In the air there hung the sharp, fresh scent of ginger, lime and tamarind.

All at once, above this cheerful bustle there floated the sound of tranquil, golden music. The *Gamelan* with the Great Gongs had arrived. Exempt from other work, the musicians sat in the shade of a pavilion playing the music appropriate to ceremonial occasions—the stately Beat of Eight that lasted half an hour; the Beat of Four, the lively Beat of One. They rested for a while; began again: Clucking Cock, with its curious rhythm; the tuneful Snapping Crocodile. Throughout the morning the air was filled with sound that gladdened the hearts of all, causing the temple to ring with "festive noise."

In and out the women came with their offerings, to arrange them by the shrines of the inner temple, until the sun was overhead and, by what seemed to me a miracle, the cooking was suddenly over.

While in the temple the village elders banqueted ceremoniously, the rest of the food was carefully divided and taken home, but not before the tiniest of servings, each meticulously complete with microscopic portions of rice and hashes, shreds of chicken and all the rest, were set aside for the gods.

A temple feast is a complex ritual, an anniversary, a three-day honouring of the gods. On the evening of the first day the gods are invited to descend and enter the shrines prepared for them. For three days they are feasted and entertained. Before they leave, advice and favours will be sought; they are then informed the feast is over, and ceremoniously requested to depart.

Late that night I walked down the road with Made Tantra to

witness the arrival of the gods.

The inner court was filled with silent, expectant men and women. They sat there on the ground, quietly waiting. Below the shrines the offerings were spread out, and before them sat the priest and three elderly priestesses. Incense burned. In the silence the priest prayed, rang his bell, began a new prayer. Eyes closed, the priestesses swayed ever so slightly.

From a pavilion came the faint chime of a *g'ndér.* In the shadow I could barely make out a few instruments from the *légong gamelan.* A single musician played softly, waiting for the others to arrive.

A long, slow chant began, faintly at first, then growing in volume as others joined in. The priestesses swayed more violently, tossing their heads from side to side.

Have the gods come? I asked Madé after a while.

Not yet; soon, perhaps.

How will you know?

When one of them begins to speak.

But presently the priestesses stopped moving. They sat there very still. The priest got up.

Madé murmured. It did not happen.

What now?

Later they will try again. Sometimes you must wait a whole day.

Outside, in the clearing before the temple, all was light and movement. A crowd had gathered, waiting for the entertaining *arja* play to begin. The actors had only just arrived, said Made. They were still dressing.

We sat down by one of the little gambling-tables where a noisy card game was in progress. The tiny cards were marked with symbols, and as Made explained, it seemed very much like *mahjong.* The players cheerfully invited me to take a hand. For the sake of sociability I joined them, but the combinations were endless, the rules involved, and in a little while I got up, to return inside the temple.

Once more the priestesses had given themselves up to the soft chant of women's voices. Soon after we came in there was a sudden cry from the oldest, and she began to toss wildly about. In a low intimate voice the priest questioned her. At first she would not answer, and cried as though her heart were breaking. Then at last she spoke, and we knew that the gods were here.

Where did the gods actually stay while here on earth? In the tiniest objects, apparently; in stones, in bits of wood, in little golden figures. These precious objects were kept locked in the temple, to be taken out, purified and set in the shrines for the three days of the feast. At one moment this feast seemed scaled for the propitiation of giants, at the next it was like a dolls' tea party. Images and stones were wrapped in the brightest of cloths, tied with golden sashes, set on silken cushions, while their food was set out for them in the smallest of dishes. Yet woe betide the community if the gods felt slighted and grew angry. Now, suddenly, they were titans; in their anger they spread disaster in the form of drought and epidemics of plague.

On the afternoon of the second day the dancers from Kesiman arrived, to perform with masks one of the ancient chronicle plays that dealt with the early kings of Bali. We watched an episode from the life of the King of Bedulu, whose mask was a terrifying combination of human eyes and mouth with the snout and tusks of a boar.

He had got the head of a pig in this way, explained Nyoman Kalér, as we stood watching. He had been born strong in magic power. When he was a child he often amused himself by cutting off his head and asking his attendant to put it back on again. One day his head rolled into the river and was carried away. In desperation the servant cut off the head of a boar and placed it on his neck. . . .

But in the play we only saw him defeated by a prince from Java, whose name was Gaja Mada, Mad Elephant.

On the third night, while in front of the temple the audience watched the shadow-play, the gods departed.

The departure had been preceded by a ceremonial dance. While, from the shadows, there came the sound of animated music from the *gamelan,* a group of women stepped forth to dance the *gabor,* the presentation of offerings of wine, oil, incense; Their shoulders were bare, their breasts bound with woven scarves, and in their hair were crowded orchids, jasmine, gardenias. I recognized Nyoman's two wives among them as they danced, seriously, tranquilly, as though in their sleep. In and out of the shrines they wove, disappearing in the shadows, emerging into the moonlight, until at last they paused before the altars, where a priestess stood, to fan the essence of the offerings in the direction of the gods.

It was close to dawn when, in the now almost deserted courtyard, the priestess fell once more in trance. In a hoarse, exhausted voice she announced the presence of the god. It was the god now speaking. There was a pause. The god called attention to the poor condition of the temple. It was in need of repair. Another pause. The priest now asked advice about certain village affairs. What must the offerings be for the next feast? Back and forth the voices went, until at last the priestess grew silent and would talk no more. In the dim light of early morning she woke, looked dazedly around, and we knew the gods had left.

KESYUR

THE HOUSE WAS NOW forever filled with visitors, who wandered in at all times of the day, to chat, or sit quietly, hoping I might be moved to play the phonograph. Made Tantra had given me a monkey, which I kept chained to the veranda post; Gusti had brought me a white cockatoo. Its wings were clipped, and it roamed the house, fought with the monkey, or sat on the back of my chair at lunch talking softly to itself, or raising its yellow crest in sudden excitement.

When strangers met at my house they were uneasy until each had discovered the other's caste. Was the other a Brahman? A Satrya? Or a plain Sudra or commoner like himself? For although the ancient caste system was borne easily enough these days, there were still formalities in everday life which must be carefully observed.

Such as the question of seating.

What distinguished my simple house as having been designed for a man of rank was the veranda, which was built on two different levels. A whole etiquette revealed itself in the way people sat.

When Ida Bagus Anom, the grandson of the old priest for whom the "Mountain of Flowers" had been built, came to visit with Made Tantra he sat on the lower step, while Made sat below, on the ground. Since Ida Bagus was a Brahman, he could actually have sat level with me, but he was twelve years younger, and as he was well brought up he was aware he owed me the respect of youth. When Sarda, who was a Sudra, came to say the car was waiting, he sat on the lower step if no one was there of higher caste. Otherwise he might sit below, but since he was proud and independent, he preferred to walk around to the back and sit with Gusti. Nyoman Kalér, who was also a Sudra, but the head of the *banjar*, chose the upper step the first night he came. He was paying me sufficient respect, for I was still on a higher level, in a chair, while he sat on the floor at my feet. As we became intimate, I insisted he sit in a chair, which flattered but did not discompose him. One day as we sat together, a tall young man strode in, came up the steps and handed me a note from the *Controlleur* in Den Pasar. He was only a Government clerk, but he was an Anak Agung, a prince, and Nyoman, who knew him, at once got out of his chair and sat down on the lower step.

For this reason strangers politely inquired of each other their caste immediately they met. In high, formal Balinese they asked the question, Where do you sit? Should the caste difference be not too great, conversation would continue in this formal language. But if a prince found himself talking to a Sudra he would immediately use the rough "low" dialect, while the other continued to address him in sweet flowery phrases, constructed, to the best of his ability, in the elliptical syntax of "high."

In the family there were also four levels. Children had their titles: Wayan, eldest-born, Nyoman, Made and Ketut, the fourth.

What happens with a fifth child? I asked Nyoman Kalér.

You begin again, he answered.

Sarda could no longer work for me, for he wished to return to his home near Buléléng. Made Tantra suggested a friend of his to take Sarda's place. We are like brothers, he said. He wears my clothes and I wear his. This is his ring, he said, showing me his hand.

Kesyur was several years older than Made Tantra. He had a dash about him, a careless elegance, and a moody temper—sulky one moment, eager the next—which seemed to have won him a widespread reputation as a charmer. Even in remote villages the girls in the market-place would cry out as we stopped, Kesyur! Kesyur is here! These cries of joy he answered in an offhand manner or ignored altogether, but I felt he was not annoyed.

The pawnshop figured prominently in his life. I had not known him two weeks before he asked for a loan. His *banjar* was giving a feast; he must have the tailor make him a new coat, and get his ring out from the pawnshop. Two days after the feast the ring was back where it belonged. In fact, all of Kesyur's property, his bicycle, *sarongs* and the kris that had been his father's, remained there most of the time.

In that way they can't be stolen, he explained.

One morning he came in looking slightly preoccupied.

What's the matter, Kesyur? You look worried.

A little troubled, but also a little pleased. . . .

He sat down on the veranda. Thoughtfully, systematically, he pulled out each finger of the right hand until he heard the bones click faintly. It's like this, he said. Once more he paused, to perform the same operation on the left hand.

It seemed that between the two adjoining *banjars* of his village there was great rivalry. Some time back the young men of Mogan (Kesyur's *banjar*) had built a new clubhouse. The men of Pagan (the other) immediately began to build one which was larger. The time had now come for the consecrations.

Two days ago, said Kesyur, the men of Mogan slaughtered the largest pig they could find for the feast. They nailed the head to the clubhouse with pride. But Pagan has shamed them by slaughtering a goat! Last night the men of Mogan met, and decided that they will kill a water buffalo, to put an end to this competition. But the head of Kesyur's village has forbidden this useless extravagance.

So, said Kesyur, Mogan will give a dazzling series of dances and plays. For a week there will be shadow-plays, *gandrung* dances, *arja* plays—all of the best! Let Pagan try to outdo that!

But the matter has not rested there, for the men of Pagan have sent word that they will attend all these performances wearing golden shoes.

Golden shoes?

Like one time in Buleléng, said Kesyur. All the men of one club appeared at *galungan-time* on golden bicycles. Frames, rims, even the spokes and pedals—all had been covered with gold. It was handsome! But if the men of Pagan appear in gold shoes Mogan will retaliate next *galungan* by dressing entirely in white.

Then we shall have won in the end, said Kesyur triumphantly, for what is brighter than white?

I agreed, although I wondered how white cotton could take precedence over gold leaf, until I remembered that white is the holy colour, symbol of purity, worn by the priests. No matter how stained the cloth, there was always that to be said about it, there was nothing brighter. I asked when the performances were to begin. To-morrow, he answered, adding that his *banjar* invited me.

I arrived next evening to find a chair and table laden with sweets, cigarettes and pink soda placed for my comfort on a platform inside the clubhouse. A large crowd watched the performance. I looked in vain for the golden shoes, and asked Kesyur about the matter. He seemed very happy as he answered.

Empty talk! They are wearing only gold headcloths, which they have had since last year. . . .

PORTRAIT OF A PRINCE

KESYUR CAME FROM SABA, a village near the sea some sixty miles away, where I had seen the little *légong* dancers with Sarda. One day I mentioned this, and he spoke proudly:

My rajah spends great sums on his dancers. Their headdresses are pure gold. There are none to compare!

But when I asked him if it were true his prince was in love with one of them he said briefly it "could be" and changed the subject.

One evening we drove by a temple near Saba, where crowds of people outside indicated a performance. My rajah's *légong!* cried Kesyur, stopping the car with a jolt. We pushed through the throng; a dance was in full progress. On a mat in front of the musicians sat the Anak Agung with a drum across his knees. He was absorbed as before, and I saw him laugh with pleasure as a dancer caught a syncopated accent with beautiful accuracy.

The Anak Agung was soon aware of my presence. He recognized Kesyur, and when the performance was over he came up. After Kesyur had accounted for me I told him how much I admired his dancers. He smiled.

Very poor! But perhaps in a year's time. . . .

He invited me to return with him to the palace. There was an eagerness about him that I thought completely charming, and I was sorry I was not free to accept. I said I should like to come to see him very soon.

On the way home Kesyur told me a little about the royal family. They were related to the most highborn Déwa Agung, ruler of Karangasem, and owned the land south of Klungkung to the sea. Once the family had been rich. But times were bad to-day, for their income derived largely from their ricefields. These had been dry for years; the stream from the mountains which once supplied their irrigation had been diverted in a completely different direction by a Government-built dam.

Where does the Anak Agung find money to spend on his dancers? I asked.

Kesyur laughed. He plays the cockfights, he said.

One afternoon we drove to Saba and stopped the car before the palace gates. In the courtyard fruit trees and flowering shrubs were set in order. The rusty chassis of a car stood in one corner; in the centre was a pool, with a fountain which no longer played. A servant approached to say that His Highness was in the far pavilion.

We had taken the Anak Agung unawares, for as we came up to the veranda we saw him descend from a step ladder, and wipe his hand on his *sarong,* which was all he wore, tucked high around his waist. He greeted me, however, with warmth and composure.

Welcome, he said. Although I am in the midst of work. I am painting.

He led me up into the pavilion. It was open on three sides, but towards the back was a door, and over the door was a half-finished fresco. It was a crowded scene from the shadow-play, depicting in lacquer and gold a terrific battle between gods and demons. We sat down at a table, Kesyur taking his place at our feet.

Tea? Brandy? Before I could answer he had called out to a servant. He was perhaps thirty, short, robust, with glowing eyes and a brusque, impulsive voice. I felt at ease with him at once, won by his sudden smile.

Attendants entered the pavilion, begging forgiveness, with trays piled high with fruit. Bottles of raspberry soda, rum and *arac* completed the refreshments. Begging forgiveness again for setting these down before us, the attendants backed away, to sit on the floor at the edge of the pavilion.

The Anak Agung wanted to know about America. Were there taxes? Was there a queen? Was it true there were white servants?

Then he asked about the temples and the gods. What were our offerings like? Our priests?

I answered as best I could.

We sat there, tearing off the crimson skin of a litchi or breaking open a mangosteen. We spat the pips on the floor, where they were immediately gathered by an attendant who, after asking permission, carried the royal discard in his hands to throw outside the gate.

Kesyur spoke up, to tell about the piano. But the Anak Agung knew all about it.

Orgel, he said. I saw one in Java. I shouldn't want one; I prefer my *gamelan*. . . .

I said that an advantage of the piano was that it took only one man.

But there are no drums! he said. How can music live without the drums? It is like the beat of the heart. It is the blood running in the veins.

He rose with me when I got up to go, begging me not to leave, but spend at least the night. To-morrow I should watch him rehearse his *légong* dancers. I should have done so willingly were it not for the thought of my house wide open, with only

Gusti to guard it. We finally departed, though not before the Anak Agung had asked me if I would take his picture. He disappeared, to return in a white jacket with a high collar and a faded sun helmet. His face turned blank and funereal as he stood there waiting. But with the click of the shutter his-smile returned, and he walked with me to the car, followed by a servant bearing a basket of litchis and emerald-skinned pomelos. His gardens were famed for these, said Kesyur later, especially the litchis. These were a sure sign of favour, for almost all the trees on the island belonged to the Chinese, who held them under contract, and would not sell a cutting at any price.

It was no secret that Anak Agung Bagus was bringing his house to final ruin with his extravagances. He bet wildly at cockfights, and when he won he simply squandered his money. When it was not on his dancers it was for something else; he would dash from one end of the island to the other in a delapidated Chevrolet in search of a trained turtle-dove, for which he would pay a hundred guilders if he thought the song of the bird was worth it.

When he lost, one more ricefield would be put up for sale. His older brother complained so bitterly at the Government office that the *Controlleur* had put the Anak Agung under oath to give up cockfighting. It was like forbidding a fish to swim, a bird to sing. He would stop for a while, but sooner or later I would find him at some great fight, miles from Saba, squatting with the rest, and trying to look incognito, with several followers to carry his vicious-looking birds and his bag of silver ringgits. When we met, he could not keep from confiding in glee if he had won. I could tell when disaster had fallen by his tragic silence, and the utter impossibility of bringing a smile to his face.

The palace was large and rambling, and badly run to seed. The gate and front courts were still imposing, though overgrown with grass and ferns, but behind the wall that hid the older part of the palace from view things were in a bad state of repair. Pavilions leaned crazily; thatch had worn thin; carved and gilded pillars were bored by beetles and gnawed by rats. Chickens roosted at night on lacquered crossbeams, and all day long the dogs wandered about, snatching unguarded morsels of food from the kitchens, and howling at the sight of a stranger. Geese descended the palace steps at dawn, stately and hostile, and ascended again at dusk, piercing the air with their loud, unmusical notes.

As our friendship grew the Anak Agung's gifts (without which I could never depart) became more personal—a ring; a handsome fighting-cock; a cutting from one of his precious litchi trees. And always three or four *gurami* fish fresh from the water, still twitching on the thong that held them by the gills.

These fish were fat and delicious, and were raised in an artificial pond that lay in the park behind the palace. Once this had been a fine garden, but now hibiscus, gardenia, jasmine and poinsettia fought among themselves beneath the confusion of palms. Orchids drooped from boughs, and the ground was black and slippery. The pond had a little pleasure pavilion in the centre, connected to the land by a rickety bamboo bridge, and here the Anak Agung often took his siesta, alone or accompanied.

One day we fished.

The surface of the pond was without a ripple, and reflected every leaf from the overhanging trees. We stood there staring at the water, while a boy tossed scarlet hibiscus into the pool. They floated, and soon the fish began to rise and drag them under. Nets were thrown; we picked the best and threw the others back. Suddenly the Anak Agung had an idea. His fishing rod was brought, and he took a fish, hooked it and dropped it in the water. For a moment he played it; his eyes shone with excitement. But all at once the fish was off the hook and gone.

We stood in silent sympathy while the Anak Agung recovered, and returned to the palace with the other fish safe inside a basket.

He had inherited his warmth from his mother. Agung Biang weighed two hundred and fifty pounds; she had an adorable smile, and eyes that could become tender and wistful. Sometimes she placed a few jasmine blossoms in her grey hair, but otherwise she paid little heed to her appearance, for she wore nothing but a wide strip of batik, carelessly tucked around her waist and falling to her feet. It was always on the verge of coming undone; every five minutes it would work loose; but with a poise that was regal indeed she would pull the cloth up an inch and tighten it once more.

She never failed to give me an intimate and maternal welcome when I arrived, putting one vast bare arm about my neck and telling me I was her son, while the other hand felt the texture of my shirt, or slipped inside to gently caress my flesh. Once more the finger tips would return to the cloth, run lightly over it. Silk, she would say approvingly, real silk. Will you give it to me? But I knew from the remote and dreamy tone of her voice that she did not want it in the least, that the question was simply to test my affection.

No, Agung Biang. Your child would catch cold driving home without a shirt. Besides, what would you do with it? It couldn't possibly fit you.

She laughed, and would say, But you must give your mother *something*, bring her *something* from Den Pasar the next time you come.

What would Agung Biang like?

She thought. Some perfume perhaps, or a cake of scented soap. Or one of those new celluloid flowers in the Japan store.

Then she would carefully peel a tangerine and put the sections into my mouth one by one.

Agung Biang supervised the kitchens herself. These were a group of pavilions in one of the inner courts, where pigs ran in and out among the piles of coconuts and mats of fish spread out to dry in the sun. She did nothing so unregal as to cook, but she directed the cooks, and assembled and spiced the more complicated dishes. I loved to watch her, now frowning and absorbed. Around her, girls grated piles of coconut, while trembling old men peeled and chopped shallots and garlic, chillies and aromatic roots and ground them to a paste. With a severe and critical air, she smelt or tasted the sauces and hashes, adding palm sugar, fish-paste, verbena or whatever seemed needed to give that final flavour. With a wide and noble gesture, she refused badly prepared coconut milk or a scrawny chicken. With noisy indignation, she condemned a duck egg that was found to be not quite fresh. And when at last the dishes were finally prepared she would invite me, as I sat there looking on, to taste and comment. Was there enough salt? she would ask earnestly. Was it sharp enough? Perhaps a little more ginger, or a squeeze more of lime juice.

Her dishes were endless: fish baked in banana leaves; ant-eater stewed and served in a bamboo tube; lobster in a sauce of coconut cream; sea turtle in a sauce of crushed peanuts; skewers of birds no larger than bumble bees (could they be humming birds? I wondered, as I took three at one bite) and, strangest of all, small green packages like cigarettes which, when unrolled, were found to contain a mixture of toasted coconut and the larvre of dragon-flies.

This repast, a strange blend of *Arabian Nights* and *Midsummer Night's Dream*, would appear after a morning of *légong* practice. For two hours Gusti Bagus rehearsed the children to the point of exhaustion. He sat on the floor, his drum in his lap, his gaze fixed on the dancers. Suddenly he would jump up to correct a position, straighten a shoulder or turn a head a little more to the side. Once more he took up the drum. When at last the lesson came to an end the children disappeared (often to return in the late afternoon for another two hours), while we retired to another pavilion for lunch. Around us the courtyard glared in the fierce light of the sun, now directly overhead. Languor descended; voices spoke softly. There was that strange noonday quiet, that moment of utter timelessness, when all life seems suspended.

Now, after we had eaten, I would walk through the park to the pavilion on the pond, which was given to me each time *I* came. Surrounded by water in this forgotten park, in this far island of friendly and mysterious people—this seemed the final exquisite isolation. In the stillness two turtle-doves called and answered monotonously, I read until I fell asleep.

The three little *légong* dancers of Saba were composed of a pair, who played the leading roles, and a third, the *chondong* or attendant, who introduced them, handed them their fans, and played the minor parts, such as the abducted princess in the tale of Lasem, or the raven that flies before his face, foretelling his death. The pair should resemble each other in beauty, form, complexion, said Gusti Bagus, as closely as possible. They should match "like two peas, like twin breasts." But the beauty of the *chondong* should be as different as night from day.

And indeed, as I watched the dance unfold, I thought how much the charm of the dance depended on the play of duplication and contrast. At the opening, before the story "emerged," the two children began to move as though, by some optical illusion, they were the double projection of a single image. From the tip of the finger, the tilt of the head, down to the position and angle of the foot, their movements were identical. Suddenly they would break away, to go off in opposite directions. They returned, but now their gestures reflected, as though one were mirroring the other. As the story began, characters emerged, yet with utmost delicacy, for even the most dramatic gesture was done with stylized restraint. A fluid motion of the hand was sorrow and weeping; Lasem was killed with the tap of the fan and a little shove.

But when the *chondong* took up a pair of gilded wings to become the raven, the drumming grew turbulent and she danced with violence. She created a strange atmosphere of brilliance and sombre mystery. She was a bird in a storm, soaring against the wind as her wings inclined first one way then another.

I never tired of watching these rehearsals, of watching the miraculous transmission of energy from the Anak Agung to the children. His restless nature found expression in feverish tempos and violent accents, and I thought he would burn them out with his intensity, his desire for perfection. Yet they responded like a flash to the slightest change of his drumbeat. They seemed as completely under his control as though they were shadow-puppets and he the operator.

As I watched I remembered Sarda's remark about the prince's love for the *chondong*. She had a wild beauty that I could easily imagine might trouble him. She was a year older than the others, and in another year would be no longer a child. Her manner was grave, and when she was not dancing she sat fingering her ring, her eyes downcast, hidden beneath long lashes. But the only indication of the Anak Agung's infatuation was the loving care he put in correcting her gestures, the relentless way in which he led her for the tenth time through a long and exhausting passage.

CHETIG

ONE AFTERNOON I RETURNED from Saba, where I had been staying for a few days, to find the house locked and deserted. I had no key, and my indignation rose as I waited until the *koki* finally walked in.

Tabé, tuan, she said with revolting sweetness.

Where is Gusti? I asked crossly.

There was a look of quiet triumph on her face as she prepared to tell me the worst.

That Gusti? He had gone on a binge. He had been drunk for

two days on my gin. Yesterday he set off the fireworks I had been saving. They went all over—into the kitchen, out into the ricefields. She described the course of a rocket travelling along the ground. She had fled. . . .

When Gusti finally came in he had nothing to say. I fired him, not for this sin, but because I was suddenly quite bored with him, his laziness, his dullness which not even this escapade could brighten. I said I would not need him any longer, and in a gentle voice he answered, Good, *tuan*, and left.

The *koki* was delighted. I even heard her singing in the kitchen, in a cracked, Chinese voice, a monotonous phrase from a Malayan song:

> *When the civet grows blind*
> *The chicken is lighthearted;*
> *When the cat loses its teeth*
> *The mouse grows bold.*

I got a boy from the hotel, a tall, brisk lad who put a high polish on the glasses and served dinner with a flourish. He folded the napkin into a bishop's mitre, and dropped a slice of lemon into the finger bowl. He was part Javanese, and whether because of his elegance or his temperament, there were no more quarrels in the back of the house. I wouldn't say that romance stirred within the koki's dark interior; that would be like expecting a blossom from an umbrella handle. Yet there was a faint warmth about her, like a pebble left exposed for a little while in the sun, when she saw Pugog remove stains from the silver, clean out the storeroom and give a new sense of order to the house.

But the *koki* was to go too, soon afterwards, because of her impossible behaviour towards Nyoman Kalér and others who came daily to see me. Was it jealousy, or plain bad temper? In any case, she could not get along with Balinese. She resented their freedom about the place; in the Dutch houses where she had worked, the scene (I knew) was quite different; there natives entered by the back door only. She could be rude and vent her Mohammedan dislike with impunity, while they in turn would accept it indifferently, as part of the established and already familiar regime of colonization.

But here in my house they came as friends, and I found her ways intolerable. The climax came after a little feast, when I had invited Nyoman and several boys and men from the *gamelan* for a roast pig. Pork was as repulsive to her as to an orthodox Jew, and for two days she went about, black as thunder, refusing to wash up or even touch her defiled pots and pans and making sharp comments on people as they went in and out of the house. She left out nothing; she dwelt on their habits, their clothes, their heathenishness, their uncircumcision. When Nyoman at last said he would no longer come to the house while she was there, I let her know that she must leave. She went back to work in a Dutch house. From time to time I saw her in the market in town. Then she would call out, her face all smiles:

Tabé, tuan! What is the news?

Pugog brought his cousin Made Reteg to take her place. It was like the sun after a month of clouds. She was young, and she sang as she worked, and she knew everyone who came to the house. She was a little shy at first, and she was both amused and confused at the idea of having to cook for me, for her only experience had been when she had worked (here she was rather vague) in the household of Abdul Bey, a Bombay merchant in Den Pasar. We now settled down to an alimentation which was constantly filled with surprise, for it was part Javanese, part Balinese, with an occasional Chinese dish and now and then an extraordinary Moslem dessert, poetically flavoured with rose-water.

I have always had a keen curiosity about food and cooking, and I would sit on the edge of the veranda making notes as

Reteg prepared some stew or fragrant *lawar* or hash. One was especially rich and elusive in flavour.

She took a chicken and split it in half, and grilled it over the coals to a light brown. Then she tore the meat into the finest shreds. These she mixed with thin coconut shavings and crushed them together in a deep bowl, so that the oil from the coconut permeated the meat. Then she added the spice, a paste of young ginger, onion, red peppers and a dash of fish-paste that had been gently fried in new coconut oil. Over this she poured freshly pressed coconut milk, thick as cream. The mixture was then kneaded to a smooth mass and finished with lime juice.

It was altogether delicious. You ate a little at a time, together with a spoon of rice. But Made insisted I must use my hand, I must *taste* my hand as I ate. It was true; the food was so delicately spiced, so fresh that if you used fork or spoon the flavour was killed at once by the chill and corrosive taste of silver.

Pugog, remembering the fine and formal dinners at the hotel, did not think these menus, which I found so fascinating in their unpredictable flavours, altogether worthy of me. For dinner he invented strange soups, into which he poured sweet vermouth. He made astonishing sauces to pour over the fish, and taught Reteg how to bake an elaborate cake. Then he suggested that perhaps I might like, as most of the residents did, to eat in the evening "out of tins." I already knew the dismal suppers of sardines, tinned ham, tinned butter, cheese and jam, that kept alive morale, but filled the spirit with gloom. They were, moreover, economically absurd, since for the price of one tin of bacon you could buy five chickens or a small pig. I had recently discovered that a six-weeks' pig roasted on the spit was a gourmet's feast, for old Réwah and Nyoman had roasted one for me at the house some time before, thus precipitating the *koki's* crisis of temper.

Réwah was the "caretaker" who had attached himself to the household the first day, but who did nothing more than sweep the yard each morning (clearing it of two leaves that had fallen from the papayas in the night) and once again in the evening. He had come as unobtrusively as the dog, and his presence had immediately been taken for granted by Gusti and the *koki*. He wants to watch the house, said Gusti when Réwah first appeared, to begin sweeping after a silent bow, without a word from anyone, and it is true I actually did find him once or twice, when I came in late at night, lying on the veranda floor with the blanket drawn over his head, sleeping so profoundly that even the rasping sound of the door as I opened it failed to rouse him.

He and Nyoman had spent an afternoon preparing the pig, stuffing it with aromatic leaves and spice. They rubbed the skin yellow with turmeric, and as they turned the pig slowly on its pole they basted it every few minutes with coconut oil. The fire of coconut husks was kept in embers and not allowed to blaze, and while Made Tantra sat gently fanning the coals, Kesyur judiciously replenished the fire around the edges. Meanwhile, other helpers were engaged in preparing the classic accompaniments: rice, of course; *pepahit*—a "bitter" dish of stewed blimbing leaves to counteract the richness of the pig; sausage, made from the pig's blood; and *urab,* a hash of finely mixed coconut, green papaya, the chopped liver and the heart.

At last the pig was pronounced done to a turn. It was placed on a banana leaf in a long wooden platter. The skin was brittle as thin glass and the meat, perfumed beyond words from the spice, melted on the tongue.

The labour involved in this little feast seemed less of an effort than when Gusti opened a tin of bacon.

Imperceptibly, another helper had attached himself to the household. This was Chetig, a friend of Made Tantra's, who played *g'ndér* in the front row of the *légong gamelan*. I first became acquainted with him when he came in uninvited one evening with Tantra and three other boys, to sit on the veranda and make music.

What prompted this little serenade I never knew. It was the softest, most nocturnal of music. There was a bamboo flute, a drum, little cymbals, and a tremulous one-stringed zither of bamboo to beat time. For an hour they played the charming and plaintive tunes from the popular *arja* operetta.

What tune is that? I asked when they stopped.

Sinom; for the princess when she parts the curtains. They began again, this time Durma, when the prince steps out.

An *arja* cast, it appeared, was made up of clearly defined character types; princess and maidservant, false princess and stepmother; prince and minister, pretender or usurper and minister, attendants—all balanced like a set of chessmen, a deck of cards. Each had his (or her) particular music, suitable to his character. Prince and princess sang in a "small" voice, high and sweet; ministers and attendants sang in the "middle" or "deep" voice. We sat there talking; soon the veranda was littered with cigarette stubs and bottles of Orange Crush.

There is *arja* to-night in Kasiman, said Chetig. If *tuan* cared to come . . .

It looked like rain, I thought. The air was damp, and the moon was sunk in clouds. But Kasiman was only a mile away, and after putting the instruments in the house and locking the door we set out down the road.

At Kasiman a solid wall of people surrounded the clearing that had been prepared for the actors near the market-place. I managed to break through to the inside. At one end hung a pair of curtains; at the other sat the musicians. Two air-pressure lamps hung down the middle, lighting up the faces which rose around the clearing in tiers. Around the edge, forever inching forward, each hoping to get a better view, sat an unbroken line of naked infants, solemn, patient, wide-awake.

The swift, light music had already begun. Two flutes rose high above the rapid, fluttering drums, now one ahead, now the other, clashing at times in casual discord, dissolving again in the

Gateway to Besakih, Mother Temple of Bali

Temple offerings

Cakes, fruits and sweetmeats for the gods

Trompong player

The deep-toned *jégogans* carry the bass

The *gangas* fill the air with ringing sound

In the Temple courtyard young girls perform the ceremonial *rejang*

The little *lélong* dancers perform
for the pleasure of both gods and mortals

In the Temple of the Dead the women of Sayan dance before each shrine

Each afternoon for a week the young girls from twenty villages
gathered to dance at a harvest feast in Tabanan

G'ndérs play the melody for the *lélong* dance

The children's orchestra

The author's *Gamelan* of Sermara, the Love God

Cymbals and little bells add shimmer to the music of Semara the Love God

The guru, I Lunyuh

The dalang opens his puppet-box

We kill a pig for the *galungan* holiday

Mask play

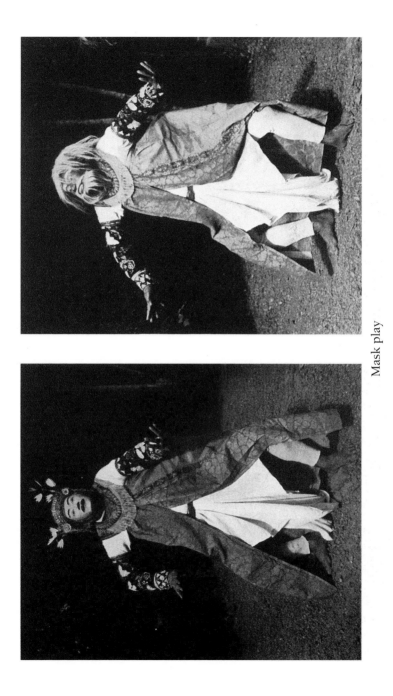

Mask play

The beloved but terrifying *barong*

The witch Chalonarang

purest of unisons. All at once there was the sound of singing; the first actor was announcing himself. The curtains quivered, opened, closed again, as though the actor could not bring himself to appear. At last they parted; the *mantri*, the prime minister, stepped forth; the play had begun.

What is the play? I asked Made Tantra.

It's not yet certain, he replied. The story has not emerged.

But it was not the prime minister after all, but his *patih*, the forerunner. He danced gravely the dance of a small official impressed with his own importance. His face was a mask of pompous indignation. Suddenly there was the sound of another voice from behind the curtains, deeper, darker in colour. Now indeed it was the *mantri*, for the *patih* immediately deferred. With elegance the *mantri* danced the length of the stage and back, followed by the *patih*, now slightly breathless. At last they stopped; a dialogue began.

This time I asked Chetig. What is the play?

It's still not clear, he replied doubtfully. In a little while, perhaps . . .

And now from behind the curtains there rose a high clear voice, feminine, yet strangely sexless and remote. A young girl stepped out. The prince! said Madé.

Clad in a tunic of white and a cape of gold, with a head-dress of flowers, she slowly advanced from the shadow into the light. Her delicate, faintly Mongolian face was a mask of grave beauty, and as she sang her voice was both harsh and sweet, something in the manner of Chinese singing. At the same time there were rapid little embellishments in her voice, light, effortless, that recalled the Arab way of singing. High above, the flutes wove around her song, embroidering on the melody. The audience watched and listened in utter pleasure.

She came at last to the centre of the stage. The ministers approached and kneeled. One spoke.

I bow at the feet of my lord. Proceed to speak, high prince of Koripan.

Ah, Koripan! said Chetig.

The locale of the play has been established for all. But is it to be the story of the prince of Koripan who was born a tiger? Or perhaps the one who was born a frog? The audience waits, listening to one formal speech of reverence unfold out of another. Slowly the plot emerges. It is the tale of two enemy princes, rivals for the love of the princess of Daha. There is also a cruel stepmother and an ugly stepsister. But all know that before dawn wrongs will be righted. Prabangsa will be slain, and Koripan will marry the true princess.

The actors left the stage. The play proceeded.

Or rather, returned to a new beginning. Once more a voice was heard behind the curtains; once more they quivered, parted.

An official steps out. It is the forerunner of the *mantri* who precedes Prince Prabangsa. We are shown another suit in *the* deck of cards. The only difference is that now the ministers are plainly buffoons, while the part of the prince is played by a heavy man, dark and threatening. The ministers kneel; the *mantri* speaks.

I bow at the feet of my lord. Proceed to speak, Your Highness. . . .

Again the stage was bare. It was time for the princess. But first her maidservant, the *chondong*, must precede her, prepare us for her luminous appearance. A frail falsetto voice was heard.

All night have I watched and waited. Day is here.

Awake, sweet lady, rise. Be pleased to come forth, step this way. . . .

Through the curtains glided an elegant figure, lithe and narrow-waisted. Her movements were seductive, her glance was melting, but something was wrong, something ever so slightly exaggerated. Her headdress was the least bit askew; the trailing skirt kept getting in the way. In a moment it was clear that the dancer was a youth, sly and sedate, who now proceeded to give a restrained but acute burlesque of the *chondong* part in the *légong* dance in a way that was found hilarious, so hilarious that the entrance of the princess herself was completely obscured.

But at this moment there was a sudden gust of wind, a few drops of rain.

Rain! called out the audience. The rain is coming!

They stirred, looked up. But in a moment it had stopped. Drums beat softly; flutes played on. The princess sang in utter despair.

Alone, forgotten, cruelly abused. . . .

Moved by the sadness of the situation, the onlookers failed to find it strange in the least that the princess was a man with a thin drooping moustache. This was the star, long famous for his finely trained voice, his grace, his special gift for female roles.

For it was not the plot that held the audience but the performance—the creation of a character by means of beautiful gesture, elegance of posture and movement, flexibility of voice and the romantic glitter in the lamplight of stiff and sequined costume. In this theatre of the imagination, free of scenery or properties, the actual sex of the performer was forgotten. Or, when transposed, served only to intensify the delineation of character. Thus a young girl, it had recently been discovered, could give the final touch of delicate grace to the portrayal of a prince of the *alus,* the "gentle-serene" type; while a man no longer young, but widely known for his finished and classical style, could give a far more feminine performance than any girl.

It was expected that the play would last till dawn. But by three o'clock, soon after the entrance of the stepmother and her clod of a daughter, it was evident that at any moment the rain would fall in earnest. Already people were leaving. It was decided to bring the performance to an end. Two hours were smoothly condensed into ten minutes; false princess was beaten with branches; Prabangsa was slain. Hearts were trumps, and with the sudden downpour of rain the last trick had been taken.

A few nights later I witnessed another play, this time by the famous company of Batuan. The night was clear, and I sat till the end taking notes.

The Prince of Koripan, said Chetig, wishes to take home his bride, the Princess of Daha. But her brother forbids this, for the day is inauspicious and the bride is pregnant. The prince insists, however, and they set forth with their attendants. Their way lies through a deep forest (a papaya tree was planted in the centre of the stage) and as it is night they lie down to rest.

In this forest lives a demon with her daughter. (They both wear demon masks, and look quite terrifying.) The daughter tells in whining tones of how she dreamt the night before of the handsome Prince Koripan. She is infatuated. As she wanders through the forest, playing tricks on innocent people (this was a rather grimly obscene bit of comedy), she comes all at once upon Koripan and his bride. With a spell she puts them to sleep and approaches.

Now she undresses the princess and puts on her clothes. She tears the fœtus from her (a doll had been concealed in the clothes of the princess) and places it inside her own body. She throws the princess in a ravine, discards her demon mask and lies down beside the prince. He wakes; he asks, astonished,

Who is this beside me, with unfamiliar face?

Your bride, Galuh Daha.

But why have the features of my bride changed so?

Alas! the air is evil, the forest is bewitched.

They set out for Koripan. (The tree is removed.) At the palace the marriage is celebrated with many offerings.

Meanwhile, the princess succeeds in reaching the court. Attendants find her weeping outside the palace gates, and she tells them she is the true bride of their prince. The preposterous story is carried inside, and she is ordered beaten to death. Now she is thrashed cruelly with branches. Singing the saddest of songs, she sinks to the ground; the audience is filled with pity.

But at the point of death she is saved by the timely arrival of her brother. In rage he seeks the prince.

Who is this, whom you have taken as bride?

My true wife, the Princess of Daha.

Indeed not! You have married a demon! My sister stands bound outside the palace gates.

But Koripan cannot believe it. Back and forth the harsh, defiant voices travel. Neither yields.

At last the Prince of Koripan calls his demon bride and asks her if she recognizes her brother. She is not clever enough to dissemble. In a new burst of fury, the prince takes her by the arm, drags her to the centre of the stage, beating her so that the branches whistle through the air. He throws her down, orders her killed at once. He tenderly unties the true princess, singing his love. Before the actors have left the stage the audience has risen and is on its way home.

Another night, as I stood watching with Made Tantra, the play was half over before he could tell me the plot. At last he exclaimed, Now I know! They have just mentioned fried onions. . . .

Once I left Chetig and Tantra looking on, and went home, for the play was unusually late in getting started. The next morning when the two came in I asked about the performance.

Oh, it was excellent. We stayed till dawn.

What was the story?

Chetig shook his head. The story never emerged.

But how could you stay till the end?

The clowns were so very funny. . . .

In the daytime Chetig would come to visit, but sooner or later he was to be found by the kitchen door, eagerly polishing spoons or wiping lamp chimneys, or in the house dusting once more the piano. This was for him the crowning jewel in a house of treasures. He never seemed to tire of standing before it picking out melodies. The strange tuning of the piano did not seem to bother him at all, and he was very quick about finding his way among the keys.

For the past month I had been at work making a complete "score" of the music to the long dance of King Lasem as the club of Kedaton played it—the slow opening music, the love-music, the farewell scene, the raven music, the battle music. I had begun by writing the "trunk tones" and the g'ndér melody, then the accents of the drums, gongs and cymbals. Nyoman had all the patience in the world. We would work for an hour or so each morning or late afternoon, to relax afterwards by driving down to the sea with Kesyur and Chetig or Tantra for a swim. As I wrote down the melody, watched it unfold, I was continually delighted by the form, the balance, the way one section followed so logically another. It seemed impossible to believe that so much beauty could be achieved with a scale of only five tones.

But the real work began when I turned to the "flowers" in the music. Chetig, who belonged to the *gangsa* players of the club, decided to teach me himself.

Early one morning, while it was still cool, he and Kejir, his inseparable friend, brought in two *gangsas* and set them down near the piano. It took two to play these flower patterns, for there were two "voices" that ran in counterpoint—two different rhythms, positive and negative, that fitted together like parts of a puzzle to form an unbroken and incredibly swift arabesque. Each part raced along in nervous electric energy. It was a fugitive duet in Morse code.

These were the patterns, so utterly Balinese (so "barbarian" in their restlessness to the Javanese) that broke the music into spangles, gave it light and fire, created tension so that the longest phrase could not die, but became instead an adventure. High and clear, they were forever changing, while below them the melody slowly uncoiled.

Wait! I would call out after a moment. Stop! *Please!* That bit once more.

With the best grace in the world the two boys would stop, and begin once more. Soon they were off again, faster than ever. I was amazed at their memory, their precision. Sometimes patterns repeated, sometimes they kept opening out into something new. Suddenly the boys would get involved, break down, to burst out laughing, each accusing the other.

Madé Tantra sat listening idly; a large bee, attached to his finger by a thread, flew round and round.

Why doesn't Tantra belong to the club? I asked.

They laughed. He can't remember a note. He only knows how to paint gold flowers on dancers' costumes.

When Chetig had nothing else to do he would sit on the floor of the veranda drawing. He would cover sheet after sheet of paper with patterns for a new jacket he intended to order from the tailor, the seams, buttonholes and lapels indicated with utmost care. One night I saw him at the *arja* play all dressed up, but instead of a flower or so in his hair, like Tantra and Kesyur, he had entangled a dozen fireflies, that shone on and off in the dark throughout the entire evening. He brought to the house his tame *churik,* a docile bird the size of a robin, that followed hopping and twittering at his heels wherever he went. The bird's name was Bli, big brother, and Chetig insisted it talked. Every now and then he would hold it near his ear, and the two would engage in the softest of conversations. When Bli finally wandered (or flew) away Chetig cried all night, and even the next day, calling through the trees as he hunted. Yet when he was stung by a scorpion he bore the pain without a sound after the first startled *Adoh!* One day he came to me in a state of excitement to say that his brother had just been found murdered on the road to Tabanan. He would have to be away for several days helping find who had done it. Three days later he was back.

What news, Chetig? Did you find the man?

Chetig's voice was untroubled. No. . . . No. . . . We never discovered. There he was, lying by the roadside, stabbed in the back by a *kris.* No one could think why.

He went through the house, putting things in order, although Pugog had just finished dusting an hour before.

FAREWELL FEAST

I HAD LOST ALL TRACK of time; I no longer answered letters; once in a while I would send Pugog to Den Pasar to ask at the hotel what day of the week it was. But one morning I awoke to remember suddenly that my six months' visitor's permit would soon run out; unless I wished to change my status to that of a resident I must prepare to leave. About this time an incident occurred which I found infinitely depressing.

The importing agent in Den Pasar handled, among other things, Oriental records, Chinese, Malayan, and even readings from the Koran. There were shelves of Balinese recordings—sacred texts, cremation music, theatre, music for the shadow-play. They had been made in Bali in the late 'twenties by two German firms, Odéon and Beka, and were rare, since only a few had been considered successful enough for the European market. You could not get them in Europe or even Java, but here they had been stored in quantities. They had been made, of course, to sell on the island—a naive project, for no Balinese had money or even the desire for a phonograph. Why should they sit and listen to disks when the island rang day and night with music? Thus one morning, when I bought two sets, the agent remarked bitterly that this was the first sale in a year. I shall throw them all out, he said angrily. They are only taking up room on my shelves.

It was a warm day, and I thought that he was perhaps infuriated by the heat as much as anything else. But later, when I knew I was leaving, I returned for another set of records, only to find that he had, in one of those quick fits of rage that can seize a Westerner in the tropics, smashed them all the week before. Not one remained.

Good riddance, he exclaimed defiantly. He seemed quite pleased at my dismay. Anyway, he suddenly shouted, how can you consider that music? You, who call yourself a musician? He looked at me through his thick glasses with sudden hatred.

I had an unhappy sense of loss. I passed the last two weeks in feverish activity, photographing musicians and instruments, taking endless moving pictures of the men as they played. I spent hours each day working with Nyoman. I called in musicians from other villages, to take down melodies and technical details. When at last I gathered my pages together and locked them in my trunk I had the feeling of storing a folio of pressed flowers. What would remain, I wondered, when I opened the pages again two months later?

All this time Nyoman Kalér refused to believe I was actually leaving, for I had postponed my departure three times already. When at last he was convinced, he appeared deeply despondent, and each day would comment on my going in phrases of poetic regret that I could not help feeling were a bit overdone.

Madé Tantra was overcome.

I keep thinking how I shall miss you, he said. I say to myself, Ten more days and *tuan* will be gone. Ten more days and I shall wonder, Where is *tuan* now? Where look for tuan?

I was touched, especially when he said one night he must have something to remember me by. A photograph.

Of course, Madé. I shall have Lai Héng make one tomorrow. How shall it be—I alone, or the two of us together?

But he only said, It does not matter if you are in the picture or not.

So Madé had his picture taken, and at his request the photographer finished the print in style by touching up the buttons of the jacket in gold before he framed it.

I wished to give a farewell feast for the men of the *légong gamelan* and for the friends I had made in the past months. I told Nyoman I would ask Gusti Bagus of Saba to bring his dancers, and the Anak Agung of Kapal to bring his magnificent *légong gamelan*. The combination of the two would make a memorable performance, I thought. I begged Nyoman to look after the details of the feast, for there would be nearly a hundred guests. Since it was impossible to prepare for so many in the little kitchen of the Mountain of Flowers, it was decided to roast the pigs and cook the rice in the kitchens of the temple across the road.

Early in the morning of the feast day, boys began to arrive with mats for us to sit on and round wooden trays off which we would eat. The high step of the veranda was reserved for the guests of honour, while mats were spread on the ground below for the others; there seemed little chance of rain. There would be pig and turtle for all; and in addition, for the more distinguished guests, steamed duck and other delicacies which, said Chetig, the club wished to offer *me* in return.

The feast was not altogether a success. I felt far away from my less honoured guests as we of the upper level were served first. Platters piled high with the crisp skin of the pig were followed by others containing the meat. Bowls of rice and pungent sauces were set down among the dishes of hashes and stews, while a large basin of water was placed near me, to serve as a communal finger bowl. We began to eat, heartily, silently; this was no time for conversation.

The dishes were rich, as feast dishes should be, rich in fat and coconut oil. We ate with our right hands, rolling the rice into wads to drop in our mouths. My fingers were soon greasy, as I was clumsy in this way of eating, and now and then I dipped them in the water. From time to time there was a brief request to hand along the duck, give a little rice. We were completely given up to the moment, eating rapidly, noisily, with deep satisfaction.

But below I noticed all at once that my other guests had begun to stir, rising and leaving; some had not yet been served. I asked the Anak Agung on my right what could be the matter.

He paused before throwing a ball of rice in his mouth. They saw you dip your hand in the water just now, he said. They think you are through eating and that the feast is over.

But I must tell them!

Too late. They are already leaving. It is nothing, he said, and before I could call Pugog they had gone.

Those around me were undisturbed. They ate till satisfied, and now began to comment politely. Gentle, complimentary belching arose, and remarks: A fat pig! A fine duck! What rich food! The belches grew louder, the remarks more earnest: Completely stuffed! A full stomach! A sticking-out stomach!

Now was the time to pass the hand basin, and Chetig poured water on the fingers that stretched over it.

That night the *légong* of Saba created a sensation. People had come for miles to see them, and watched breathlessly, completely entranced by the swift elegance and beauty of the dancers. This part of my evening at least, I thought, was a success.

When the Anak Agung was about to leave, he asked me if I would send him an alarm clock from Paris. He drew me aside and said, more seriously:

And, if possible, a bottle of medicine that is a cure for impotence.

He shook his head sadly, made a pathetic little gesture with his finger.

I said I would try, and asked him not to forget me.

The departure was to take place in this way. I had hired a bus to take the trunks to Buleléng, and fifteen closest friends would ride along to see me off. The men of the *légong gamelan* had arranged that I was to leave the village in heroic style; I was to walk in procession to Den Pasar, through the town, and say farewell at the turn of the road to those left behind. A *gamelan* would be carried along to play the pieces I had liked best.

Through the morning everyone in the village seemed to be in the house. They came and went, bringing enough presents to fill another bus. There were pineapples, mangoes, gigantic bunches of bananas, coconuts, a tiny squirrel, sugar cane and a flute. Men and women came up, and their eyes filled with tears.

Why does *tuan* leave? Why must *tuan* depart?

May I not go along in the bus, asked old Réwah sentimentally, to say goodbye at the ship? I have never been to Buleléng.

About noon the trunks were finally locked and piled in the bus, which drove off together with the car, to wait at the spot where the procession was to end. I took a last look at the Mountain of Flowers. It seemed very forlorn and empty. I had given the monkey to Made Tantra, the heron and parrots to Chetig. An old man went about the grounds gleaning little treasures.

We formed along the road outside the house. The musicians went first, and after them the women, with flowers in their hair. Then the men, and among them, like a precious object carefully protected, myself. Behind us thundered a second *gamelan*, in a different rhythm and key. It was really quite disturbing.

We walked through the town. As we passed the house of the Assistant Resident someone peeped from behind a curtain. Down the main street the Chinese and Arab merchants came to their doors and looked. Cars and pony carts turned out of the way to let us pass.

At the bus the procession broke up. To the sound of gongs and cymbals I got into the car and waved. We started off, followed by the bus, which soon passed at top speed, everyone shouting out the news that they had got ahead.

The ship was to leave at five, and when we arrived in the middle of the afternoon it was already there, gently rolling, half a mile out. On shore a second farewell now took place, this time more temperate, for I had my trunks to see to, and my friends were torn between the drama of my departure and the distracting sights of an unfamiliar town.

Nyoman, Chetig and Made Tantra rode out in the launch to the ship. We silently walked the decks, looked down at the engines. I showed them the saloon and my cabin. They turned on the taps to see the water come out, and exclaimed at the miracle of the lavatory. The whistle blew and we went on deck.

Goodbye, *tuan,* goodbye. Safe travelling.

Goodbye, goodbye.

They went down the steps that hung over the side of the ship and got into the launch.

Once more goodbye, and waving as the boat grew smaller and smaller. The engines started, there was the sound of churning water, and the ship headed for Surabaya.

From the stern I watched the island recede and grow blue. The sky took on the colours of a dying dolphin. From the deck below came the sound of singing. It was Sunday afternoon; flat nasal voices had begun intoning familiar hymns. I looked down over the railing. A group of Celebans, neatly dressed in white European clothes, were gathered together. They sang in Malay a paraphrase of the words:

From Greenland's icy mountains
To India's coral strands . . .
Where every prospect pleases,
And only man is vile—

The sky grew dark, and the ship's lights went on. A deck boy passed and I ordered a Dutch gin. I was staying with the ship as far as Batavia; there I would take another for Marseilles. In a month I would be once more in Paris.

PART TWO
THE HOUSE IN THE HILLS

PARIS IN 1932 SEEMED much more on edge than when I was there the year before. Even the taxi-drivers spoke with a new impatience, appeared preoccupied, as though continually listening for some distant sound. In subways and restaurants there still hung the placards from last year, *Il ne faut pas gaspiller le pain*, and in every bookshop *La guerre est pour demain* was pushed to the front of the window. I had barely been there a month before the papers announced in great headlines the electoral victory of Hitler.

I took a small apartment in the Rue de Fleurus and phoned Erard for a piano. It was high time to return to composing. But I found it difficult to get into the mood for work; the weeks passed and the pages on the piano were filled with no more than scraps of themes. I went to concerts only to listen with restlessness, for the programmes of new music that I once delighted in now seemed suddenly dull and intellectual. I cared even less for the eloquence of the romantic symphonies. As I sat in the concert halls I thought of the sunny music I had listened to in the open air, among people who talked and laughed, hearing yet not hearing the musicians, but cheered and exhilarated by the sounds. Here, as I looked about me in the hall, I felt suddenly shut in, and I could hardly wait for the end of the concert. The huge orchestras sounded torpid and mechanized. The basses dragged, the drums were heavy as lead, and I could no longer listen to the endless *legato* of the violins.

There was no doubt about it. I was already homesick, both for the life and people I had left and the music, which now seemed more filled than ever with magic. I unpacked my notes and put them in order. In plain black and white they had the lifelessness of harmony exercises, yet for me they were filled with meaning. Each complemented the other. I began to see a wider design, and I wished I had taken many more. One afternoon, as I idled away the time on one of the river boats along the Seine, I realized with sudden clearness that the only thing in the world I wanted to do was to return to Bali and make as complete a record as I could of the music. Some inner compulsion to preserve in some way this fugitive art made it seem important and urgent. It was only too clear such music could not survive much longer. A thousand forces were at work to destroy it; at present the people of the island still lived in an illusion of freedom, but they had long since been caught in the net that was now being slowly dragged in, and their fate was the fate of the Eastern world.

One day I received a letter from Nyoman Kalér which said, among other things:

When does *tuan* return? I am building a new pavilion, so that there will always be a place for *tuan*. It needs only thirty guilders more. Chetig was killed in a bus that overturned coming down the road from the mountains.

Two months later I was in Marseilles, waiting for the boat which would take me back to the Indies. I had decided to build a house in Bali and live there. How long, I had at the time no idea; it would depend on my work.

Nyoman Kalér and Kesyur were waiting at the barbed-wire gate by the Custom House. We strolled down the streets of Buleléng while I savoured the moment, hardly daring to believe I was back. On the way to Den Pasar I asked Kesyur to turn off to Saba so that I might give the Anak Agung the alarm clock I had brought back for him. Near the market I found him watching a cricket fight, and on his face was that intent expression which told me there was money at stake.

His face broke into a smile.

Béh! Tuan! Why so long away?

I have just come off the boat from Europa.

Indeed? he said vaguely. . . . He looked up. To-morrow I begin to train new dancers. Perhaps you have heard: I have got water for my ricefields.

And the cockfights?

A little loss, a little gain.

I gave him the clock, and he immediately rang the alarm. As for its use as an instrument to measure time, I knew it would never enter his head.

The Anak Agung wanted me to live in Saba; he offered to build me a house by the pool. Nyoman Kalér hoped I would come back to my old house. But I had made up my mind to live in the hills, for I had found the climate of the lowlands exhausting, especially in the hot and humid days that preceded the rainy season. In the hills it was always cool at night. It was also less populated; villages were more primitive, farther apart, and you had less the sensation of teeming life, which for six months had fascinated me, but which I knew I should not care to be in the midst of over a long period of time. Some quiet village would be the ideal spot in which to live and work, undisturbed; when I was in need of fresh material I had only to get in the car, for the ceremonial and festive life of the island continued through the year without a break. Kesyur and I drove about looking for the perfect village, off the beaten track, far from the sight of tourists, yet near enough to some centre of music and dancing.

One day I found the place I was seeking.

The village of Sayan stretched along the top of a narrow ridge that ran up into the mountains. Every three days a crowded bus rattled down from the Chinese coffee plantations to Den Pasar, choking and stalling as it climbed back again at night. The land I wanted lay at the end of the village, next to the graveyard, on the edge of a deep ravine. Far below ran the river; across the valley ricefields rose in terraces and disappeared in the coconut groves. Behind these ran the mountains of Tabanan, and far off to the south a triangle of sea shone between the hills. The land had once been terraced to grow rice, but now was covered with grass and shaded with coconuts. It descended in several steps to the edge of the cliff, where it dropped four hundred feet. From below came the faint roar of the river as it rushed among the rocks and stones.

The village belonged to the district of Gianyar, ruled by the detested Anak Agung Ngurah, who was eating his heart out at colonial restraint. His attempts at ancient tyranny were constantly foiled by the *Controlleur*, whose tiny office across the square from the palace in Gianyar was a constant and infuriating reminder of another regime.

Sayan was a peasant village, not very old, but running according to old Balinese law. There was not even a village school, and very few men spoke Malay, which meant I would have to learn Balinese. There were three *banjars,* with an assembly hall where on rare occasions the elders of all three *banjars* met for matters of grave importance. There were half a dozen small temples, and a crumbling palace which belonged to the Chokorda Rahi, a poverty-stricken prince from the ancient and highborn family which once ruled in Pliatan, across the valley to the east. The rest of the village were simple farmers; when they heard a white man was coming to live among them the signal drums beat loudly, and there was meeting after meeting of the village elders.

Rendah, the owner of the land, was a shy, frail man of fifty; he was plainly startled when, as he led his cow through the bamboos one afternoon, he found me sitting under his trees. It was only after Kesyur told him that I was merely walking for pleasure that he relaxed. Then Balinese manners prevailed. I was welcome! Would I not like some coconut water? He tucked his dusty *sarong* around his loins and began to climb a palm with surprising agility. In a moment there was the double thud of two

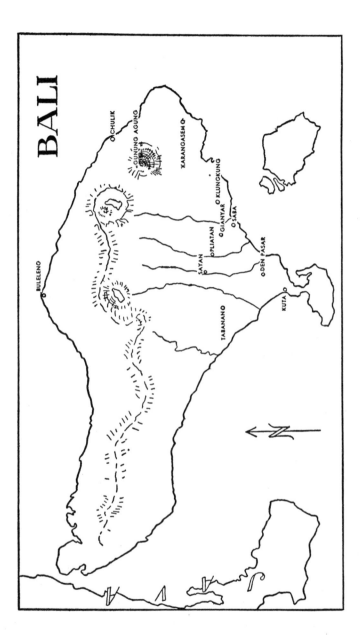

nuts as they fell, and he descended, to open them with a neat blow from his heavy knife.

We sat conversing. I made no mention of my plans, as I knew the idea that I wanted to build a house on his land would have to be broken with caution. Kesyur was soon embarked on a synopsis of where I had come from,. where I was going, my finances and my character, while I was already thinking of the kind of house to build.

I saw Rendah twice before I ventured to tell him what I had in mind. It was clearly a shock, and there were many conferences with his older brother, who was headman of the village. He spoke in disapproving tones, but finally the two broke down and consented. I offered to lease the land for ten years, with a lease to be drawn up legally before the *Controlleur* in Gianyar. But before this could be done, the *pipil* or deed would have to be found. This was a bit of writing scratched on palm leaf. No one had seen it for ages, and it took a month to find.

In the meantime the village heard of the amazing news, and soon found out that Rendah would profit considerably. This was too much! A long and bitter dispute arose over the ownership of the land. The village claimed it had always been village property. Chokorda Rahi, the prince, suddenly appeared, all smiles, to say that the land belonged actually to him, had been given to him long ago by his father, in the palace at Ubud. The land had been merely loaned to Rendah, he claimed, adding sweetly that I was welcome to it, I must please accept it.

Rendah, however, insisted that the land had been given outright to him by the Chokorda in return for money he had once loaned, and the day the *pipil* was found the Chokorda had to retreat, baffled. This *pipil* on examination turned out after all to be made out in favour of Rendah's older brother, the *klian*, with items—the coconut trees remained the property of Chokorda Rahi; the crop was his; one-fifth of it went to Rendah in payment for watching the trees. At last it was agreed that the *klian* should receive the rent, while I would engage Rendah as gardener and watchman, and give him a similar amount. Both were pleased; this maintained a balance, was justice.

The village, however, was far from pleased, and immediately began a lawsuit against the *klian*. Two months later the verdict was given at the Courthouse in Gianyar, and they had lost. Angry meetings now took place in the pavilion of the elders. Kesyur told me they had vowed to take the case to Buleléng; then to the Governor-General in Java, and later, if necessary, even to Queen Wilhemina herself in Holland.

But Jacobs, the *Controller* in Gianyar, assured me the village had no claim, and that I could begin to build. I did not like the idea of breaking into a hostile community. I already had a feeling of guilt about the disruption my mere presence in the village would inevitably cause, but I had hoped I might be able to move in peacefully. However, I felt that this quarrel was not mine, and I decided to let matters stand until the time when I actually came to the village to live. I was determined not to ruin things at the outset by the simple solution of offering a bribe of money, and I had lived on the island long enough to feel that things would soon quiet down again, especially if I made the village a present of two pigs at next galungan-time, which was soon approaching. This was a ten-day season of bright celebrations, when the spirits of the ancestors came down to earth to be honoured and entertained, and the opening day in particular was one of great feasting. It was also a day for giving presents—chiefly food, it seemed, for everyone who killed a pig for his own use sent the choicest parts to those to whom he felt indebted in some way. On this day I gave new batik *sarongs* to Kesyur, Nyoman, Made Tantra; a bottle of brandy to Gusti Bagus in Saba. The unexpected arrival of two additional pigs for slaughter (as large as I could find) could not fail, I thought, to soothe the village elders, especially on a morning when all were in the best of humour.

Since my return I had been staying in Ubud, a few miles from Sayan, with Walter Spies, a German artist who had lived in Java and Bali for a long time, and who painted enchanting and dreamlike pictures—half Persian miniature, half Rousseau—of the island. We now went every day to Sayan, to walk around the grounds and discuss the best position for the house. Sometimes we were joined by old Rendah, who would invite us to "pay a call" at his house down the road, where he would offer us sweet rice-cakes and coconut juice. Rendah's household and I were on the friendliest of terms, for I had already won over the youngest children with a mechanical Mickey Mouse. I had also found my neighbour, Gari, whose fields and house lay to the south, as willing to make friends. But when I called on my other neighbour to the north I ran against a wall of cold unfriendliness, of stiff, unrelenting politeness that I never succeeded, the whole time I lived in the village, in thawing to the slightest degree.

Gusti Lusuh, the contractor, was a honey-voiced noble from Gianyar who smiled and bowed at every suggestion I made. When he spoke, he always referred to himself by the Malayan word hamba, your servant, slave, which I found too affected for words, especially when he constantly spoke of the coolies who would work on the house as his vassals. When we discussed prices and materials he would grow suddenly distraught, and I could read in his eyes rapid calculations in which he planned to profit outrageously. For a week we haggled energetically, and when at last a price was reached that was about half the first quotation I thought I probably was not going to pay much more than I ought.

The house was to be built native style. There would be several buildings—a sleeping-house, a main house, a kitchen, bath-house and garage. There would also be the house temple, a little group of shrines for my ancestral gods in the north-east corner of the land. All buildings would have thatch roofs; all materials except for the floors, which would be of polished Borneo cement, were to be found on the island. I wanted the house built quickly, but Gusti Lusuh dismissed so foreign an idea immediately: it was the wrong season for cutting bamboos; good *lalang* grass for thatch had not reached full growth; both ironwood for the pillars and teak for the bookshelves would take time to find. Moreover, the foundations could not be begun before a propitious day had been sought, when permission to open the land would have to be asked of the gods.

I went to the *pemangku*, the priest and temple guardian of the *banjar* in which I would live, to consult the calendar for a favourable day. It seemed as though I must wait a long time for all good days for beginning to build were dominated, it seemed, by evil forces for months to come. But I said I could not wait that long, and at last we decided to risk everything on a day not far off, when bad omens barely overbalanced the good.

Work began one bright morning while the grass was still wet with dew. When I arrived from Ubud the *pemangku* had already set up a row of bamboo shrines, in which he had placed the offerings for the gods. On the ground below were spread the offerings for the demons. For a long time he sat murmuring chain after chain of magic verses, but at last he rose, saying his work was finished and that we might proceed.

Gusti Lusuh had brought twenty-five coolies to work, and they had already built a sleeping hut and a kitchen, for they would live on the place until the house was finished. They laughed and called out as they set to work, while Gusti Lusuh walked about, thoughtfully tapping his chin with his ruler. Each time a tree was cut down, a little branch was planted in the cleft of the trunk, so that the tree-spirit might have some place to go, and I wondered where the spirit finally went when a few days later the trunks were dragged away by the family of Rendah, to be cut up for firewood.

I went to see Pugog, but he could not work for me, as he had become head boy at the hotel. He suggested his younger brother, Pugig. A week later a tall and serious youth arrived in Ubud to see me. He was rather startled at the prospect of living in what seemed to him the wilds, and in a thatched house, so unconventional for a *tuan*. He had been trained in the neat new bungalows of Den Pasar, and to take charge in Sayan, in a house, moreover, built on the side of a steep valley, filled him with dismay. At the first earthquake, he announced as we stood looking out over the valley in Sayan, this will all surely slide down the hill. I liked his appearance, for he seemed both earnest and responsible, and I finally induced him to come.

I now went to Java for a week to look for a piano and furnishings for the house. I chose a used Steinway grand which was offered for sale in the *Soerabajaasche Handelsblad*. It was described as built for the tropics, but this was not so, and later I had a great deal of trouble with it, especially in the rainy season.

I did not stay this time in one of the large and frigid European hotels, but went instead to a Chinese inn. It was friendly and crowded, and noisy as a zoo. Through the open transoms of the rooms came the sound of singing and laughter, the music of fiddles, the click of *mahjong* bricks, kept up from early morning till far into the night. All day long boys knocked on doors with fresh tea and hot towels or trays of covered dishes. Around three in the morning the halls grew silent, but for a brief hour only, for at dawn life began once more where it had left off. I opened my door to find incense burning over a little heap of offerings on the cement floor of the hall. One by one the guests awoke, and soon all was noise and sociability again.

The afternoon the ship sailed I strolled through the bird-market where you could buy parrots and cockatoos, hornbills and tin finches, wood pigeons the size of young geese. A cage of brilliant doves caught my eyes. Some were saffron, some rose or emerald green; others were iridescent bronze. I took a dozen back to the ship, for I thought they would make astonishing presents for old Rendah, Kesyur and Made Tantra, who was in Ubud to help Pugig until I got settled. But that night it rained. The cages had been left on deck, and the next morning I found a sad transformation, for my birds had been dyed, and now I had only a dozen bedraggled domestic pigeons.

What are *these* for? asked Kesyur as he came on deck from the launch to help me off the ship.

Oh, nothing . . . I answered. I could not bring myself to explain.

In the tropics it is the plants that live intensely, thrusting up and flowering overnight, while the work of man proceeds so slowly as to be at times quite imperceptible. It was thus with my house. I gave up hope of ever seeing it finished as I watched the coolies work five days and stop for ten. Once they were away for a month to help prepare for the cremation of Gusti Lusuh's grandfather. Back they came to work for ten days, only to stop for another month, for the week of *galungan* was near, the time when the gods came down to earth, and long after they had departed the island would remain in a holiday mood. In the daytime strolling actors and dancers would travel from village to village, to perform from morning to dust. At night there would be shadow-plays, *arja*; no one could possibly think of work.

At the end of *galungan* a period of rain now set in, but a day came at last when the sky cleared and the sun shone once more. There was a strong wind blowing, and it seemed a fine day for work. I drove to Sayan, only to find the coolies, too exhilarated to work, absorbed in making toy windmills. The place hummed; boys and men ran back and forth with little ones that turned on the ends of poles, while on the roof of the sleeping-house the master carpenter was busy fixing a large one in place.

From the veranda two Chinese carpenters surveyed the scene with placid superiority. They had been engaged to build the cupboards and shelves. Steeped in opium, they worked in a Nirvana of peace, leisurely and accurately fitting drawers, shaking their heads at each instance of inferior Balinese workmanship. After an hour's contact with reality they would lay down their planes, light their pipes and retire once again into a more Confucian world of the spirit.

However, the time finally came when I could move in. All but the main house was ready, but before the house could be entered, beds slept in, fires lighted, the ceremony of consecration would have to be performed. Once more the *pemangku* and calendar were consulted for a favourable day. The women of Rendah's household prepared the offerings, the endless ritualistic cakes, flower arrangements and objects of fresh green palm leaf. In addition to this there must, of course, be music, and in the evening a theatrical performance to end the day in style. Kesyur's mind was immediately at work with the idea of a great three-day festival that would include the *légong* dancers from Saba, the *arja* company from Batuan (at that time the most famous and the highest in price) and finally *jangér,* a sort of modern vaudeville that was very popular and which I found incredibly dull. In fact, it was to be an unforgettable event that would startle everyone for miles. There must also be a display of fireworks, and a long row of decorated bamboo poles along the roadside by the gate.

Rendah listened open-mouthed. But Madé Tantra was for a shadow-play, and Pugig for the *jogéd* dancer from the next village. This meant he could dance with her, and he rather fancied himself as a dancer.

Kesyur listened impatiently. What? Only the *jogéd* from Kengaton? A poor affair indeed that cost only two guilders at the most; besides, all had slept with her long ago.

But to Kesyur's disgust I explained that this was to be a small celebration. The house was only half finished and half paid for. Time enough to be reckless when the main building was ready.

The others agreed, and we decided on a shadow-play.

But at least call a good *dalang*, pled Kesyur, who did not want to see me disgraced, for it would ultimately reflect on him, and I promised to engage the one from Mas, an elderly Brahman of great scholarship. His performance was famous for its eloquence, and it was said that in the pathetic parts he could move his audience to tears. I went to see him, and it was arranged that for twenty strings of Chinese cash he would play from midnight till dawn. I was to furnish the oil for his lamp, and tea and betel for his assistants, who were each to receive, in addition, the gift of a Chinese paper umbrella.

Kesyur now soothed his wounded feelings by ordering a number of fine bamboo poles on his own account to decorate and set up along the road. He took pains to inform everyone that this was only a preliminary; we would not kill a turtle now, only pig. There would be few guests. Later, a real feast, conducted properly, could be expected.

The month had been full of sun, but the rainy season was near, and every afternoon the clouds now gathered more darkly. By night they disappeared, but the moonlight was no longer brilliant. The day for moving in began bright and steaming, but by noon the clouds had piled the dense layers. There was silence in the air, a brief drumming of rain, and again silence.

It's finished, said Kesyur in relief, as we turned the road to Sayan. There will be no more rain to-day.

By the gate a crowd had gathered, and as I drove in there was a glorious burst of firecrackers, set off by Pugig and Tantra. Nyoman Kalér had come on bicycle, bringing a fighting cock as house-warming present.

On the veranda of the sleeping-house four shadow-play *g'ndérs* played soft animated music. The offerings had already been set out on the floor, and before them the *pemangku* now lighted his sticks of incense and closed his eyes. He prayed for the safety of the house, for the protection of the gods. A halfhour passed, and then he rose, to go from house to house smearing the lintel of each door with the three magic colours, black, white and red, composed of soot, lime and fresh chicken's blood. From each lintel he hung a square of white cloth covered with magic diagrams. As he sprinkled each house with holy water (brought all the way from the volcano lake), he intoned the spells that were directed against all devils. For my land was magically dangerous. It not only lay next to the graveyard, but was not completely surrounded by walls; no precaution could be considered superfluous in protecting me from evil.

The *pemangku* had barely gone before there was a faint rustling sound far up the valley that within a few minutes rose to a roar, and suddenly in a gale the rain fell, furiously, taking the breath out of you. Palms tossed; nuts and branches crashed to earth; bamboos strained against each other, groaned and shrieked like primeval monsters. The terraced land was turned to waterfalls and ditches of foam.

This was a bleak beginning. I felt lonely and dispirited as I watched Madé Tantra come in from the kitchen, drenched and naked beneath a broad coolie hat. The wind blew out the lamps as he lighted them, and the house creaked like a ship in a heavy sea.

But in an hour the storm had passed. The moon came out, washed clean. In the lean-to beside the kitchen the pig was already turning on the fire, and from the kitchen came the cheerful sounds of chopping and laughter.

Suddenly I heard singing. A young, nasal voice, languorous, insolent, and at the same time mysteriously filled with a veiled radiance, rose in the air. The singer, I later learned, was the poet himself.

Were I rich I would take you to the Bali Hotel
There the beds are covered with fine silk

We would lie down
And when we had made love we would leave
In a fine Chevrolet
Blowing our horn loudly along the way.

It was Durus, said Kesyur, a boy from the company of *arja* players in Batuan, who had come here with the *dalang*. He sometimes acted, sometimes wrote the verses for the songs.

At the end of the stanza there were cries of sardonic approval; the voice grew thinner, more derisive, then stopped, submerged in a shout of laughter. Another voice, now harsh and strident, took its place. Back and forth the voices answered each other, burlesquing a scene from some play, until the cooks called out the pig was done.

The booth for the shadow-play had been set up outside the gate, and by ten there was the familiar scene, the lamps glowing on the little food tables, the crowd wandering about or sitting gathered before the screen. The *dalang's* lamp was already burning, and the music had begun.

The story was from the first book of the Hindu epic *Mahabharata*, the Wars of the Bharatas.

The gods have assembled to produce *amrita,* the food of immortality, by churning the sea. They use the great mountain Meru for churning-stick, Naga the great serpent of the underworld for rope; for pivot they use the turtle on which the world rests. The demon Kala Rahu has joined them in disguise, and in the course of events slyly manages to steal some of the *amrita* and eat it. But before he has time to swallow, Sun and Moon denounce him, and Vishnu cuts off his head. But the head has become immortal, and in revenge swallows the sun and moon, causing the eclipses. . . .

Such is the bare outline of a play that went on all night. I sat there, between Nyoman and old Rendah, until I could hardly keep my eyes open. I was too tired to wait for the end, and finally I got up and left. I stood on the veranda of the sleeping-house and looked out; across the valley the moon was low in the sky, and its light streamed through the open windows over the bed. I could hear the music from the road, and the voice of the *dalang* as it rose and fell in the half-chanted dialogues. As I fell asleep the sounds merged with the soft roar of the river below; it seemed hard to believe in the violent tempest that had taken place so short a time before.

It was about a week after I had moved into my house that the village decided to barricade me. One morning Kesyur rushed up to the veranda with the dramatic news that the elders of the four *banjars* had held a meeting the night before and had now gathered and were dragging trees and bushes to pile in front of the entrance. I could hear sounds of disturbance out on the road, the voices of many people like the humming of angry bees, and I walked up the driveway to find that it had been blocked completely. A thick wall of shrubs, branches and pineapple plants lay piled at the gate, and in front boys and men, wearing their *krises* or knives, came and went or squatted by the roadside, their faces dark with determination.

The reason? It seemed that the drive I had made to connect my land with the village road took in a foot or so of land belonging to the graveyard. Also belonging to the graveyard was the pandanus thicket which I had partly cleared in order to make room for the mud wall which ran along the driveway. This was village property, and there they had me. Not allowed! They do not give! I am to be sealed in!

I knew I had only to drive to the *Controlleur* in Gianyar, but I preferred to arrange things if possible according to village law. I asked Gusti Lusuh to speak for me.

He stood on the wall and used his suave and disarming eloquence. *Tuan* regrets! *Tuan* did not know! *Tuan* has come as a friend. If it is given, *tuan* would like to become a village member and pay annual dues with the rest. In addition, for the privilege of using a foot of village property he offers to contribute two pigs each year to the village feast at *galungan* time.

The effect of his words was immediate, like a funeral oration on a Shakespearean mob. Within five minutes hearts had melted and men were dragging off branches so laboriously brought a short time before. Only a few older men remained. The leader, a scarlet hibiscus in his grey locks, spoke with dignity:

Tuan's thoughts are gentle and considerate. His attitude is noble. Indeed, he is welcome to the land, and the men of Sayan beg forgiveness.

In this way the village forgot all grievances and accepted me.

DURUS

I SOON DISCOVERED THAT I had chosen a more austere village to live in than at first I had thought. Already Pugig and Kesyur were complaining of the silence after nightfall. Not one sound! Not one light! It was a *wilderness!* It was true. No music filled the air at night, no voices sang along the road. By nine the village slept; rarely did a feeble lamp burn in the clubhouse down the road, to light a drowsy group around a gambling-table, or a still drowsier conversation between two or three village elders.

The village possessed a very out-of-tune ceremonial *gamelan,* but only on feast-days were the metal keys and gongs unlocked and set up on the rough wooden stands that lay piled in a corner of the temple. This *gamelan* had a thin disagreeable sound, for some of the instruments were missing, and one of the great gongs had once fallen and cracked, and now gave only a hoarse rattle when struck. It never occurred to the men whose part it was to play at the temple (they did not call themselves a club) to gather and practise, or make music for pleasure. They had been playing the same four or five ceremonial pieces that their fathers had played before them; these were sufficient to honour the gods with music, and there was no need to learn any others.

This collection of aged instruments belonged to my own *banjar*, Kutuh. The *banjar* of Mas to the south had two more *gamelans*. One belonged to the *légong* club, but there had been no dancers for years. The musicians, however, played from time to time at ceremonies in the temples of their own *banjar* only, for it seemed that even in Sayan there was unfriendliness between *banjars*. Chokorda Rahi, the prince, had trained a troup of *arja* players for a while, but the prettiest girls had married, there had been a quarrel among the actors, and the club had disbanded. There was, however, the *jogéd* dancer whom Chokorda Rahi had also trained. She was no beauty, said Kesyur, and her dance was mountain style. But it was at least entertainment.

The reason for this apathy lay perhaps in the fact that Sayan stood on the very outskirts of the old kingdom of Gianyar. It was a new village, said Rendah, only recently settled. In the time of his grandfather the ridge had been covered with heavy jungle. Young men who had wished to establish households of their own had come from the crowded town of Pliatan, a few miles to the east; they had been given grants of land when they married in return for their services in the palace of the old Chokorda as *parakans*, temporary slaves or attendants. Slowly they had cleared the land, terraced the slopes of the valley for their rice and corn, built further canals and conduits to bring water into their fields.

At the river they went no farther, for across the valley to the west began the kingdom of Tabanan. The slopes had once been the scene of occasional skirmishes between the two enemy rajahs. Rendah could still remember. How many times had he seen the foe pursued across the valley! With gongs and banners the warriors marched from Gianyar, armed with spears and blow-pipes, even guns. The priests came too, while the rajah rode on a white horse. You could hear the drums for miles. Once they had fought on this very land, here where my house now stood.

I asked him if many were killed in these battles. He shook his head. He could hardly remember two he had seen with his own eyes. And one was drunk, he added seriously.

Little by little, as they had in Kedaton, people began to wander in from the village, to sit politely on the edge of the veranda and gaze at the complicated structure of the house. Sometimes they were strangers from far away with something to sell, a *kris* or mask, or newly woven pandanus mats and homespun of whitest thread. Sayan was on a road which ran far into the mountains, and soon boys from the hills began to appear with the most surprising objects. One day I had bought a couple of young monkeys, and now, within a month, there were brought to the house jungle-fowl, a flying fox, an iguana, a small python, tiny red and green parrots that slept hanging upside-down from their perches and a young hornbill, still without feathers and looking like a goose ready for the oven. From the sea, twenty miles away, a frail old man now made a weekly call with his basket of fresh salt. Sometimes, with a crafty smile, waiting for my exclamation of surprise, he would slowly remove the cover to disclose a few lobsters or crabs lying on top of the salt. Long and leisurely bargaining was the very essence of these transactions, and I soon learned not to destroy all pleasure in a sale by bringing it quickly to a close and accepting the first price mentioned.

Often my visitors arrived with a present—*a* hen, a few eggs, a basket of mangoes; but although these gifts were set down with the briefest of words indicating their presence, they were (I soon discovered) usually to be considered as payment in advance for something wanted in return—an empty kerosene tin, a glass jar, or medicine which might possibly help the giver's rheumatism. One afternoon an old man sat down, to make a polite request for a sheet of fine paper, white, and with, he added, a star for watermark. This I did not have, but among my things I found a writing pad that had been marked with a large crown, and I asked my visitor if this might do. He held the sheet of paper to the light, looked at it searchingly, but after saying it was not what he was seeking, he made a final bow and departed as mysteriously as he had come.

One day a visitor from the other *banjar* came in and sat for a long time in silence. He looked the house up and down. His wrinkled eyes took in the other buildings.

Béh! Now we have *two* palaces in the village, he finally remarked. One to the north, one to the south. Only the Chokorda's is falling, he added politely.

I had not thought till now of how my house might be considered in Sayan, and I found this comment far from agreeable. It would not leave my mind. I thought with regret of the Mountain of Flowers in Kedaton, and the easy friendliness of the village. But gradually the remark lost its sharpness. For the relationship between palace and village had long been recognized and accepted; my role, already cast for me by the people of both *banjars*, was, I realized, the only natural one for me to play. Fortunately, I could remember the Anak Agung of Saba perched on top of his step-ladder, or seated among his musicians with a drum in his lap. I thought of the Anak Agung of Lukluk applying with loving care the make-up on the faces of his dancers; of Chokorda Johni, who drove a truck. I was grateful for the flexibility of the part assigned to me, and I only hoped I might be able to play it with imagination.

One late afternoon as I sat reading, there was the sudden clatter of a bicycle coming down the gravel road, the sound of a rusty brake, and a boy of perhaps seventeen got off his machine, leaned it carefully against a tree and came up to the house, to sit down on the veranda floor with a quick smile and bid me a slightly breathless good day. It was Durus, whose singing I still remembered coming out of the darkness the night of my arrival, above the sound of other voices as the men roasted the pig. He was here now, it seemed at first, to sell me a ring, for he was from Batuan, a village of goldsmiths. But as he sat there it soon developed that the real object of his visit was to ask if he might work in my house. He could write, he said. He could read. He could polish lamps, be my secretary, learn to be useful.

He spoke eagerly. There was a bit of the startled deer about him in his nervous grace, and also a candour, an impulsiveness in his voice and manner that I thought very charming. The idea of a poet in the house amused me, but I said I did not know yet if I needed anyone else, and that I would think about it. I asked him about himself.

No, he had not gone to school. His father had taught him to read and write. He had read as much as he could find that was written in the Balinese language; but he knew only a few words of Kawi, old Javanese, in which most of the ancient literature was written. He belonged to the newest *arja* club in Batuan, wrote verses for the singers and sometimes acted. What role? Oh, he was best as Kartala, one of the comic attendants.

Batuan was only ten miles away, and it was not long before I began to expect the sudden and always slightly excited arrival of Durus every few days as he came to tell me of a feast or play he had just heard of, that would take place somewhere near his own village, or else to announce that he had no news whatever, but had simply come to pay me a call.

He was very good at explaining the plot of the play when we went to a performance at night, and would often appear a few days later with the story we had seen acted written out in great detail. He now began to bring me palm-leaf books which he said had belonged to his father, who had been something of a seer and scholar as well as goldsmith. How this collection had come together I could not imagine, for the titles were strangely varied—The Laws of the Smith; The Creation of the World; Of Objects to be Buried on Building a Temple; Means of Detecting a Thief; The Tale of Birds Who Formed an Actors' Club. But I could make nothing of the texts, since they were in the old

Kawi language, and I now made arrangements with Madé Gria, a scholar and *dalang* whom I already knew in Ubud, to come to the house a few days a week and translate into Malay these ancient writings that seemed to me so full of mystery.

Soon Durus had become one of the household, for Pugig had decided he needed a helper. He sang as he polished the silver, and he was forever writing verses for some imaginary *arja* play. These verses were in the strictest classical style, I discovered, although the subject was often a considerable surprise. One day he commemorated in verse an account of an agreeable excursion we had made the day before, complete with the route we had taken, Kesyur's bad temper at the blow-out he had had to mend, our picnic in the mountains, and the town where we had stopped to buy cigarettes and ice-cream. Durus had composed this little poem in the metre of Durma, which has seven lines of different length to a verse, and I was amused to find his stanzas coincide exactly, down to the number of syllables and the vowel endings to each line, with the verse by that name as it was given in Raffles' book on Java, published over a century before.

This is a handsome poem, I said. You must read it.

But instead of reading it he sang it to me, in the chant proper to the metre. Poetry could not be read, it seemed; it must be sung.

One day he returned in triumph from Batuan with a rare text he had discovered in the home of the *klian* in his village. It was a book of recipes and ingredients for the different feast dishes, written in verse. But when I gave it to Madé Gria, the *dalang*, to read, he looked at it for some time, and at last, finding the stanzas unfamiliar, he said:

I cannot read it, for I do not know the tune.

But never mind the tune; just read the words.

But he only repeated: I can't; I do not know the tune. . . .

To-day you may not write, announced Durus as he brought in

the coffee early one morning and found me beginning a letter. Nor read. . . . That is, if you intend to follow custom as you say. It is the day of the books. . . .

It was the last day of the *galungan* festival, a day of general purification, when all who could made a pilgrimage to the sacred pool of Tampaksiring in the hills to bathe. It was also a day dedicated to Saraswati, goddess of wisdom and learning, a day of peace, and quiet visiting among friends.

That afternoon, together with old Rendah, Durus and Kesyur, I drove up the road that led to Tampaksiring. As we approached we could see in the valley below the long rectangular pool of clearest water. The bright holiday clothes of men and women as they came and went were shining specks of pink and green, yellow, blue and orange.

We arrived at the gates, to enter the men's side of the bathing-place and undress. Beneath the spouts of water that ran out from the pool we stood along with strangers who had come from far away, men and boys who spoke and laughed softly among themselves, their voices half drowned by the cheerful sound of falling water. It was a sunny afternoon, with a clear blue sky, and the air was filled with a quiet Sunday peace. On the way home Durus wished to go on to Batuan, to his house, in order that Rendah and I might visit and be served with "yellow rice," the dish which was made on this day only, in honour of the gods, particularly the goddess Saraswati.

The same atmosphere of peace hung over the household of Durus. With smiling words of welcome we were led to a pavilion, and from where I sat I could see over the walls into the little house temple, with its shrines now filled with flowers and offerings of rice. As I sat there, tasting the faintly scented rice which had been placed before me, piled in a silver dish, I felt indeed that I was nourishing the divinity within me. Its flavour was enchanting, for among the grains of rice stained with turmeric to a golden yellow, the colour of the gods, there were scattered shreds of verbena and the pink, waxlike petals of the *kechichang,* a blossom with a taste acrid and utterly strange, like the taste of coriander leaves.

On the way home, as we passed through Ubud, I stopped to pay a call on Walter, since it was visiting-day, but he was not at home. We returned to Sayan, to find on the table by my bedroom door a large silver bowl of yellow rice, buried in flower petals. It was from Madé Gria, the *dalang.* Beside the palm-leaf books which he had been working on the day before there lay a little fan of blossoms.

How do you honour books in America? Durus asked as he set a lamp on the table. A large mantis flew out of the dark and settled in the circle of light.

I found it hard to explain.

THE TEMPLE OF THE DEAD

DURING THE *galungan* holidays, the island was suddenly filled with magnificent masked beasts. With glaring eyes and snapping jaws, with elaborate golden crowns, great hairy bodies bedecked with little mirrors, and tails that rose high in the air to end in a tassel of tiny bells, they pranced and champed up and down the roads from village to village to the sound of cymbals and gongs, as though they had newly emerged, like awakened dragons, from caves and crevices in which for months they had been lying dormant.

This was the *barong,* a beautiful composite animal, lion, said some, bear, said others, Ruler of the Demons, said still others. Parasols of white were held above his head in honour as he travelled along the road, and in the villages he danced and snapped his jaws obligingly before each gateway to clear the air of demons, while children gathered courage to approach and pluck a hair from his body for luck. Adored and terrifying creature, sacred pet filled with magic and protective power, his mask and shaggy hide were kept within the temple, and carefully guarded by the priest.

I could never quite understand his changeable nature. In some villages the *barong* departed at *galungan* time, to roam at large for a month, accompanied by his club of attendants and musicians, to play for a few pennies in village after village, revelling in his freedom like some beast escaped from a zoo. Yet in Sayan he seemed a captive, rarely leaving the village or even emerging from the temple, except to be taken to some sacred spring for purification. He remained there, unseen, his presence felt by all, referred to as the Great Sir when one wished to pay him special respect.

At festive afternoon performances these creatures were high-spirited and full of whims, dancing a strange ballet, coquettish and playful one moment, rolling on the ground like a puppy, and suddenly and unaccountably ferocious the next, snapping and stamping in fine fury as the two dancers within the body synchronized their steps and movements with beautiful coordination.

But when, late at night, towards the end of some play, the *barong* made a dramatic entry, looming out of the darkness to the sound of agitated drums, it was no longer the friendly, agreeable creature. It advanced slowly, with strange menace, its gold and mirrors shining dimly in the lamplight. Now it had become the mystic and supernatural form of king or saint about to engage in battle against the forces of evil, a conflict in which the last ounce of magic strength would be needed to put to flight the witch or demon foe. This was a dark moment in the drama, a moment of hovering on the borderline between reality and the unseen, for more often than not the dancers, carried away, identifying themselves perhaps with the beast whose body now enveloped them, fell into trance. Here a new drama might begin, for the *barong* often left the stage, to run quite wild into the night.

In Sayan, it appeared, the *barong* was unusually *sakti*—

charged with magic. Its body of white chicken feathers and its ancient mask were kept in the Temple of the Dead which stood just outside the village, to the south, along with the equally *sakti* mask of the Witch, the terrible widow, Chalonarang. Wrapped in cloth, protected with charms, the two masks were locked away until the time of the temple's anniversary feast. Now they were taken out, to lie side by side among the offerings, two complementary symbols for two magic forces—the magic of right and left, of light and darkness; positive and negative, protective and destroying.

There had been no temple feast in Sayan since I arrived, but one morning Rendah remarked as he came in that the Temple of the Dead would begin its celebration at the time of the next full moon.

The temple was a small one, and as there was to be little in the way of entertainment, it was not until the third night, the right of the departure of the gods, that I walked down the road late at night to watch the shadow-play that was taking place under the trees before the temple. It was a noisy play from the Ramayana. Prince Rama had called the apes and monkeys to help him wage war on the demon King Rawana and recover Sita, his stolen bride.

But one saw little of the noble Rama or the princess. Instead, the audience watched with enthusiasm an endless series of battles between demons and monkeys, for a *dalang* who specialized in this play was popular according to the realism with which he could imitate the sound of monkeys in rage and howl like a thousand demons great and small. The *dalang* that night was amazingly clever, and what with the sound of gongs and drums and the banging of the *dalang's* gavel during the fights, you could have heard the din a mile away. But in spite of all this commotion I began to yawn, and soon I fell asleep.

I awoke to find it close to dawn. The play had already stopped;

only a few boys remained, to watch the *dalang* put away his puppets. From within the temple there rose the long-drawn-out chant of women's voices.

Inside, the temple was half empty. Resting on their instruments, lying flat beneath the gongs, the musicians slept. I recognized the *gamelan* in the shadows as the one belonging to the south *banjar,* and among the men there were some whom I already knew—Sekan, a surly youth, head of the *jogéd* club; old Popol, the stone-carver; Klepus, son of the ironsmith; several boys who were always to be seen about the marketplace.

The *pemangku* finished praying and rang his bell. He got up and gently woke the drummer, for it was time to begin the *gabor,* the final dance with offerings. Slowly the men awoke and picked up their hammers. The light, animated music began, very softly.

In the darkness of the dimly lit courtyard (for the moon had sunk; there were only the stars) the women who were to dance stood waiting. Soon they began to move—in line, in pairs, in fours, breaking suddenly away to scatter over the courtyard and meet once more before the shrines and altars. They danced simply, with great dignity. I recognized old Koti, the hunchback sister of Rendah, among them, now beautiful as the others with her hair filled with flowers, her shoulders bare, her tightly wound black skirt trailing behind her as she danced.

But now the light began to change; in the east the sky had turned a faint yellow. Imperceptibly the music grew quicker; drums became more agitated. Suddenly from among the onlookers the priestess darted into the midst of the dancers in violent trance, waving in her clenched hand a *kris.* The dancers scattered. For a moment she seemed scarcely to move, but with a cry she clutched it in both hands and pressed the point to her breast. Tossing and writhing, her hair loose and flying, she now began to dance frantically, aimlessly.

As though her appearance were a signal, the music had changed with unbelievable violence. A new rhythm began to sound from the drums, heavy and ominous, as drumsticks now beat in rising fury. The hypnotic phrase of the music which had been repeated over and over for the last half-hour became a single reiterated note that rang, rang, rang above the clashing cymbals. Only the priestess danced.

All at once there was a commotion in the *gamelan*. One after another the musicians grew rigid, and fell with a crash over jangling keys. Youths and men rose panting, eyes staring as though answering some dreadful summons. *Sarongs* rolled to their loins, they stepped like somnambulists out into the centre of the court, *krises* high, bodies tense, until, with a sudden thrust of the blade against his chest, each threw himself into a frenzy. With wild stabbing motions they attacked themselves. I wondered at the strange resistance which kept the blade from entering the flesh, for I thought they must surely kill themselves. One by one they collapsed shuddering and sobbing to the ground, to lie with outstretched arms, flexing their backs, thighs braced, writhing in spasms both tortured and ecstatic.

In the early light the white form of the *barong* was now clearly visible. It stood at one end of the courtyard staring and motionless, but now two men entered beneath the body to bring it to life. Its little bells jingling softly, the beast came out into the centre of the court and stood there. Offerings were brought and set before it.

The light grew stronger. Bodies relaxed; the sobbing died. One by one the boys and men awoke or were awakened by the priest. They looked about, rose, and silently walked away.

Sometime during the night the gods had left.

Soon the only sound to be heard inside the temple was that of an attendant sweeping the empty court. A single dog sniffed among the offerings. The sun rose higher, shrivelling the fallen flowers, filling the temple with a blinding glare. In the village, by this time, daily routine had once more been resumed.

PRIMEVAL SYMPHONY

IHAD BEGUN TO GROW restless at the slow progress of the coolies on the house, for I was impatient to commence work. The piano had not yet arrived, and on the veranda of the sleeping-house the crates from Java stood unopened. One morning I called Kesyur and Durus and told them to strap the tent which I had brought from Europe to the back of the car, get together provisions and be ready to leave within an hour, for I had decided to go off on a trip of exploration.

The territory I had in mind was far at the eastern end of the island, beyond the last great town of Karangasem, where the villages lay scattered around the base of the sacred mountain, the Gunung Agung. Hot, glaring, this bleached, arid land suggested the primitive sunshine of Crusoe's island. In the tangled *lalang* grass iguanas met and fought with the fury of dinosaurs, and when at last you came to a village you were blinded by the reflections of the whitewashed walls that crumbled in the sun, unrelieved by any shade.

Here, it seemed, mysterious and ancient *gamelans* were to be found, unlocked only on the most solemn occasions. Antique musical instruments, long since discarded elsewhere as too simple and crude, were said to be still in use. I was particularly curious about one, a strange affair of bamboo, known as the *angklung*, which I had seen in the museum at Batavia. It was an early Indonesian instrument, used long before the coming of the Hindus. But although in Bali, even in Sayan, there were to be heard at feasts sweet-toned *gamelans* which bore the name of *angklung,* they did not include these ancient primitive instruments, nor did anyone recall a time when they had been used, or even what they looked like. But I remembered that once Nyoman Kalér had vaguely said he had seen them at a cremation in Karangasem, and now I decided to go and see for myself, for not only did I hope that these *angklungs* were still used; but I was eager to discover what kind of music they might make. I told Durus to pack my cameras and plenty of film, and said to Pugig that I would be away a week or even more.

Durus was elated. *Plesir!* he called out to Rendah in Malay; Off for pleasure! *Melalli!* he shouted triumphantly to Pugig, who must remain at home to guard the house—Off to forget! This charming word not only meant to "forget," but also indicated any expedition which had no clear or practical objective—a stroll, a visit without asking a favour, or to drive all over town at the *galungan* holiday in a dog-cart. Pugig uttered a sardonic farewell to Durus as he got into the front seat, and we drove off to Rendah's polite hope that we would have no accident.

Two hours later we were sitting in the Javanese restaurant across the square from the great palace of Karangasem. This was the last town for a hundred miles, and as we sat at the counter eating fried rice and skewers of goat's kidneys which the cook gently grilled over a charcoal fire, I studied the map. The road now ran along the stony edge of island until it reached Buleléng. Countless small roads branched inland towards the mountains, to join one another or simply come to an end. I decided to keep off the main road as much as possible, for it was in the villages of the hills that I thought I should be most likely to find what I was looking for.

It was late in the afternoon when I told Kesyur to stop the car just beyond a village on the slope of the mountain. Here at last were some trees beneath which I could pitch the tent, and after searching for a while I found a level place a quarter of a mile from the road. The tent went up without any trouble, and before it was dark Kesyur had already found wood and started a fire. Durus unpacked and began putting things in order—an air mattress, a folding chair and table, the dominoes and the gramophone. It was very much like home.

This activity was not long in attracting an audience. Out of nowhere appeared an old man, two youths and a small child, to watch in blank wonder. I offered the old man a glass of *arac,* but he shook his head.

But I ask for a cigarette, he was finally able to bring himself to say. He sat down on the ground near the table. The others gravely sat down behind him.

Tuan is from where? *Tuan* is proceeding where? asked the old man politely.

Melalli, I replied.

Ah, was all he said.

Conversation would have died had it not been for Durus and Kesyur. Now was the time for the gramophone, I thought, for I had brought it along for just such moments. I opened the machine and put on a *gamelan* record. With incredulous delight, they listened, too amazed to speak. But by the time the record was finished they had already accepted the surprising object as a charming plaything, incomprehensible indeed, yet no more wonderful than the tent or my transparent oilskin raincoat that hung from the tent line. One of the boys asked softly if the box knew any songs from the *arja* play. Whatever only! said Kesyur importantly as I put on the requested record. A thin, tremulous voice rose in the air above the faint sound of drums.

What style! remarked the old man. What a beautiful voice! Like honey!

The high, nasal voice had been well trained. It was the famous singer from Buleléng, Ni Limon—Miss Lemonade. Her voice was graceful, flexible, and full of little runs. I had not expected to find such keen appreciation in this remote spot, so far from anytown. As we sat there listening to the records, relaxed and friendly, I thought I might now begin to ask for information. I said I had heard that in these parts men still made bamboo *angklungs* in the ancient way.

They thought. Not here, but it was said that in the village of Chulik, far away to the east. . . .

How far? Oh, at least ten miles. . . .

As we talked I thought I heard the sound of a gong, the beating of drums in the distance. The men were practising in the village, said one of the boys. They were training a new *gandrung* dancer. Durus and I left Kesyur to watch the tent, and walked in the direction of the village.

In the clubhouse the men were startled to see me appear out of the dark, but they did not stop playing. The dancer was a listless boy of fourteen, with apathetic eyes, and feet out of time with the drums, and he went through the ambiguous, effeminate gestures of the dance as though his mind were far away. The musicians too seemed strangely apathetic, while the *gamelan* sounded thin and out of tune. It was an incomplete *Gamelan* of Semara, the Love God, never intended for dancing to, and as I watched the boy I wondered how he could move at all. The gaiety and bold sensuality of the dance depended on the light brittle tones of an orchestra of xylophones; here the echoing tones of the gongs simply slowed down the dancer's motions.

I had not been standing there long before a man came up and introduced himself as the village *perbekel*. Just arrived? he asked politely. I was from where? he wanted to know. On my way in what direction? He apologized for the *gandrung's* performance, saying they had no teacher. But when I asked him why the men used the *Gamelan* of Love for such a dance, he looked surprised, and said, What other *gamelan* could you possibly use?

I sat watching, and thinking how unmistakably the pulse and temper of a whole village were revealed through its musicians. Some *gamelans* were all flash and fire, some filled with mystery. Some were completely matter-of-fact, lacking any quality whatever. In this distant village the musical impulse that was so intense in the centre of the island had all but spent itself. The *perbekel* himself seemed a mere shell of a man, polite, correct, but dry and bleached as the soil of the surrounding country. I was delighted to find, however, that he knew of at least three villages nearby where I would find the *angklungs* I was looking for. One I had already passed through, while another lay farther up in the hills; the third was in Chulik, down by the sea, and this last, he thought, was the best, for the men knew the greatest number of melodies.

It was after eight when I bade the *perbekel* goodbye and left. At the tent we found Kesyur fanning the fire and talking to the old man, who apparently had not been able to tear himself away. The others had gone. Kesyur astonishingly had prepared a meal; he had killed one of the chickens and broiled it; he had made a stew of breadfruit and steamed a pot of rice. He and Durus would not eat with me, but insisted on serving me as though I were at home. Kesyur received my rather elaborate praise (I had never seen him so much as slice a piece of ginger) in injured silence. He had turned morose, suddenly depressed at being far away in a strange and quiet land. He disappeared with the old man, saying he must guard the car.

Durus, on the other hand, was in high spirits. He found the expedition an adventure. He set everything in order, and carefully put out the fire before he came into the tent. He lay there beside me, refusing to go to sleep and softly singing verse after verse of plaintive melody from the beloved *arja* play. The words were ineffably sad—the lament of a deserted princess, cruelly abused by a wicked stepmother; of a prince, beautiful as a golden god, sick as a wounded deer for love of the princess who loves him not. He paused. From a corner of the tent a cricket chirped. Outside a breeze stirred. He began again, about a princess who chased a golden dragonfly into the forest and was carried off by a demon king. But at last Durus' voice died out and he fell asleep.

Chulik lay at the edge of the stony wasteland that ran along the north-east coast, between the mountains and the sea. It was a tiny village, dry and dusty, and when I stopped at the market to ask the way to the house of the village *klian*, men and women stared and small children ran to their mothers. I told Kesyur to ask about the *gamelan,* but this was impossible for him to bring himself to do. Pride, as usual, interfered, and he would willingly have died rather than show the least ignorance of anything before a stranger, above all before these barbarians. It was Durus who finally got out and spoke to a market-woman. His voice was soft and disarming.

Jero, I offer my ignorance. They say there is a *gamelan* with *angklungs* in this village.

There is.

Durus paused to consider how to continue.

Jero, I beg indeed your pardon; but perhaps you could tell me where this *gamelan* is to be found.

She had no idea; but a boy standing by informed us it was kept in the house of the *klian.*

But the *klian* had gone to Karangasem and would not return before nightfall. It was late morning, with a searing sun, and I thought longingly of Sayan, where at this moment the skies would be overcast with heavy rainclouds. I looked on the map for the possibility of a more inviting place to spend the night. We took the road that turned down to the sea, and soon came to the little fishing village of Ahmed, a cluster of huts in an oasis of mangoes and palms. Here on the shore, just beyond the village, Durus and Kesyur opened the tent beside the fishing *praus* that lay drawn up in the shade. There was nothing to do now but wait for evening, when I could return to Chulik. I sent Durus to the market-place to buy some food already cooked, but all he could find were some little charred packages of baked fish, very dry and salty, a few preserved duck eggs and some cooked fern shoots. This, however, with a handful of cold rice, formed a repast that was sustaining if austere. Durus mixed a glass of coconut water and rum, and I settled back in my chair facing the sea and opened a torn volume of Proust.

But I was not to have the afternoon to myself, for it was not long before a deputation of three elderly men from the village approached to pay a formal call. They ceremoniously introduced themselves and sat down. In the course of the most leisurely, the most gentle of conversations it was disclosed that they had come to find out who the stranger was, his origins, his intentions. That I was here in search of *gamelans* only half satisfied them, but they politely passed to other things. Soon they were talking of ancient Bali and their own ancient lineage; of local adat, or law and custom, of equal antiquity and so different, it seemed, from elsewhere. They were Bali Aga, *real* Balinese, they stated with dignity, descended from the mountains. They could trace their ancestry back, back, to a time long before the coming of the Javanese princes, of the Hindus even.. ..

And Durus?

Of the guild of smiths, he said. His father had been a craftsman in gold.

They nodded. A smith, whether he worked in bronze or iron, was of the same remote and honourable ancestry. Even a rajah must use the "high" language, speak formally when addressing a smith. . . .

It was during this peaceful conversation that I learned of the sacred *gamelan* in the ancient village Tenganan, so holy that it was forbidden for an outsider even to touch it, for it had come from heaven long ago, beyond the memory of man.

But in Bungaya, it seemed, there was one still older, the gift of the God of the Sea. The oldest of the three men related its miraculous origin.

Long ago the men of Bungaya, far up in the mountains, were walking by the sea. All at once, from beneath the waves, they heard the sound of music like nothing they had heard before, and as they listened, the instruments appeared above the surface of the water, still sounding. One by one they were washed ashore by the waves, although they were of heavy iron. But the men of Bungaya did not dare to touch them and went back to their village. Their priest told them to return, make offerings on the shore, and bring the instruments to Bungaya.

The instruments were placed in the temple and honoured. Time passed, but they were never used, for no one knew how they should be played. One day, as the village elders sat in the temple, a white raven flew down from the sky and perched in a tree above their heads. From this bird the elders learned the five different modes, and the melodies of these modes, whose names and tones it is forbidden to reveal to strangers.

Even to-day, said the old man, the people of Bungaya must sit in reverence as the instruments are carried out of the temple. These instruments may not pass beneath bridges or even telephone wires. When, during a procession to the sea, the people of Bungaya come to these wires they cut them down, and pay without complaining for the cost of reparation. One day, as they passed through a neighbouring village, the men and women stood in doorways and laughed at this ancient *gamelan*. But they were sorry later, for not long afterwards their village caught fire, for no apparent reason. . . .

The shadows lengthened. The fishermen began to drag their boats to the water's edge. The old men rose and departed, and as Kesyur had found a boy to watch the tent, we got into the car and drove back to Chulik.

The *klian* was drinking coffee at the market-place. I told him why I had come, saying I had heard of the most excellent *gamelan* in this village, and that I was sorry there was no feast at the moment where I could hear it, as I had come from far away. Would it not be possible, I asked cautiously, for the men to assemble and play, if only for a short time, since in my part of the country there were no *angklungs*. . . . Perhaps if I offered them five guilders to buy *sirih*?

The *klian* was thoughtful. This was something without precedent. There was no law to forbid, but he must first consider all possible dangers. He finally agreed. To-night, of course, was impossible; it was too late. (By that he meant, too late to break the news; too late for the men to grasp the situation; too late for them to come to an agreement, take out the instruments, get in the mood to play.) But if I would return to-morrow, when the sun stood there (he pointed) in the sky, the men would be waiting in the clubhouse pavilion. I thanked him. But I had one more request. Might I see the instruments before I left?

My impatience for immediate action was both unnatural and incomprehensible. He clearly hated having to make up his mind, then and there. But courtesy prevailed, and after hesitating a while he assented.

It was now night, and the courtyard of the *klian's* house was pitch-black, except for a feeble lamp that hung in one of the pavilions. He unlocked the door to the *gedong,* a small building with four stone walls, and I turned on my flashlight. Drums, gongs and instruments I had never seen before lay piled together on the floor. And the *angklungs?* I asked.

The *klian* disentangled a strange object. It vaguely resembled a harp in shape; within an upright frame hung three bamboo tubes of different lengths, and when the *klian* shook the frame to and fro the tubes produced a strange hollow rattle, soft and musical. A more primitive instrument could hardly be imagined, and yet, as with so many primitive implements, there was both ingenuity and science, for the tubes diminished in mathematical ratio to create a harmony that was surprisingly pure. As I listened to the sounds the centuries fell away; a golden age echoed in the bamboo tubes.

Kesyur and Durus looked in blank astonishment. They were not impressed. The *klian* locked the door, called into the darkness for another lamp, and led me to the main pavilion.

The *gamelan,* which belonged to the village, was taken out and played only when there was "work in the temple," or during the rites that accompanied the cremation of the dead. The rest of the time it was stored. It was the same in other villages near by, added the *klian*; Prasi, Mega Tiga, Poh. . . .

But are there no other music clubs in the village?

None. There is an *arja* company in Kangkang, a shadow-play in Ngis, but that is all. We are simple people.

He walked with me to the gate. Once more I reminded him of to-morrow. Agreed! It is certain! I said good night and left.

Béh! It's empty in this country! exclaimed Kesyur. I would die here! Durus agreed. In his village by this time all would be animation. The *arja* club would be practising. The square in front of the great temple would be filled with twinkling lamps; the women would be there with their tables of food; the little gambling tables would be crowded. We drove along in silence.

The tent was deserted. It was up to me to keep the two boys from being attacked by that sudden depression and boredom that can descend on a Balinese without a moment's warning. We built a fire, turned on the gramophone. To the strains of Mood Indigo the chicken fought as Kesyur slit its throat. Two or three strangers appeared from out of the dark, to sit at the edge of the circle of light from the lamp and silently watch. They looked on in uncomprehending sympathy as Durus, then Kesyur, won a little pile of cash when later we played a few hands of rummy.

As we drove into Chulik the next afternoon I heard the sound of strange wild music down the road, so different from anything I had yet heard on the island that my heart began to beat with the anticipation of discovery. An unbelievable array of instruments filled the pavilion—angklungs, xylophones, *g'ndés,* gongs and cymbals. The men had already given themselves up to the music, lost in the reverberations of sound that eddied and swirled about them.

It was a barbaric symphony, an unheard-of blend of primitive sonorous materials, of metal, wood and hollow reeds. The melody rose ringing and metallic from the g'ndérs, far above the other instruments. Cymbals clashed, little gongs murmured; the dry notes of the xylophones clicked like hail. But it was the strange notes of the angklungs which gave the music its primeval resonance. One after another, in rapid but irregular succession, they trembled as the players shook them, creating a mysterious tremolo background, insistent, soft, like the low sound of wind in the lalang grass.

Over and over, like a record caught in a groove, the melody repeated, relentless, without the least change of expression. It had a very narrow range, for there were only four different notes in the scale of the instruments, and the completely strange relation of these tones to each other, the strangeness of their tuning, gave the music a quality I cannot describe, created an atmosphere of incredible antiquity. It was like tracking music to its source.

Once again I felt that exultation I had suddenly known the day I first arrived on the island, when I stood listening in the Chinese temple in Buleléng. On and on the men played, on and on swept the melody, carrying you along with it in the reiteration that was both mechanical and hypnotic. Suddenly, without warning, the music stopped. What brought the men to a final halt I could not determine at all.

Crow Stealing Eggs, said the klian.

But when I asked him the meaning of the title, Ah! He could not say. It was old, very old! Perhaps from the very beginning. . . .

Once more the men began. I thought I could hear a slight difference in the melody, but I could not say where. It might as well have been the same piece as far as change went. And yet I could not find this music monotonous, for there was something which kept urging it on, some inner rhythm, far below the surface, which the ear began to follow instead. As the melody returned to its starting point, to repeat once more, there was a sudden agitation of drums, an accent from a gong, causing each time a feeling of suspense and a new release, like the endless flow of waves rolling one after the other to break along the shore.

White Horse, announced the *klian*.

But again he could not account for the title. On the men played, with tireless energy. Toad Climbs Pawpaw; Cow Drinks; Burning *Lalang* Grass; Hibiscus Flower. I had taken out my notebook and was writing furiously. It was not difficult to note the melodies as they were played by the *g'ndérs,* for I could fill in and correct during the repetitions.

It grew late. The last rays of the sun shot through the pavilion, lighting up the players, casting fantastic shadows. Suddenly I felt I could not listen to another note. I was completely exhausted. I told Durus to offer the money I had promised to the musicians, and to tell them that a few leaves of *sirih* were poor return for the pleasure they had given.

As the *klian* walked with me to the car I asked him if the performance could be repeated the next afternoon. I wished to listen again, hear more of this wild music, take moving pictures of the musicians as they played. The *klian* agreed; the instruments could be left out overnight, and there would be no difficulty.

I spent a happy hour the following day making pictures. When at last I was satisfied we moved the *gamelan* back in the pavilion, to begin where we had left off the night before. I wished to hear again one of the pieces I had written down, and asked for White Horse. The men looked blank. They consulted. White Horse? *Was* there such a piece? Only after several false starts were they able to begin, but the melody was that of Toad Climbs Papaya. Then I asked for Drinking Cow, but what I heard was Burning Grass.

At last I spoke, saying that yesterday they had played differently for White Horse. They looked astounded. Could it be? They began again. But now the tune was Hibiscus Flower.

I took my notes and sat down by a *g'ndér.* I felt professorial indeed as I said, But yesterday White Horse went like this! I picked up a *g'ndér* stick and began to play, reading from the page beside me on the floor.

A miracle! Mystification! Delight! They burst out laughing. Of course; indeed; the superior writing! Soon they had joined in, soon we were playing together as though we had been doing so all our lives.

It was clear the titles were mere labels. It mattered little, after all, what the tune was *called,* for the men took their cue from the soft brief introduction that was first heard on one of the *g'ndérs.* This most casual of suggestions was enough. The tonal sequence had been outlined, and now they had only to fall in, unquestioningly, at the right moment, and the air became filled with music.

The pieces they played resembled each other as the leaves on a tree; no two were identical, yet to discover variation required the closest scrutiny. As I sat there that night outside the tent, watching the play of moonlight on the sea and thinking with satisfaction of the last two days, I could not help smiling a little at finding myself suddenly absorbed in noting deviations with the eagerness of a naturalist. By the light of the lamp I looked over the sheets of paper spread out on the table, comparing the minute irregularities I found so charming in each melody. I knew I would not be satisfied until I had written down the last phrase of music the men could remember. I wanted to hear every *gamelan* in the countryside. Each leaf of the tree was precious; one could only know the tree by tracing the contour of every leaf.

What can you do with all these notes? asked Durus as he came into the tent.

I shall write a book some time, I said.

He was quiet for a time. Then, when I thought he had fallen asleep, he suddenly asked, Could I sell this book, would it bring me money?

But I was too sleepy to answer. Perhaps, I said. . . .

I passed a week among the villages scattered around the foot of the mountains, listening to *gamelans,* taking photographs, talking to musicians. Poh, Muntig, Kebon, Babi, the story was the same. The instruments were unlocked only at the time of cremations and temple anniversaries. Sometimes the men were friendly and eager to answer questions; sometimes they were shy and remote, refusing to respond, doubtful of my intrusion.

Flying Fox; Fighting Cats; One Hundred Cash and Some False Silver. They seemed strange titles for music intended for the gods or the rites of death. As I considered this I thought of a funeral procession I had once seen in a Mexican village. It was raining, and as the line slowly wound its way to the cemetery a small band followed in the rear, playing, in the same curiously detached way, on a tune that seemed equally irrelevant, The Darktown Strutters' Ball.

Kesyur was sulking. Durus had grown restless. We had stayed away too long. But their spirits immediately rose to a peak when one morning I announced the welcome news that we were going home. By way of Buléléng, I added, where we could go to the Bioscope that evening. This had the intended effect. Once more the excursion had the air of *plesir.* Objective had been attained, no longer existed. Once more it was *melalli.*

We drove sixty miles to dine festively at the Chinese restaurant and sit through an interminable Tom Mix film. The audience scented the plot in the first three minutes. They recognized at once the prince, the princess and demon king. They cheered the fights and flights as though they were at the shadow-play. They rose jeering and slightly scandalized at the final embrace and laughingly filed out the doors into the night.

THE REGENT

THE MAIN HOUSE WAS now finished. It had been built in the style of a theatre pavilion, and the long veranda was large enough to hold both *gamelan* and dancers. A wide lower step ran around the entire pavilion where an audience might sit and look on. It would also make possible the etiquette of caste should I have visitors of different rank at the same time.

At one end of the pavilion, where the curtains that concealed the actors might have hung, I had closed off a room for my piano and books. Above was a little balcony which overlooked the veranda. Here I wrote. The pavilion stood at the very edge of the cliff, and as I looked out from the balcony through the break in the sloping roof, out and down over the ravine and curving river, it was the looking out from a plane.

News of the house had begun to spread, and strangers passing through the village now wandered in, ignoring Pugig completely, to sit on the lower step and contemplate the construction. One afternoon Durus came up to the sleeping-house in a state of excitement. The Regent of Gianyar was below. I was barely awake, and as I splashed myself with cold water in the bath I wondered what could be the object of this visit.

I found the Anak Agung striding majestically up and down. He greeted me as a lord might his highest vassal, saying he had come to look at my house. Short, heavy, incredibly overbearing, he had the air of melodramatic tyrant, with a face that was a masterpiece of sensuality, cruelty and cunning. His *sarong* and headcloth were arranged in extravagant folds. Enormous moonstones buttoned his white official jacket, and his fingers were heavy with rings.

On the lower step of the veranda sat three old and obviously highborn attendants with his wallet of betel leaves, his golden box of betel nut and his golden-handled *kris*. They sat in aristocratic silence, clasping their hands and bowing in a *sembah* each time the Regent tossed a word in their direction.

Nothing escaped the speculative glance of the Anak Agung. His eyes narrowed as he asked the price of the piano or the peacock-chairs. He approved the floor, which had been polished with pumice and now shone like green marble. He found the carving in the pillars good, though the lacquer was too thin. The bamboos beneath the thatch would have wormholes within five years, and I had been done on the thatch, but he admired the long board above our heads which hid the angle of the roof, carved with astronomical figures that Madé Tantra had covered in gold. He turned to the doors. They came from an old palace, and were carved in the Chinese style with leaves, flowers and birds. They had been gnawed at the bottom by rats, and the Regent could not understand why I did not have a door like the one at the District Office. He suggested a motor to pump water from the ravine; it would also give me electric light. Once more his gaze swept the place, resting for a moment on Durus as he set the tea on the lawn.

His eyes met mine in a glance of insolent penetration.

The air is salubrious, he remarked, looking across the valley. He turned to leave, adding unexpectedly that if I wished to hear one of his palace *gamelans* at any time I had only to let him know. Followed by his attendants, he strode up the road to his car, holding the trailing end of his *sarong* off the ground like a king in the *arja* play.

He was still feared to the very borderlines of Gianyar. His spies were everywhere, said Rendah. He knew of every nubile and attractive girl in every village. He had many devious ways of extracting money or seizing property, and only the most courageous and "advanced" thought of taking these matters to court before the *Controller*, for the revenge of the Regent, continued Rendah, was like water that ran under the earth.

Soon after my arrival in Sayan the news spread in hushed delight that thieves had broken into the palace at night and stolen the Anak Agung's three most precious *krises*. This, said Kesyur, had clearly been done from a double motive. The *krises* were of great value, for the hilts were thick with jewels. At the same time the Regent had been disgraced, for the *krises* were full of magic power, and were carefully guarded. Yet the guards must have slept, the *krises* could not have been so charged with magic, Kesyur said scornfully, if thieves could steal them so easily.

When at last the thieves were discovered and brought to trial they insisted they had thrown the *krises* in the sea (though everyone knew they had buried them), and cheerfully went off to serve three years in jail. The Regent had first pled for confession by torture, but the *Controller* had refused. He had then demanded their death, and on this too having been refused, he had cried in anguish, But at least allow me to have their ears cut off! In the old days, said Durus, they would certainly have been put to torture. How? Oh, stuck with needles, perhaps. . . . Or impaled, added Rendah, in a palm tree. The shoot of the new leaf grew two feet a day, he amplified, and in two days would open, scattering their arms and legs . . .

The Anak Agung, it seemed, could not bring himself to part with a grain of rice. When for some gala occasion he hired a troupe of actors from another district (thus being forced to pay them) he gave them the minimum fee and offered them the meagrest of left overs from the feast, so that more than once I heard the crowds scream as, in front of the palace during an arja play, the comedians exposed the Regent under his nose.

Little brother, why are you so sad? Why do you look so ill?

Alas! older brother, how can I be gay? How can I act? I am weak from lack of food. I shall die. A handful of yesterday's rice! A single dried fish! One miserable shred of garlic for seasoning! Do you call that a supper for a poor man to dance on? Here the clown collapsed completely, while the other searched frantically in his wallet for food to revive him.

But in the palace of the Anak Agung stood a *gamelan* I had long wished to hear. It was one of the few *gamelam* of Semara, god of love, that still remained on the island. I had once heard this *gamelan* for a short time, as it was brought out of the palace for some event on the great square before the gates. Carved with dragons and fantastic blossoms, shining with lacquer and gold, the instruments rang with an elegant, sweetly poignant music which I had found enchanting. I was now glad of the Regent's invitation, and intended to take advantage of it as soon as possible. In Sayan I had begun to miss the sound of music at night, for only rarely did the deep note of a gong or the beating of drums disturb the silence, and then only from a great distance.

Above all I missed the activity of Kedaton and the sound of Nyoman Kalér's *gamelan* rehearsing, and I had begun to wonder if it might not be possible to form some such club in Sayan: I must try to think of some way to bring music back once more to the village and set the boys and men practising again. Yet I still felt a stranger in Sayan, and could not make up my mind exactly what to do.

One morning, as I sat in the little coffee-stall under the banyan at the market-place, chatting with Chokorda Rahi and watching the women bring in their wares, for it was market day, I said that if he would call his musicians together again to practise, I would ask Nyoman Kalér to Sayan to train new *légong* dancers. Didn't he think, I asked, that the village was at the moment rather lacking in diversion?

He agreed. But when Nyoman came he could not find three children whom he could possibly teach. To choose the *chondong*, the little girl who would take the part of the attendant, was easy enough. But for the two others, who must be supple, and delicately formed, he searched in vain. We could not find a satisfactory pair that matched. One was too tall, another too stiff. Another was pretty but clearly too absent-minded. A fourth would have done, had she not squinted. He gave up. If you had only built a house in Kedaton, he said, instead of going far off among mountain people. . . .

The whole problem was soon to be solved almost without my knowing it through Sampih, a small boy who had already been living *in* my house for some time.

SAMPIH

I HAD FIRST MADE his acquaintance not long after the coolies had begun work on the house.

One afternoon I had gone down the hillside to the river and waded to the other side to walk along the edge of the ricefields which ran down to within a few yards above the level of the water. A crowd of smallboys splashed in midstream, leaping from rock to rock. Their wet brown skins shone in the sun as they danced up and down in the ecstasy of nakedness. They were completely wild, agile and delirious as a treeful of monkeys.

The river was shallow at this spot, but farther up it ascended in a series of cascades and disappeared between two walls of rock. These rivers have quick floods after sudden heavy rains in the mountains; they are normal one moment, and the next, with a rush and roar, an unexpected tidal wave may sweep down, cutting a deeper gash into the land, and carrying with it trees, cattle and even men.

It was while I was walking along the river's edge that one of these floods occurred. The skies in the mountains were black, and now, suddenly, there was a warning rumble in the gorge. The children heard it at once and leapt for shore. It was not a big flood; it merely raised the river a foot or so as it rushed down in muddy, swirling eddies. I started back, for it seemed easy enough to cross by wading and jumping, but I soon found myself in deep water where the current was far too strong. The children shouted excited directions from shore, but I could not hear what they were saying. It was then that one of the more boisterous, one whom I had already noticed as the leading spirit, threw himself into the water, swam to a boulder and jumped over to where I was struggling. He knew by heart every shallow and hollow in the river bed, for he quickly led me ashore by pointing here, shouting not to go there. I understood one word in ten, but the inflections of his voice were enough. When we reached land this naked, dripping youngster and I stood facing one another. He was perhaps eight, underfed and skimpy, with eyes too large for his face, daring and slightly mocking. I offered him a cigarette, but he suddenly took fright and was off into the water before I could say a word.

It was a week before I saw him again. I had gone over to talk with Gusti Lusuh about the house. Several children stood watching the coolies; they fled the moment they saw me, but not before I had recognized my guide of the week before.

Who is he, the largest?

A small man from the ravine below; he lives in a field hut.

Gusti Lusuh pointed to a cluster of tiny huts down the valley, adding morosely, A little thief!

What is his name?

I Sampih.

The next time I saw him he was alone. He lingered a moment as I came down the path, watching me, estimating each step. When I got nearer than his nerves could possibly bear, he was off over the side of the cliff. It was like approaching a small wild animal. But one day he stood his ground, returned my glance, and cautiously approached to take the cigarette I held out.

It wasn't long before we were friends and he found himself daring to do the coveted thing, ride in a motor car. He sat beside Kesyur, terrified and delighted. We drove to Den Pasar and his eyes opened wide at the smooth lawn of the Assistant Resident's house, the line of shops on the main street. An explosive *Béh!* burst from his lips. I gave him a ten-cent piece, and he walked down the street hand in hand with Kesyur to buy a dubious-looking ice and five packets of Javanese cigarettes.

This excursion marked a step in our relationship, for I had taken him to a foreign land and brought him safely back. The experience had not been too terrifying. But the next time, as we crossed to the north side of the mountains on our way to Buleléng, he was nearly frightened out of his wits as we descended into this strange country. Where's north? he cried. I pointed straight ahead. Kesyur pointed backwards.

Kesyur was actually right, for "north" has a flexible meaning. It refers to the mountains that run across the centre of the island. "South" means seawards. Once you have crossed over the mountains these directions are automatically reversed. Only east and west remain unchanged. Thus a southerner in the north is hopelessly confused. More than confused—actually ill with uneasiness. It is worse than being drunk. For Balinese are so conscious of themselves in relation to the points of the compass that they are helpless if they lose sight of them. A road does not turn left; it turns west. You move a table to the southwest; a pen on the table lies north-east of the ink bottle.

The experienced Kesyur explained, but Sampih would not be convinced. He slumped in the seat, miserable, joyless. Suddenly as we came to the sea he cried out once more,

Béh! What's that?

The ocean.

What's that, the ocean?

Ach, stupid, it's water.

Look, look! It's coming up all over the land. We'll be washed away!

What simple talk! Those are only waves.

Béh!

What a number of things to talk about once safely home! From now on, in spite of these dangers, Sampih was sure to appear sooner or later, when I came to Sayan, to stand near the car, silently begging to be invited into the front seat. One day I asked him if he would like to work at the house when it was finished;

he could take the ducks to the ricefields, peel onions for Rantun the cook. This proposal frightened him so much that it was a week before I saw him again. There was no further allusion to the matter; but soon there grew a tacit agreement between us, and it was taken for granted by everyone that he would become one of the household.

Sampih's father scratched a living from a few acres that jutted between the cliff and the river. He raised a little rice and a few banana plants. He was a handsome man, shy and smiling in public, brutal at home, often away for days on some amatory expedition. His wife was a small thin woman, no more shrewish than another, with an elfin face and eyes that reflected craft, trouble and pathos. The household was completed by two small girls, still of the age to run naked, and an old man, a vague relative, who sat all day uselessly whittling. The family was startled indeed when I appeared one day to ask if Sampih might work at the house. The dog howled; the children hid. Sampih's mother stopped dead as she saw me. It was Sampih who led me to sit in a place of honour and called out for bananas for my refreshment. But we grew at ease, and on a later visit it was agreed that Sampih should work at the house. He could sleep there or come home at night as he pleased.

I thought you a demon at first, Sampih confided one day; that is why I was afraid to come and live in your house. At first I did not dare.

A demon? But why?

Béh! Your round eyes! Your great voice! Your white skin!

Since when does a demon have white skin?

He considered this.

But you live beside the graveyard, and there was word that you dared to eat fire.

This, I discovered, referred to the fact that I had taught Rantun to make pancakes with burning rum. As she watched me show Pugig how to ignite them and serve them still in flames she was frightened half to death. Later, however, she would often send word around the village when she planned to make them, so that people might come and see. They sat in the dark, outside the veranda, silent and wondering.

It was not long, however, before Sampih was begging Pugig to let him light them himself and bring them to the table.

Soon after Sampih came to live at the house his parents made a formal call. Sampih's father wore *sarong, kris*, white shirt and an old train-conductor's cap. His mother had on a black winding skirt, with a new bath towel wound above her breasts. On her head she carried a stand piled with fruit. They sat on the floor at the edge of the veranda and thanked me for taking their child. Sampih's mother did the talking, uttering long cliches of politeness in an affected voice; her husband said nothing at all after the opening words, I crave indulgence.

They relaxed somewhat after Pugig placed cigarettes and the *arac* bottle on the floor beside them. Sampih's mother now began a long tale of family connections across the river in Bangkasa. Her voice cracked and cackled, and when at last she paused for breath I asked her about Sampih.

She drew in her breath and began again, this time in a new voice, whining and rhetorical. Up and down her voice trailed, steeped in sudden self-pity.

Trouble . . . trouble. . . . Difficult from the time he could walk. Naughty . . . disobedient . . . daring . . . . One day his father beat me. Sampih grew very angry. He hit his father. Then his father beat him, hard, hard. When his father was not looking, Sampih stole his purse and ran away. I cried . . . cried! He was still so *small*. No one knew where he had gone. When I went to sell at the market in Mengwi I asked, Is Sampih here? No one had seen him. When I went to sell in Ubud I asked, Have you seen my child, I Sampih? But always no! Lost . . . lost. . . . After a month he came home. Hard . . . so very hard!

Sampih listened to this narrative indifferently.

How did you live while you were away?

I hid in the house of my uncle. I went as far as the mountains. When the money was spent I came home.

How old is this Sampih? I asked.

Mother and father looked at each other. I heard bits of phrases; died of fever—before the earthquake . . .

The father spoke at last. I offer my ignorance; perhaps four years.

Sampih's mother was indignant. Indeed not! Eleven, most likely.

It was a few months later that I came home unexpectedly one evening to find the phonograph on the floor, playing the loudest and most syncopated *gamelan* record, and Sampih seated beside it improvising a wild *kebyar* dance. He was showing off to Durus and Pugig, and although he stopped the moment he saw me it was not before I had a glimpse of melodramatic gestures, coquettish eyes and flashing hands that caught with surprising precision the violent and abrupt accents of the music. But nothing would induce him to go on. This little performance was for his own private amusement, something intended for the two boys, but not for me.

That night I questioned Durus.

Oh, he often plays the phonograph when you are away. He is always dancing.

But can he?

He could. . . . His eyes are beautiful, and he can make his face very sweet. It is too bad his skin is dark and rough. . . .

Durus spoke with the cold appraisal of one raised in the theatre. It was not for nothing that he came from Batuan, famed for its actors and dancers.

Each night I played the phonograph, hoping to lure Sampih back into another mood of exhibitionism. One night, in an overflow of high spirits, he suddenly begged,

Play a *kebyar* record.

As it played, I said slyly, Try dancing this one.

He had been laughing, but he stopped, looked astonished, falsely incredulous.

But I can't dance!

Ach, try! You did for Durus and Pugig only a week ago.

I'm too *ashamed*!

This I refused to believe. I started the machine again. All at once he decided to please me. With head bent forward, eyes on the floor he listened, waiting for the approach of a certain accent when, without warning, he plunged into a fury of movement, as a diver might plunge into a torrent. He sat there on the floor, swaying this way and that from the waist, his arms outstretched and his hands, reflected in the lamplight, flying about like birds. He smiled, opened wide his eyes, narrowed them, grew stern and threatening. He was an absurd little whirlwind, but I was fascinated to see his unmistakable feeling for the feverish music as he drooped with it or sprang into a theatrical pose on a ringing accent.

Suddenly he stopped. His voice broke into high, excited laughter.

I can't go on: I don't know how.

Where did you learn this much?

Alone. I saw Gusti Raka once, at the big temple feast in. Bangkasa.

Would you like to dance like him?

Perhaps . . . I don't know.

His voice fell. He sat there, suddenly depressed, silent, once more remote, negative. He went out; but a few minutes later there were the familiar sounds of shouting and laughter from the kitchen, Sampih's voice high above the rest. His mood had reached another phase.

I thought about this little scene for a week. One night I watched him as he brought in the lamps; he was singing to himself, and as he went out he struck the heroic pose of the *baris* dancer, striding down the veranda to the sound of an imaginary *gamelan*, and indicating the gong-accents by chanting—

Gong . . . Pur-r-r . . . K'mpli . . . Pur-r-r . . .

It was then that I had the sudden idea of an experiment. I wanted Sampih to study dancing. I had several reasons: I wanted to see what would happen; I was curious to know if his instinct for drama held any real germ for development; I also wanted to watch the process of teaching.

The problem lay in the choice of a dance-style. Kebyar has no tradition, has very little formality; moreover, most of the dancers I had seen seemed to suffer from a lack of any classical background or training. Yet what was there for Sampih to study at his age? *Nandir* had long since disappeared. *Légong* was for girls. He was too young for *baris*. There remained only *gandrung*, and here I anticipated a scene, for the dance was that of a boy dressed and dancing as though he were a girl. After a solo which displayed the dancer's skill, partners stepped forth, and the performance was one of flirtation. It was unusual in this part of the island, and for that reason unpopular, though old Rendah came out with the surprising news that he had been a *gandrung* dancer when he was little older than Sampih.

I went first to Nyoman Kalér. I told him the tale; he was not impressed. But he agreed to return with me to Sayan. He tightened his headcloth before a mirror, took up his *sirih*-pouch and, after calling to his wives that he was off to Sayan, followed me to the car.

Who is that person? asked Sampih suspiciously as he brought my coffee next morning.

The teacher of *légong* in Kedaton. How would you really like to learn to dance?

Béh! Where is Kedaton? I would not dare.

A boy your age? Kedaton is a fine village, near Den Pasar, with shadow-plays every night.

I would not dare!

If I gave you a flashlight. . . .

This he considered, so that when Nyoman appeared to say, disarmingly, *Tuan* says you like dancing, he only answered,

I offer my ignorance; I am stupid; I know nothing at all.

Nyoman stood up. Come over here!

The boy went to him, and he took hold of a hand, turned it gently, felt the wrist. He drew out the arm, bent it at the elbow, felt the bones. Then he took hold of the head and turned it from side to side, up and down.

Stiff as a nail! A real farmer's child! Smile!

A pathetic, drooping expression appeared around a mouth that yesterday had done nothing but tease and shriek with laughter.

Well, he has a dimple, said Nyoman.

The face went blank.

Nyoman sat down on the floor and told Sampih to sit opposite. He called for the phonograph. The music began, and with the signal accent he began to dance. He narrowed his eyes, smiled with pedantic sweetness; his hands postured correctly. Dance! he said; follow me; and Sampih began to move, mirroring him at first, then going his own way as the music grew rapid.

The record stopped. Nyoman reached for his *sirih*; he spread a leaf with lime and slowly rolled it. Then he put it in his mouth, chewed a moment and spat.

It's like this, he began at last. He is not what you might call stupid. But he has the body of a peasant. He will never be really graceful. Think of Rindy, who is about the same age, and who is already a good dancer. He is slender, supple; his skin is smooth as silk. This one is like a wild animal, rough like a strong wind. But his mouth is good, and his eyes are beautiful. He will never dance well, but he could be perhaps an actor of strong parts. If you wish, I will teach him for a while, for an actor must know how to dance.

Sampih had listened to this summary as though we were discussing someone else, and now he got up and left.

I went down the hillside to break the news to Sampih's mother. As she saw me she rested her pestle in the mortar she was pounding and came forward.

Tuan! she said, speaking through the wad of tobacco that stopped her mouth like a cork. She took it out. *Tuan!* she said more distinctly. *Tuan* comes! she shouted over the pigsty into the palms. Fetch a coconut!

Her voice sank to polite sweetness.

Welcome, *tuan*. My house is too unclean. I am poor, so poor! With a polite thumb she indicated the hut with the highest elevation. Please ascend; please be seated!

I gave a brief synopsis of the project.

She burst into tears, but she cried less with tears than pathetic and picturesque lamentation. Her grief was not deep, but rather the instantaneous reaction inspired by a remembrance of the past, of her small child once more in a strange land, alone among strange people, demons and unformulated dangers.

It is not what you might call far, I said. Kedaton is near Den Pasar where you walk twice a week to sell rice. I will bring him home often. Try to think: if he learns well, he will know how to look for money when he is older.

The magic word brought her immediately to her senses. Things became clear and practical.

He is tuan's child, she declaimed. I gave him and I asked nothing. The great priest of Bangkasa has claimed him as *budak* (serf-attendant) but *tuan* desired him and I have given.

Her voice modulated by degrees from the depths of sorrow to ecstatic enthusiasm. As for Sampih's father—he had nothing to say. He agreed to everything with a smile and a bow.

When *tuan* buys the flashlight I want one from Europa with a ship trademark. Those from Japan are cheap and soon broken.

Sampih's yielding came at the end of a three-day battle, and shortly afterwards I took him to Kedaton, bewildered but self-possessed. I left, saying I'd be back in five days.

I had hoped I might interrupt a lesson when I returned five days later. But Nyoman had discouraging news. No sooner had I left than Sampih had lost his sense of direction. Although Nyoman had pointed fifty times to the north, he simply could not remember. It was impossible to teach him; to say, take three steps east, bend south-west, was simply talking in vain. He can't even follow directions when I send him to market, said Nyoman. When he turns the corner he is lost, and has to be brought back.

At that moment Sampih appeared, pathetic, lifeless, almost sick, and as he saw me a look of utter relief came into his eyes. I took him home, but he was silent as we drove back. The road wound this way and that through groves and valleys. At last we came to the broad ricefields. The landscape grew familiar; to the east rose the great cone of the Gunung Agung, misty, unreal, yet strangely reassuring.

There's north! cried Sampih suddenly, pointing straight ahead. He began to laugh. He was a different child.

The first thing he did when we reached the house was to run to the cliff, look down the valley towards home. Far away a man ploughed in the field; two midgets followed a line of ducks that shone white in the later afternoon sun. All was well. He ran down the hillside, to remain at home for several days, until his sense of safety had been restored.

The same thing happened all over again a week later. Nyoman was baffled. I was about to take Sampih back in the car when I remembered that down the road past the temple there were some open fields. I told Sampih to follow me.

What mountains are those? I pointed.

Tabanan.

And what is that over there to the east?

The Gunung Agung.

Then north. . . .

Straight ahead.

Now you can't possibly forget again!

No, *tuan*.

Surely?

Surely.

Once more I left him, and the next morning he began his first lesson.

If you watch a Balinese dancer in a film without music you receive a strange impression. The dance seems to be taking place in slow motion. For a long time nothing happens. Suddenly, for no apparent reason, the dancer is seized with an outburst of energy, strikes pose after pose in rapid succession; whirls and spirals in a frenzy, hands flying, shoulders quivering; as suddenly falls into inertia. What is happening in the dancer's mind? What muscular life, if any, is at play beneath the dancer's stiff costume?

But look once more at the film to the sound of music. It is at once apparent that a mysterious energy is sweeping through the body of the dancer. Gestures that appeared relaxed and casual are seen to be at a peak of tension. The rhythm of the body, the halting of the hands, even the last movement of the eyes—all coincide to the last fraction of a second with the syncopated accents of the music. The dancer is the music, made visible.

This is particularly true of the long introductory dances, before the story "emerges." Here the metric construction of the music, even more than the melody, controls every progression, every movement. The dancer, it is true, creates a mood that prepares for the story which is to follow, but his movements, his gestures and postures must be considered before all in relation to the musical phrase. Sudden flurries of movement take their impulse from the sudden flurries in the drums, whose accents are now seen to be essentially quantitative. As the drums scan the phrases so the dancer scans the music, and the beauty of this part of the dance lies in the restraint, the abstract movement, pure, impersonal, which fits the music like a glove.

As the story emerges, the dancer is freed. He now occupies the foreground, while the music recedes, to supply a warmer accompaniment, soft or agitated, playful or violent, depending on the dramatic action which is taking place. But even now the dancer's movements are conceived and learned in closest relation to the phrase, while his hands, which form the "flowers" of the dance, his eyes which give the "accents" must be rehearsed until they and the flowers and accents of the music are one.

It was clear from the very beginning that Sampih preferred those dances which told a story or portrayed a dynamic character. He took forever in learning the opening dance, before the story began. He was impatient with its slow unfolding, its measured tempo, the restrictions which governed each movement of the hands or eyes, each position of the foot. On the other hand he learned with rapidity the violent and agitated dance of the raven that foretells disaster as it flies across the path of king Lasen, and in a short time he could give a spirited performance of *bapang*, the dance of an official preparing the way for a noble.

At first Nyoman would stand behind him to hold him loosely by the wrists, guiding him, impelling him, now this way, now that. Humming softly, Nyoman managed to give an impression of the whole *gamelan* as he went first from melody to gong-accent, or muttered a *kepuka-puk-DAG!* in imitation of the drums. Indeed, as I watched Nyoman with Sampih, it seemed as though he were playing some instrument, executing some languid *g'ndér* phrase as he slowly drew the arms out, or thinking of the drums as he agitated the hands in a series of rapid and intricate designs.

All this, however, was preliminary. *It* was only after Sampih was able to go through the outline of the dance by himself that the teaching really began.

Nyoman had two other pupils at this time: Rindy, a graceful lad, somewhat older, who had been studying several months, and Gatra, small, awkward, with the face of a good monkey. One after another they would dance, while the other two looked on. Stop! Nyoman would cry, to walk up and correct once more the position of the dancer, turning the hand this way, the body that, gently altering, modelling the pose until the body was a sculptural unity, invisibly framed, as though filling the panel of some temple relief. Once more he would begin to hum, take the child by the wrists and start him on his course. But soon the body would be flying off in all directions, elbows above the shoulders, hands clenched instead of gracefully opened.

Little by little the dance "entered." The positions of the body grew more clearly defined; the hands became more precise. These formal positions of the hands, these "flowers" of the dance, derived from antique gestures of the priest. But now no inner meaning, no mystic symbolism marred the purity of their beauty. They told no story. Abstract and ornamental, they brought each gesture to its ultimate fulfilment and gave the dance its final elegance.

Nyoman began planning a gala début for the three boys. A day auspicious for the launching of dancers was sought, and a theatre pavilion set up by the roadside. By nine in the evening of the performance the road was blocked with people. The pavilion was a blaze of lamps; the overture music had begun, and the bright sound of xylophones filled the air. But the dancers had not yet arrived. They were still in the temple, praying to Panju, hero and god of dancers and actors, that their "attempt" might be successful. We drew up by the pavilion where we could sit in the car and watch. The car was full: old Rendah, Durus, Sampih's mother and two small sisters had come along. All sat staring in silent wonder. Rendah spoke.

Which way is north?

Kesyur pointed, and he settled back to enjoy himself.

We waited. The music continued. At last, through the crowd, the dancers appeared and made their way to the chairs in front of the musicians. Their new costumes shone in the bluish light of the air-pressure lamps that hung from the roof. Their faces were white with powder, their eyebrows shaved and pencilled, and they sat there in the light, inanimate, the folds of their costumes stiff and graceless.

There was a pause in the music. Nyoman entered, to sit down and pick up a drum; the rapid *bapang* music began. Sampih stood up. He looked incredibly small as he stood there listening for his cue. His headdress was a bit too large; his winding skirt dragged slightly. I knew he was thinking of this in shame.

He opened his arms with the sudden thrust that meant he was parting curtains. He stepped forth, eyes wide, "searching for danger." He began to dance, slowly advancing, darting suddenly from side to side. No one considered it strange that he was a small boy, in girl's costume, doing a girl's interpretation of a high official. The audience watched as though they were watching a puppet in the shadow-play.

He was nervous. But his nervousness was beautifully concealed by the stylization of the dance, and he managed to give an adequate performance. Yet where, I wondered, was the wild child who had danced so ecstatically that night to the sound of the gramophone? I could recognize his temperament, now so subdued and hidden, only in the last few bars of the music, when all at once, as though from bravado, he seemed to open up, expand defiantly, and come to a triumphant end. It was now Gatra's turn.

Sampih's mother had been watching in silence. *Béh!* she finally exclaimed. That Sampih! She gave a rusty little laugh and fished in her sash for a leaf of betel.

Rindy was now dancing. He was very sure of himself. Slender, tall for his age, hidden coquetry in every glance, he moved with a cool grace that charmed the onlookers. Golden wings were attached to his arms, but instead of an ill-omened bird you had the impression of a flirtatious peacock.

The music stopped; the dancers left. There was to be no performance of the actual *gandrung* dance, when partners might step forth from the crowd. The audience dispersed.

As Sampih, followed by Nyoman, came up to the car, he gave me a look of utter disfavour and reproach. He silently got into the front seat, holding tightly the small suitcase that contained his costume. He was to have danced a second time, but this, said Nyoman, he refused to do. We said good night and Kesyur started the car.

Why wouldn't you dance again? I asked.

I was too *ashamed!* My costume was all wrong! I hate dancing! Besides, Nyoman Kalér would not let me dance the raven!

But why?

He was jealous! He thinks only of Rindy!

Nonsense, I said.

But how can *tuan* know? he answered fiercely. If *tuan* does not believe . . .

He went home that night to spend a week recovering from a complexity of emotions.

As for Nyoman Kalér, he was remote and evasive when I went to see him. He had done his best, he said. To please me. But Sampih's thoughts were elsewhere. Neither in his mind nor his body would the dance enter. It was vain to spend time on this mountain child.

I did not agree. I had no intention of giving up, especially when one day Sampih said, very gently, Am I not to dance any more?

But do you think you really want to?

Whatever *tuan* wishes. His answer was almost inaudible.

I resolved to find a teacher with more patience, someone younger and less pedantic. Someone, moreover, who would come to Sayan, where I would be able to watch the lessons from day to day. But who? There were many teachers to choose from. Chokorda Rahi, right here in Sayan, had indicated he would be only too pleased to continue Sampih's training, but I had no wish to bring down elaborate court culture about our heads. There was, moreover, too great a disparity in both age and caste. The lessons would be dreary. It needed someone young and lighthearted to draw this boy out, someone of his own class and temperament. All at once I thought of Champ-lung, one of the *légong* dancers of Bedulu. I had heard she had stopped dancing, since she was now almost fourteen, and had begun to train new dancers for the club. Already there was word of their excellence. I thought that if I could persuade her to come to Sayan, she would be the perfect teacher for Sampih.

But other preoccupations caused me to postpone plans for Sampih for the time being. Matters more urgent at the house now needed my attention.

IDA BAGUS GEDÉ EXPELS THE DEMONS

ONE SUFFOCATING AFTERNOON, as I lay in bed numb and stupefied from sleep, the house suddenly began to creak and shudder, to swim unaccountably before my eyes, slightly at first, and then with violence. I was out of bed and on the veranda in a flash. Outside the scene had become unreal and agitated. Palms waved, the ground rippled; the outlines of everything were blurred with movement. Almost immediately there rose a clamour up and down the valley, the sound of voices shouting, of many people beating on signal drums and gongs, on pots, bamboos, kerosene tins—anything to increase the din and frighten the demon that was causing the earth to shake. The tremors ended; began again; ceased as suddenly as they had commenced. The earthquake had lasted perhaps a minute. A lifetime had passed. Soon the valley was quiet once more, but long afterwards the cockatoos were screaming from their perches, the monkeys still jumping on their chains.

In the graveyard the altar to the Sun God had been cracked down the middle, we learned. Damage in the village had been otherwise slight. A tree had fallen, and one more wall to the palace of Chokorda Rahi had crumbled to the ground. But when Rendah brought up the water to fill the bath tank he said the earthquake was a bad omen. It had occurred in the wrong month (there were favourable months for earthquakes, it seemed), one already marked by drought and a plague of rats in the fields. Already there had been in Tabanan a great ceremonial burning of the rats. The land was "hot," demons were abroad, and illness would surely follow. Once more he urged me to complete the walls that ran only part way around the house.

But *tuan*, perhaps, has no need for walls, he added in a small and questioning voice. After paying this indirect tribute to the mysterious power of resistance of a foreigner, he shouldered the pole from which hung his water cans, and went down the path once more to the spring.

Like the magic rectangle drawn on the ground by a sorcerer, the walls surrounding a Balinese household protected those within from evil forces, forever lurking outside and working to bring misfortune. The one vulnerable spot in the magic barrier was the entrance, and here the gateway had been reinforced by a strip of wall inside the courtyard, which blocked the view from without and deflected the assault of demons.

So too the entire village must be protected against the outer world. In the mountains the more primitive villages were actually surrounded by walls. To the north and south, where the two gates broke the magic circle, the entrances had been reinforced by simple mazes, constructed for the special bewilderment of evil spirits. Sliding gates, narrow lanes that turned back on themselves were part of the puzzle, so that the village was actually laced in, isolated as a fortress.

But in Sayan, as in most villages built in later times, the walls had become an invisible abstraction. Boundaries existed chiefly in the imagination. That they did exist, however, was suddenly clear at each return of *nyepi*, the yearly day of silence. Now the village was suddenly aware of itself as a unity. In the evening, after the priest had summoned the evil spirits to a feast at the crossroads of the village, and then put them to flight with magic formulas, the road was barricaded at either end with a pile of branches. Visible walls now joined the invisible. No one might come in nor go out; for twenty-four hours the village was sealed.

For a day people remained at home. Fires were extinguished; lamps might not burn. On that night I would sit in darkness without even a cigarette. The village was now *sepi*, empty and silent. The demons, wishing to return, would surely think it had been deserted and pass it by.

It was only too clear to all that my land was exposed to every kind of danger, since it not only was unwalled, but lay outside the village circle. Worse still, it was situated between the graveyard and the ravine, in whose dark crevices dwelt an endless tribe of sprites and monsters.

In the daytime the graveyard was not too intimidating. It was overgrown with trees and shrubs, a wilderness, recalling an earlier time when the dead were left unburied in the forest, to be devoured by wild beasts. Even now the dead were buried hastily enough, with a hilarity even, that seemed to conceal the same aversion. A show of grief was forbidden; a weeping child was sent out of the graveyard. From my house a funeral sounded like the liveliest of picnics. Once the mirrors had been placed in the dead eyes, the body lowered into a grave which was left unclosed for three days, the funeral party broke up with shouts. Laughing, singing, yelling at the tops of their voices, youths and men rushed down the hillside, followed by the women, to bathe and forget in the river below.

But after nightfall the graveyard was transformed, a haunted spot that no one would dream of entering. On moonlight nights the solitary *kepuh* tree, sacred to Durga, goddess of death, glimmered high above the palms. Imps and demons gathered in its branches; in the shadow-play this dreadful tree was seen to be filled with evil birds, hands and legs with faces, while the branches were festooned with entrails. Cauldrons caught the dripping blood, and the roots wound in and out of bones and skulls. Here the pupils of the Widow met at midnight, to dance and feast on the living blood of dead brought back to life. . . .

The graveyard, moreover, was a natural meeting-place for witches and sorcerers, for every village had its suspects, owners of books of spells that enabled the reader to change himself into a *léyak*—a ball of fire, a giant rat, or even a riderless motor cycle that travelled backwards. In this magic state sorcerers were indeed dangerous; they could send a man out of his wits or bring him to a lingering death.

No one was surprised, then, when all at once things began to go wrong in the house. Misfortunes occurred, one after another, and as they accumulated everyone began to have a worried, hunted look. Rantun the cook slipped on the kitchen floor and broke her arm. Pugig stepped on a thumb-tack and got an infected foot. The cat fell off the roof, actually fell, for no reason at all, and was killed, while Kesyur and Sampih declared the garage was haunted. Night after night they would wake, they said, unaccountably rigid, jaws clenched, unable to make a sound. They heard the bicycle bells of Durus and Pugig ring out in the darkness, although there was no one else with them in the garage. Voices called their names from outside, but they opened the doors to find no one. And late one night, as Kesyur walked up the road alone to the garage, he saw, sitting silently among the bamboos, a great bird, large as a horse.

This, however, was not all.

In the morning, as Pugig brought up the coffee, he would point to drops of blood that ran in an unbroken line all around the outside floor of the sleeping-house. A fight between two *tokés*, the great lizards that now hid and croaked in the thatch, I suggested; but Pugig did not agree, for he would wash the spots away, only to find them again the following morning. One night I awoke to hear the loud ticking of a clock almost in my ear. It was rapid and metallic, like an alarm clock, and seemed to come from outside the wall. As I reached for my flashlight it began to travel quickly around the four walls of the room. I ran outside, but there was no trace of anything at all.

Everyone agreed, as I related the experience in the morning, that all this was the work of *léyaks*. Kesyur urged me to consult a seer at once. He suggested the older brother of Chokorda Rahi, whose spells and amulets were known to be unusually powerful. But Rendah was wiser. He reminded me that although the house had been blessed by the priest when I first moved in, I had, however, never made offerings for the demons that inhabited the land itself. Disasters would increase until I had done so. I must make a *mecharu*, a purification ceremony, when the demons would be called to a feast and then expelled from my land, and he advised me to seek the help of the great priest of Bangkasa across the valley, Ida Bagus Gedé.

This was one of the ten great priests of Bali, and his holiness and magic power were known throughout the island. He was able to summon the *léyaks* and dispel the demons. He knew all the entrances and exits to this world, knew the mysteries of the microcosmos and the macrocosmos. He was, in addition, famed as a *dalang*, but he only performed for the most solemn rites, and the only story he ever performed was that of Chalonarang the witch—of how, long ago, she spread plague upon plague in the land of Java, and was finally destroyed with a gesture of the hand by the holy saint and recluse, Mpu Bharada. It was clear that Ida Bagus Gedé identified himself with this ascetic.

We already knew each other. He was a benign old man, often slightly drunk by ten in the morning, dignified and austere and frowning severely one moment, smiling with paternal warmth and tenderness the next. He wore his long white hair tied up in a knot on the crown of his head, and when I met him on the road, chubby and crumpled, piled high on top of a slow-moving pony and holding over his head a paper umbrella, I could not help thinking of some Chinese portrait of a Taoist monk.

Once I passed him in a dog-cart and stopped to ask if I could not take him where he was going in the car. He got out, while his attendant transferred his paraphernalia: a red-and-gold mitre two feet high, his prayer beads, his bell, his bronze insignia, a large wallet stuffed with betel, two hens, and several baskets that might have contained anything at all.

Our progress as we drove along was constantly impeded by obstacles, for each time we came to an overhead bridge or water conduit he would call out dramatically,

Stop . . . ! A priest such as I may not pass beneath where men have walked or water flows! Kesyur would open the door, and out he would get, staff in hand, to clamber up the bank and join us on the other side.

As for an aeroplane, he scowled at the very thought. It was the ultimate insult for men to fly above his head, dare to dishonour the gods by crossing over their temples. He shook his head. But now we had come to another bridge. Once more we stopped for him to get out, and by the time he rejoined the car he had forgotten what he had been saying.

The morning I called to consult him about the purification of my land he was not yet visible, for he was still at prayers. I knew his morning programme. So holy a man might not speak before he had bathed, brushed his teeth, put on clean garments and recited many prayers. Then only was he in a state fit to utter the sacred words within him. He would come out of the house temple at last, to sit cross-legged in his highest pavilion, ready to receive, and his first request would be for *arac*. He also appreciated (I had already discovered) brandy, especially the kind that had three stars clearly outlined on the label.

I had not been waiting long before Ida Bagus Gedé appeared. I sat down before him, taking care to remain on a lower step, and greeted him. He gave me one of his gentle smiles, pronounced a word of welcome, blessed me theatrically and asked the object of my visit.

I replied that I had come to seek his help. My land was full of demons; I wished him to make a *mecharu* at my house, and wanted to know what the offerings would be. He straightened himself and drew in his breath importantly.

You need the great ritual, he began, the highest one, and it will take many offerings, and a month to prepare. For this you will slaughter one young bull, one goose, one goat, one dog with a three-coloured hide, one duck with similar markings, one young male pig, one chicken with feathers growing the wrong way, five hens of five different colours, and twenty-five ducks. You will also need six hundred duck eggs, six hundred bananas, and five thousand Chinese cash. The offerings prepared in advance will include two roast pigs, ten roast chickens, ten roast ducks, five baskets of rice, flowers and cakes, and five skeins of thread in the five colours.

He paused, to think what he had left out.

These were only the main items which I wrote down. When at last he could go no further he paused, looking at me severely.

That is what is correct, he said.

I was so impressed with the solemnity of the moment that it

took all my courage to murmur, Father, I am not rich; is there no other way?

Yes, he said. You need not slaughter the bull.

But where am I to find such a dog? And who will prepare the offerings?

Yours is a large house, he answered sternly. And your land has always been dangerous land. He poured a little glass of *arac* and drank it. He spread a betel leaf with lime, rolled it carefully, and put it in his mouth.

I did not feel, however, that compromise was impossible. I suddenly thought of a scene from the story of Chalonarang. After the holy man has rid the land of the witch, the time comes to make fitting celebration. King Erlangga seeks the saint. "The king asked further concerning the cost of the ceremonies. 'My lord, tell me. How great must the sum be that I should give? Tell me the cost of the lowest, the middle and the highest ceremonies.' Bharada answered: 'It matters not, the cost, if a man is a good man, and a seeker of the Way. And. if he is not, it also matters not. The lowest ceremony requires a sum of 1,600 pieces of silver, the middle 4,000, and the highest 8,000. There is also the ceremony which is the highest of high, requiring 80,000. Give, O king, what seems fitting and right.' The king replied, 'I will take the 8,ooo ceremony.'"

Guided by the remembrance of this situation, I begged Ida Bagus Gedé to reconsider the offerings. For there was also the matter of musicians I must engage to play during the ceremony, and also some dramatic performance at night, to bring the day to a festive conclusion. He called to his grandson to bring a pencil. A small boy now sat on the ground below us and began to write.

On no account, it seemed, could the dog be omitted, but eggs, coconuts and bananas were reduced considerably. Everything mentioned in fives remained, for these were for the gods and demons of the four directions, and also Him of the centre. It was decided that the women of Ida Bagus Gedé's household should prepare the offerings and I would pay the cost.

Sampih, who had come with me, had been sitting silently all this while. But now he spoke up.

Father, I crave indulgence. But is there not to be a cockfight?

Of course! It was understood! How could a *mecharu* be effective without the sacrificial shedding of blood! He turned to the difficult problem of determining an auspicious day. He asked for his almanac and with a frown began to study it.

I thought of the mounting disasters at home, and begged that the ceremony take place as soon as possible, before, perhaps, the house caught fire (already the thatch had blazed one night from a flaring lamp) or I was killed by one of the wild, swaying buses that missed my car each day by an inch. But no; it must be on a Saturday, a *sabtu*, when the moon was dark. In five weeks' time, he said at last. I rose, saying, Father, I now take leave.

His face grew serene. He gave me a smile of great kindliness, and said, Go home in peace, my son.

At the house no one could talk of anything but the cockfight. Pugig went home for two more birds. Kesyur and Durus brought two more. On the kitchen veranda a line of cages now stood, a restless cock in each. Every day mock fights were staged to exercise the vicious-tempered birds. The whole village, it appeared, looked forward to the event. Every boy, every man, said Rendah, who owned a cock would surely be at the fight.

A *mecharu* is not complete without a performance of the tale of the witch, Chalonarang, either danced and mimed, or given as a shadow-play. I had decided on the latter, but only after long pleading was I able to persuade Ida Bagus Gedé to act as *dalang*. It was too dangerous! So strong was his magic power that when, in the play, the witch calls all *léyaks* to her aid, many *real léyaks* from the neighbouring countryside had been known to come out at the call of Ida Bagus, unable to resist his summons, and filling the night with flickering lights. He could not answer for consequences, and he had not performed since the time in Marga when, the next morning, many people in the village had been found dead. He did not want this to happen in Sayan, he said.

But at last, as I insisted, he reluctantly consented, saying, Let a place then be prepared for me and my musicians by the graveyard, high up from the ground and facing east.

Early on the day of the *mecharu*, members of the household of Ida Bagus Gedé began to arrive with the offerings. The lawn in the middle of the garden was chosen as the best place for the ceremony, and now the men proceeded to set up the shrines and altars of bamboo. Soon the rectangle was divided like a compass. A shrine stood facing each of the four directions; in the centre rose a fifth. To the north-east a high and tottering altar swayed in the breeze, laden with offerings to the Sun God. To the south-west stood the correspondingly low altar to the God of the Sea.

A rather grim banquet was now set out on the lawn for all the demons of the five directions. A slain white hen, white rice and white foods were spread to the north. A black hen and black-stained foods lay to the south. Yellow offerings to the east, red to the west, all four colours merged for the centre. The little puppy which had spent last night whimpering so sadly had been disembowelled, split open, and now lay flat upon the earth below the altar to the Sea God. At last the table was set. The assistants rested. We waited for the arrival of Ida Bagus Gedé.

The sun was nearly overhead when Sampih called out, Look! There they are! He pointed across the valley.

A procession of tall white parasols and people dressed in bright clothes shone through the distant palms and slowly descended the hillside in single file, winding along the edges of the rice terraces until it reached the bottom of the valley and was lost from sight around the bend of the river.

At last they appeared over the edge of the lawn. Ida Bagus Gedé entered the veranda and looked about. His practised eye detected at once which chair was the highest. He made for one with a tall peacock back, and although the space was small, he managed to tuck his legs beneath him and sit there, cramped but upright, and framed like a Bodhisattva in a niche. At his feet an attendant immediately began to prepare a leaf of betel to refresh him.

I asked him if he would like tea, or perhaps a cool syrup.

He smiled at me affectionately.

Brandy, my son. With three stars. . . . If there is any, he added considerately. He nodded with satisfaction at the label when Durus brought the tray before him, and drank a small glass as though he were feeding his soul.

But now his wife, who had been carefully examining the arrangement of the offerings, sent word to say a skein of yellow thread had been forgotten. Someone must return and fetch it. (For without it the rite would not be complete; there would be a weak spot in the magic of the offerings.) While an uncomplaining *budak* departed on a five-mile walk, Ida Bagus went inside to change to his ceremonial garments. He would not go in by the front door, for he had noticed the balcony above.

My son, I may not enter by this door.

I know, father, I answered. Will you proceed to the door made especially for you? I led him to a door which opened on the lawn. He was immensely pleased.

When he appeared again he was an imposing figure. Folds of white cloth enveloped him from waist to knees. Around his bare shoulders hung a string of prayer beads, and on his head rose the tall scarlet mitre, egg-shaped and trimmed with gold, of the high priest. He walked solemnly out into the garden and climbed on to the special platform which had been raised for him, to sit among the offerings and pyramids of flowers. Incense rose from a salver before him, on which were arranged his bells and his bowls of holy water filled with blossoms. He folded his hands, closed his eyes, and was soon lost in meditation.

Om, he intoned in a deep voice. Om, Om, Om!

He took his bell in his hand and began to pronounce the holy *mantras*. He prayed to the five directions, to the Five Guardians of the Universe, chanting on the five sacred tones. When at last he had completed the divine cycle he paused for breath, before turning his attention to the demons.

From the direction of the garage there now came a confused murmur of excited voices. The cockfight was already under way. In quiet bliss the ring of men watched round after round. Three rounds were sufficient ritualistic bloodshed, but the fights, I knew, would go on till sundown. I loyally placed two guilders on Kesyur's cock, but lost them to Chokorda Rahi, for within thirty seconds it was dripping blood, sliced open by a lightning slash from its opponent. In vain Kesyur tried to revive it. He blew in its ear, stood it on its feet and pushed it forward. But the other bird rushed to meet it. There was a second flash of the steel spur, a flurry of feathers, and Kesyur's cock lay dead. Another round began; the morning passed.

The missing thread arrived, and Ida Bagus Gedé could now proceed. As he uttered each magic verse his hands turned, folded and opened in hieratic gestures. They wove invisible geometric designs, paused now and then in some symbolic position, holding one hypnotized like the silent communications of a mute. From time to time a single star-shaped blossom shot into the air, expelled from the tips of his fingers. His voice grew strained with exhortation. Louder and fuller it rose, above his bell, above the sound of the *gamelan*, filling the universe. At last he stopped.

In the silence which followed I felt something of great importance had taken place, that evil must surely be allayed, dispelled once and for all.

He returned to his chair on the veranda, tucking his feet up under him once more. He looked very old and tired as he took off his mitre and handed it to an attendant. The *sari*, the essence of the offerings, consisted of a few dozen strings of cash, piled on a plate, and Durus now thoughtlessly brought them in and set them on a table. Ida Bagus waved them away, offended by their sight. He brightened, however, as Sampih knelt before him with a small glass of brandy. Soon he was smiling once more and commenting on the ceremony, above all on my astuteness in having sought his aid. With his magic power the ritual took on the maximum efficacy and I was now safe.

He sat there sipping his brandy. He was not through talking, however. He must explain still further the respect due a great priest. He began to tell of how the famous holy Sage of Java, Mpu Bharada, once came across the water on a breadfruit leaf to Bali, to visit and learn from the greatest Sage of all, Mpu Kuturan. At last the time came for him to leave. He departed from the cloister high in the mountains and returned to the sea. But when he stepped on to the breadfruit leaf it sank. How could this be? What force greater than his was at work? All at once he remembered that he had neglected to take formal leave of the Sage of Bali. He turned round and journeyed back to the cloister to beg the holy one's pardon, asking to be allowed to leave. The Sage bowed (here Ida Bagus looked very gracious). Proceed upon your way, little brother. Once more the Sage came to the shore. This time the leaf did not sink. It bore him safely back across the sea to Java.

In spite of his holiness he was wrong, said Ida Bagus, looking stern. He was younger; he had not reached perfection; he still owed great respect. . . .

He rose to leave, to rest before returning that night for the shadow-play. This would demand a fresh display of force and he was at present exhausted. He went home to be recharged, reanimated with sleep, magic formulas and *arac*. Following him down the hillside, the procession bore home the roasted meats left over from the offerings.

That night at dinner, Pugig uncovered the serving-dish with a flourish. A rich smell of wine and herbs swept into the air.

The fighting-cock of Kesyur, he announced.

It was really quite excellent.

There is no meat more fortifying, said Durus as he brought the cigarettes. Unless, he added thoughtfully, ant-eater.

But why ant-eater?

He is the strongest of them all. Not even a tiger can kill him. He rolls himself into a ball you can't open. His scales are like iron. . . .

He set the bottle of brandy on the table.

Ida Bagus Gedé seems able to drink much arac, I said.

He is old; he needs it to keep his strength, said Durus.

I thought priests might not drink strong drinks.

Ida Bagus is very holy. He may do as he pleases. . . .

When Ida Bagus Gedé returned that night he was already in a state of exaltation. He would not speak. His mind was fixed on the play he was to perform. He rested for a moment, and then walked up the road towards the graveyard, followed by his musicians and men bearing the heavy box of puppets. Soon the sound of shadow-play music filled the night; but now drums and gongs had been added to the little orchestra for this dark tale of witchcraft, and the music sounded strange and ominous.

The audience was tense. Rarely was there the chance to see this great priest perform. The site chosen for the play, the edge of the graveyard, created an additional atmosphere of mystery, producing a mood of subdued excitement. Anything might happen. The road was crowded; children sat along the high base of the altar to the Sun God, waiting.

From the first moment that the voice of Ida Bagus was heard

behind the screen, chanting the opening words of invocation, all knew he had fallen in trance. His voice was like some powerful call from the underworld. I watched him while he took the puppets as though in a dream from the hands of his assistants, shoved them against the screen and sombrely declaimed their lines. Back and forth he swayed beneath the lamp, inspired, possessed. A battle of good and evil was taking place within; he was both sorceress and holy man, and the conflict on the screen was mirrored in his distorted, tortured face. Even the clowns were frightening. The audience could not understand the strange humour of Ida Bagus, his satanic obscenity, and watched with growing apprehension.

Léyak! Léyak! he shrieked, as on the scene the sorceress summoned her pupils to her side. *Léyak!* Come out! He dimmed the lamp; the screen turned murky. He drew the puppet back from the screen so that the shadow suddenly magnified and filled the stage. The gongs beat softly; the drums throbbed.

What is that out there, in the fields? a voice cried sharply from the crowd. In the distance a pale light was seen to waver unsteadily. The audience began to stir. But soon it was recognized as a flashlight.

Léyak! Léyak! screamed Ida Bagus. His voice had grown hoarse and utterly inhuman. Veins stood out in his forehead and neck. His face was beaded with sweat.

But no flames came out of the night in answer to his call. He went on with the play. At last the final scene was reached. The air was rent with furious cries as Chalonarang sought to overpower the holy man with incantations. Calmly he stood there, unharmed. He raised his arm and pronounced the sacred words that destroyed her. The play was over; for the second time that day evil had been averted. The audience rose and drifted into the night.

Slowly, almost reluctantly, Ida Bagus Gedé returned to consciousness. But his mind remained far away, and he did not seem to hear me when I spoke. He covered the puppets with a white cloth and pronounced a final prayer. He put the lid on the box and with an effort rose to his feet. In silence, followed by his attendants, he set out for home.

No *léyak* dared appear! said Sampih as we walked back to the house. They here probably too afraid. . . . Of *tuan*, he added, half to himself.

But in the morning Rendah came with the news that the child of Kejir had died in the night. A ball of blue fire had been seen glowing dimly through the trees back of the house. It had floated off in the direction of the graveyard and disappeared.

THE STORY OF SAMPIH CONTINUED

THE MOOD OF ANXIETY which had hung like a raincloud over the household had now completely evaporated. There were no more accidents, no more mysterious calls or visitations in the night. All felt protected and secure after the departure of Ida Bagus, and we were able to settle down once more to a life of untroubled peace.

One afternoon I drove to Bedulu, to stop at the marketplace and ask the way to the house of Champlung. A small boy guided me down the narrow lane that ran between mud walls, softly shaded by the cool green of bamboos and banana plants. Champlung's door was the last, where the road came to an end at the edge of the fields. From over the walls came the rhythmic thud of rice poles.

In the courtyard the sunlight fell through the trees on two women threshing. Beside them, Champlung stood with a winnowing tray, and as she tossed the grain in the air the chaff floated down around her bare shoulders in a luminous shower of gold.

The *tuan!* she exclaimed. *Tuan* Sayan is here! All work came abruptly to a stop; I must be made welcome.

It was some time before I made the suggestion which I knew would astonish everyone, that she come to Sayan a few days each week to give lessons to Sampih. She burst out laughing. *She?* Teach a boy? She would have no idea how to begin.

But we were no strangers, and I was prepared to spend the afternoon in wheedling and insidiously undermining the resistance of her parents. We talked till sundown.

In the end I had my way, as I expected, though only after it was decided that for a small sum in addition to the one I proposed her father should come with her to chaperone her. For Sayan was too far for her to return home each evening. She would often sleep there, and she had a snub-nosed prettiness, a husky voice and bright gaiety that was, it seemed, already too attractive. Her father watched her like a hawk; it would be unfortunate if some accident occurred which might definitely mar her reputation and lower her marriage value.

She must, in addition, bring with her two musicians; a drummer (without which no dancer could move, no gesture have any form of meaning), and a *g'ndér* player to outline the melody of the music.

It was growing dark. We had talked ourselves out, and I got up to leave.

In two weeks, then, I said.

Yes, it was understood.

But I could not depart without having to take with me a basket of mangoes and little rice-cakes. She carried them down the road to the car, where we said goodbye.

She will stay in Sayan? said Kesyur, as we drove along.

Yes. . . . Why?

Oh, nothing . . . I simply asked. He seemed preoccupied and thoughtful the rest of the way home.

She arrived early one morning in Sayan with her musicians. For a moment she sat on the edge of the veranda, demure and correct, inhaling her cigarette and slowly blowing out the smoke, replying all the while in the most distant of monosyllables. But this reserve was too much. She suddenly broke down, and soon she was giggling with Sampih like a child of ten. As for her father, he simply sat there, on the lower step of the veranda, bowing in silence when Pugig brought him a cup of coffee.

Champlung looked at Sampih as he went through the *bapang* dance with a severe and critical air that I could not help finding amusing. But soon she began to smile, and then to giggle, holding her hand politely before her mouth.

Den Pasar style! she exclaimed at last. Nothing apparently could be more absurd. She got up to show how it should be done.

It was two years since I had last seen her dance, and I was amazed at the change. I remembered her for her tense, animated performance, her rapid movements, timed always, it seemed, a fraction ahead of the beat. Now, suddenly grown-up, newly feminine, she had taken on a serenity and restraint, a new grace, which gave her dancing an altogether different quality. It was charming and completely unexciting. Gone was the sexless beauty, the abstract sensuousness; gone the lightning speed, the miniature-like perfection. Now each movement seemed too ample; the delicate frame of the dance was broken.

She stopped. Like that, she said. "Breaks," "flowers," "progression"—all were different. Sampih must start once more from the beginning.

If Champlung no longer danced with the light fleetness of childhood, she was still able to suggest it in her gestures. Her style had sweep, imagination, a fluidity that made Nyoman's teaching seem dry and superficial. It was charming indeed to see the way she passed her knowledge on to Sampih. She was no analyst, indeed had no experience other than to train the new dancers in her village. But she put all her youthful energy into these lessons, difficult, moreover, for her to give, for she had a wilful and far from supple boy to deal with. She solved each problem in her own way.

Sampih adored her. Their bright peasant natures understood each other. Suddenly thinking he had rehearsed long enough, Sampih would begin to complain, but she refused all sympathy.

Béh! I'm tired! My neck hurts! Sampih's voice had become small and dismal. But she merely laughed.

Three steps north-east! Turn! Bend backwards! Further! Keep the fan waving. . . .

One day Nyoman Kalér arrived unexpectedly during a lesson. He surveyed the scene with detachment. He watched Champlung as she moved as though she were a curious insect.

Bedulu style! he remarked acidly after a while. He got up to go. He had just dropped in, he said, on his way to the mountains to look for bamboo for a flute. His glance rested once more on Sampih. He turned away.

Rindy has made much progress, he remarked. He is already very much in demand. He is to dance each week for the tourists at the hotel.

I recognized this as intended to wound, in return for my disloyalty. I felt a wish to soothe him. Could I not drive him to where he was going? No, he had his bicycle. But I insisted it could be carried behind. As we drove along, sitting side by side, he grew more and more subdued and dispirited. We reached the village at the end of the road in silence. It was clear he had no objective whatever, but he got out, saying goodbye, mounted his bicycle and rode up the narrow path, disappearing in the mountain drizzle. I did not see him again for several months.

Madé Lebah, Champlung's drummer, had a lightness of touch, a swiftness and delicate fire in his playing that was breath-taking. I soon discovered he was a remarkable musician; he not only played the *g'ndér* with unusual grace, but he was one of the leading *gangsa* players of the famous *gamelan* of Pliatan, a few miles away. He was famed most of all, said old Rendah, for his drumming in the *arja* play.

He was a high-strung, rather fragile youth, perhaps twenty, filled with some mysterious nervous energy, for even when he was not rehearsing, his long, slender fingers were forever drumming lightly against some vibrant surface, and when he laughed his voice was high and excited. He had the most agreeable nature in the world. In a short time we were fast friends, and when Sampih's lesson was through for the day he would patiently play through some *légong* melody for me to write down, or else show me the different styles of "flower parts," the Buleléng way, the ways of Den Pasar and Pliatan.

He knew a vast amount of music, and soon I began to wonder how I had got on without him. He had not the cultural background of Nyoman Kalér, but there was a clarity and precision about his information which delighted me, for it was before all practical, based on experience, very much up-to-date and not blurred by theory. He knew the island very well, where the best *gamelans* were, in what villages the best gongs were made, and where to find the best tuner. He also had his own ideas about how my garden should look, and was constantly surprising me by filling in some corner with jasmine, a gardenia bush, or a row of flamingo-coloured lilies. He would spend a day on his bicycle, off in the mountains, to return with some great fern or clump of orchids that had opened that day. He was also an expert in the art of spicing and roasting a pig.

But I valued him most of all, perhaps, for the easy way he had in making friends in a strange village. His gentle assurance made it possible for him to give a simple and disarming explanation for my unlooked-for appearance and my strange curiosity in *gamelans*. This Kesyur could not do. He either introduced me with the air of a high official preceding a Chokorda, or else he retired into himself and refused to speak at all. One day, after I had quarrelled with Kesyur about this and he had gone home for a couple of days to sulk, Lebah unexpectedly offered to drive the car. He drove well, and I could not keep from asking, then and there, if he would not care to work for me all the time—drive the car, be my guide, instructor and friend. He smiled.

But Kesyur?

I said that Kesyur was tired of driving me about. He was not happy so far from Den Pasar. He agreed then, and a few days later he had taken Kesyur's place.

Kesyur, I said the morning he left, as a chauffeur you are impossible. I much prefer you as a friend.

He admitted this with a smile. We parted on the best of terms, each promising to visit the other's house next *galungan* time.

With Lebah part of the household, I now settled down to several months of uninterrupted work. I had built a hut for rehearsal under the trees just inside the gate, and people from the village now began to wander in and out, to sit and gaze contemplatively as Champlung gave Sampih his lessons. At the gateway a few women set up their tables of cigarettes and little bowls of sweetmeats, and the place began to have an atmosphere of quiet sociability. Lessons took place each morning, and for several hours the air was filled with the sound of drumming and the intermittent chime of the *g'ndér.*

In the afternoon Lebah would sit down near the piano, to play phrase by phrase some *g'ndér* melody while I wrote. Or he would pick up a drum to show me the rhythm in a certain part of the music. Seriously, leisurely, we worked together till sundown. At last we would decide to stop. We would walk down the hillside to bathe in the spring halfway down, or else in the pool far below, where through the ferns the water fell from overhead.

In order to give some objective to Sampih's lessons with Champlung it was necessary to "try out" the dances from time to time. Chokorda Rahi offered his own *gamelan*, and once in a while Sampih would dance in the square before the palace. But there was always a conflict in these performances, for Chokorda Rahi dearly loved to play the drum, and Sampih insisted he could not follow the Chokorda's beat. It was too slow, too old-fashioned, he said loftily, and he refused to dance without Lebah.

When Sampih first appeared, his solo dance aroused much admiration, but when the time came for partners no one stepped forth from the crowd. He was too small; they were used to a dancer almost full-grown, and a girl, moreover. He circled disconsolately around the lamp that flared in the darkness, waving his fan to no avail. At last with an extravagant gesture, Pugig stepped out, raised his long arms and began to dance.

He was six feet tall, and Sampih came only to his waist. A crane with a rice-bird! Durus called out. Pugig gave him a look of cold fury. But then old Rendah stepped out nimbly and Pugig retired. Rendah's dance was agile and full of humour, at times sardonically obscene. All at once Sampih came to life and accepted the challenge. He had an instinct for comedy, and the crowd roared at his glance of disdain and the deftness with which he evaded Rendah's sly advances, the dexterity with which he slipped his fan before his face when Rendah's had drawn too near.

Encouraged by this, two boys shyly ventured forth, one after the other. Soon it was the turn of Chokorda Rahi himself. He danced sedately, elegantly, as befitted a highborn prince. But after him no one else dared. The performance now came to an end.

When may I begin to study *kebyar?* Sampih kept repeating with growing insistence. This was forever in his mind. This I had promised. For this he had worked. He had learned a great deal from Champlung. It was now a pleasure to see him dance. Lebah, Durus, Chokorda Rahi, Rendah—all were delighted. But it was clear his heart was not in it. Suddenly, overnight, the interest of both dancer and teacher seemed to die. Champlung could give no more; Sampih could absorb no more. It was time to bring the lessons to an end.

It was also high time I began to think of the next step, the *kebyar* lessons I had so rashly promised. Where to find a *gamelan*? How to found a club in Sayan? It was Lebah who had an inspiration. His own *kebyar* club in Pliatan, three miles away! They had no dancer, and for some time had been talking of training one.

The Pliatan *gamelan* was one of the most famous on the island. It had been to Java; had gone to Paris for the 1931 Exposition. I had always found their playing rather impersonal. It had a cold brilliance that was spectacular but not moving. But their technique was perfection, and they played the latest *kebyar* pieces, learned directly from the foremost composers of North Bali.

What was the powerful spell of this new music, the meaning even of its name, *kebyar*? No one could give a precise translation. Kebyar was the crash of the cymbals, said Lebah. An explosion, said Nyoman. As for Chokorda Rahi, he said it was like the sudden bursting open of a flower. It was release, escape from the calyx of the past. It was, before all, a style, *the* new style, all flame and radiance, tense and syncopated to a degree I had never imagined.

But form suffered. Gone was the solidity of structure of the ceremonial music, the delicious melody and balanced metre of the *légong*. Instead a new composition was a medley of fragmentary themes and patterns from cremation music, mask dance or shadow play. Episodes rarely reached completion, for they were continually broken off in the middle, to proceed to another tune, as though the players could not wait to begin something new. Forever changing, brilliant and sombre by turn, the moody music seemed to express a new spiritual restlessness, an impatience and lack of direction, for it was unpredictable as the intermittent play of sunlight from a clouded sky.

As for the dance, it was as capricious as the music. The face was no longer a mask, as in the older dances, but had become mobile, human, sensitive to the slightest change in the music. Yet at the same time the motions of the dancer were more limited, for the dancer now sat, reverting to the ancient position of the ritualistic seated choruses. The dance had been created, it seemed, by the famous Mario of Tabanan, who now no longer danced. Tabanan was in close contact with the villages of North Bali, the source of the new music. Had Mario, I wondered, been inspired, not only by this music, but by the elegant and flamboyant style in the north of playing the *trompong*, a row of little gongs on which a soloist performed, touching the knobs of the gongs before him with long thin sticks in wide and sweeping gestures? The performance itself was almost a dance, and when Mario pretended to play *trompong* in one of his earliest and most beautiful dances his gestures were identical.

Although as yet there were perhaps no more than a dozen performers of this newest dance on the island, the music itself had already taken the villages by storm. Clubs formed, practiced furiously for a year, lost interest and broke up. Others continued for a longer time, one year burning with enthusiasm, the next year bored and indifferent. The psychic state of the club was as unpredictable as the music itself.

But the *gamelan* of Pliatan was firmly established and the musicians took themselves very seriously, although the club existed purely for pleasure. When they went to Paris they took with them their *légong* dancers. Now, their dancers over-age, they were in a state of suspended activity, undecided what to do next.

Thus it happened they were willing to consider my proposal of Sampih. They saw him dance; all agreed with Lebah that he was indeed a find. His smile had charm, his eyes threw light; they admired his energy and synchronization. It was decided to begin his training at once. But first he must become a member of the club.

Here a difficulty arose. For Sampih came from a village several miles away. Could he be counted on to attend rehearsals which, at first, would take place every evening? The situation was without precedent. It was only after Sampih promised solemnly to "follow" the club in all activities that they agreed to accept him as a member. It was now the moment to discuss finances.

The club was wealthy. Part of the money made in Paris had been divided, part had been invested in coconut plantations. At present the books showed each member to be worth about a hundred guilders. In order to enter the club, Sampih too must contribute this amount. This would entitle him to share in the profits from coconuts, divided each *galungan* season. He also became part owner of the handsome instruments of the *gamelan*. He could never ask for this money back, but should the club break up, all assets were to be divided equally. There was, moreover, a fine of a quarter of the guilder for absence from rehearsal.

One evening I paid the entrance money, and Sampih's name was written into the books, before witnesses. The club celebrated by giving a little feast, during which it was announced that they had decided to make me an honorary member. I was begged to come often to rehearsals. I had only to ask, and the club would come to play at my house in Sayan.

Gusti Raka, who agreed, although he had never taught, to give Sampih lessons, was Mario's foremost pupil. He was a vivacious youth of eighteen, wealthy, highborn, spoiled, and it was a problem to get him to come from Tabanan, twenty miles away, to spend even three days in succession in Pliatan. But he was a superb dancer, and he was attracted to Sampih from the very beginning.

Why, he can already dance! He has been well trained! Gusti Raka exclaimed on the first day. He will learn quickly.

The past six months were justified, they had been worth the effort, I thought, as I watched these lessons. Champlung's classical style gave both depth and elegance to Gusti Raka's more glittering gestures. The club was already delighted.

Sampih seemed to learn over night. Gusti Raka's first concern was with the gestures, the rapid, trembling movement of the hands which were never still, and as I watched I could see how tightly interwoven were the "flowers" of both dance and music, shattering simultaneously the melody and movement, so that the phrases had a glittering tension that was never allowed to die.

Sampih threw himself into these lessons with feverish intensity. After a lesson he would be completely exhausted, nervously and physically, for neither teacher nor club spared him in their enthusiasm, and they would rehearse for hours. Most tiring of all was the curious hopping glide on crossed feet, and one ankle, dragged as a sort of rudder, was soon calloused and inflamed. But he only complained when he was forced to stop for several days to recover.

The Pliatan *gamelan* was to play at the great feast in Gianyar when the Regent and a number of leading families would cremate their dead. There would be dazzling performances of all kinds for days, attended by enormous crowds, and the club had decided that on this occasion Sampih should make his first public appearance. This was to be a memorable event. The *gamelan* was tuned and covered with a new coat of gold. The most lavish costume was ordered for Sampih. The rehearsals grew tense and irritable.

One of the great gongs of the *gamelan* had been cracked for a long time and the club had ordered a new one from Java, for the smith of Bali had never known the secret of casting these enormous gongs. It arrived shortly before the day when the club was to play in Gianyar, but before it could be used it must, of course, be blessed. Early in the afternoon, before the club set out for Gianyar, the men carried offerings to the little temple of Panji that stood on a hill a mile away. There we sat watching, while both gong and Sampih were cleansed with holy water. We returned to Pliatan where a bus was waiting, for this elegant club would not be seen carrying their instruments. One by one, clad in new silk shirts and brightest of *sarongs* and headcloths, they got into the bus that was already piled with gongs, *g'ndérs* and drums. There was a cough and an explosion from the motor, a moment of anxiety and the bus started with a jolt. I followed behind in the car with Sampih and Lebah.

The début was an unmistakable triumph. Sampih was in one of his exalted moods. He could hardly wait to begin. He danced as though the wind were blowing through him, and his assurance and theatrical sense enchanted the watchers, from the first proud moment, when he sprang into life with a crash of gongs and cymbals, to the final almost self-effacing pose.

Where did you find him? A handsome dancer! A smile like honey!

It was the Regent himself. I was rather astonished, for he rarely looked on at a performance. He had already heard, he said, of my "presenting" a dancer to the Pliatan club. He had wished to see for himself.

In two years' time, I said modestly. He has only begun. . . .

A farmer's boy, I believe, said the Anak Agung.

From Bangkasa.

He will be very spoiled, said the Regent. He stood looking a moment longer, then picked up the train to his *sarong* and walked back towards the palace.

The next week Sampih danced at the feasts in the great temple at Pliatan, the following week in Blahbatu. In a month's time his name was known in Den Pasar and Karangasem. The club was in raptures.

Sampih's success was due in part to his youthfulness, his undeniable charm, and above all his vitality and fine sense of timing that made you overlook any momentary flaw of gesture. This rhapsodic dance, so moody and so flashing, so full of bright display, suited his temperament to perfection. He clearly loved to dance, loved the excitement of a performance in which he was so focal a point. Yet as I watched, his dancing seemed to have the pathos of something doomed to a short life. For a few years he would delight audiences with his precocious brilliance, but this violent dance offered little to build on. Already Gusti Raka at eighteen was bored by it. Would Sampih, I wondered, continue to even that age?

For the moment he was secure in his alliance with the club of Pliatan. But a club which exists for the sake of pleasure only may dissolve in the night. I could see no stability in the future, and I was only able to take comfort in the thought that at present the mood of the Pliatan club was one of unity, and that the members showed no signs of breaking up.

I was away in Java for two months, to visit friends and attend a series of plays given by the court actors in the palace of the Sultan of Jokjakarta. The performances were unforgettable for their exquisite finish, the beauty and incredible refinement of the dancers, the strange, mystic atmosphere created by their languor of movement and the soft velvet tone of the *gamelan*. I returned to Bali half under the spell of this dreamlike experience, yet eager for the violence, the shock, the exuberance of the performances that took place each night, not in palaces, but underneath the trees, surrounded by an audience of villagers.

Sampih's dancing had improved amazingly. It had a new brilliance, a sureness and authority that it had never had before. There had been many performances, said Lebah. The crowds were huge wherever they appeared.

Sampih seemed suddenly much older. At first he was shy and rather distant when he returned to Sayan, but in a few days he was as at home in the house as ever. Yet there was a new tone in his voice, a new expression in his eyes. He had suddenly become aware of his charm. He tried it on Rantun the cook when she scolded, on Nyoman Kalér when he came one day to the house, on the Anak Agung of Saba, on me.

He must now wear sandals, and have a coat made by the same tailor as Lebah. He began to let one fingernail grow long. He longed for a gold tooth. It was clear he had become a star.

LAPSE OF TIME

MEANWHILE THE CALENDAR of feast days slowly unrolled. One after the other the six temples held their anniversaries, disrupting private life and throwing the village into a state of agreeable turmoil.

Long before a feast the elders met to determine the number of offerings, the scale of expenditures. They sat in a circle at the crossroads, answering in turn as their name was read out by the *klian*.

Tiang! I!

This word had a second and not unrelated meaning, for it also meant pillar of a building, an upright post that supported the roof. When a silence fell after a name the *klian* scratched a marginal note with his knife in his palm-leaf book: fined ten *képéngs* for absence.

They now discussed the coming feast. How many pigs should they slaughter? How many chickens and ducks? What should they have in the way of entertainment? The priest consulted his book of directions. Each household would give a measure of rice, ten eggs, six coconuts. . . .

When at last the meeting broke up, each man knew down to the last detail his contribution, from the number of sticks of firewood to the exact amount of coconut oil and salt.

A day or so before a feast Rendah would politely beg to be excused from work, for at home there was now *repot*, much business to attend to. The tone of his voice implied that he did not know how he could possibly get through with it. But if I went to see him at this time I was pretty sure to find him actually doing nothing at all, and I could find little sign of anything unusual other than his wives and sisters preparing in all tranquillity the offerings of cakes and woven palm leaf. Yet if I asked Rendah to return with me to the house for even the briefest moment, he would insist it was quite impossible. So much repot! Such urgency! He sighed, paralysed at the thought.

At home it was Rantun, the cook, who prepared the little offerings which must be made every few days for our welfare.

She was very young and very pretty, and Pugig had soon fallen quite in love with her, and they now slept together in the little house among the trees by the kitchen that had been built for Pugig. She never forgot to make the offerings for demons every few days, setting them on the ground before the gates at sundown. Every fifteen days she burnt incense in the house temple and placed tiny fans of flowers and betel for the gods in all the houses—on the beds, beside the bath, on the piano, the car, and beside her braziers in the kitchen. Each day she placed a little portion of the food she cooked on a shelf above her pots and pans for Batara Uma, and dropped blossoms and betel leaves beside the little pool in the rocks down near the river (from which we got our drinking-water) for the spirit of the spring.

Once every five weeks Daria the priest came to the house to bless my different possessions. On the day of the coconut palms he placed an offering at the foot of the largest tree, and went about sprinkling the trees with holy-water. On the day for blessing the pigs and domestic animals he indulgently sprinkled water on my pets as well, the monkeys, the parrots, and even Chéngchéng the dog. There was the day for cattle that ploughed the fields; the day for weapons, but I had none; for books, and then the day for blessing the puppets, masks and musical instruments. When these six sacred days had come and gone, the cycle was complete; it was now time to begin once more.

It was all very charming and peaceful, giving the house an indefinable feeling of protection and security. When, on the morning after the day of silence and fireless hearths, Pugig lighted the fire again in the kitchen, it seemed to burn with a new warmth. Voices rose brightly; people set about work with animation. A fresh start had been made once more.

One morning, as I returned after a week spent in the wilds along the western tip of the island, I found lying on the table a long envelope. Inside, a typewritten mimeographed announcement informed me that the Regent of Gianyar was to receive a decoration from the Queen of Holland, and invited me to the palace to attend the ceremony when he would receive the Golden Star. A programme was outlined. At eleven-thirty the ancient guard of warriors, bearing spears, would form a line along the road at the entrance to the town. In front of the palace would assemble the Padvinders—the Boy Scouts. At twelve the *Gamelan* of Carnal Love and the *Gamelan* of the Great Gongs would begin to sound. The Star would be affixed by the Resident. We would lunch, and afterwards witness a performance of the ancient *gambuh* play, performed by the actors from the court of Tabanan. I was requested not to come in shorts. With Honour, the Anak Agung Ngurah Agung, Regent of the District of Gianyar.

I wondered how he had wangled the decoration. I knew the utter pleasure he would take in this ceremony, a pleasure intensified by the thought that he had advanced a step ahead of the other agents. It would be hard for them to refuse with face his invitation, and their compliments would add the final touch of joy to the event. I was delighted to go, for I could hear once more his lovely-sounding *Gamelan* of the Love God.

It was a bright warm day as we drove into Gianyar. Several hundred small, barefooted Padvinders stood in line before the palace walls, clutching paper flags. As each car passed and entered the palace gates the flags were momentarily agitated, as though stirred by a gust of wind, to the accompaniment of vague cheering. All at once the Padvinders began to sing in despondent unison, a song composed for the occasion by the Indonesian schoolmaster. To the tune of God Save the King rose the words, regardless of stress or quanity:

Slamat trima bintang
Slamat trima bintang
Anak Agung

Happily receive star
Anak Agung—

A few guests had already arrived and we were seated in the great pavilion on chairs arranged in a row. Conversation was bored and languid, and I finally gave up trying to talk to the wife of the *Controller* from Tabanan. I suppose we must talk English, she said. Americans never speak another language.

Mais si ça vous plaira de parler français. . . .

But this only seemed to irritate her the more.

I sat counting the clocks on the wall, that hung on either side of the door leading to the inner palace. Suddenly, in an outburst of chimes, a little symphony began as the clocks in turn struck twelve. At that moment the door opened and the Regent stepped out.

He was arrayed in all his glory. He bowed stiffly; his eyes narrowed and there was the faintest shadow of pleasure in the corner of his lips as he noted the presence, one by one, of the other regents.

There was another pause, a stir, and the Resident arrived, to sit down beside the Regent and converse. We waited. Music began. In this formal atmosphere I listened with keener pleasure than usual to the complex blend of dissonance as the two *gamelans* rang out at the same time. The Resident rose, pronounced a few brief phrases and pinned the decoration on the Regent's dilated breast. Boys poured champagne, which rose warm and sweet in the glasses as we drank a toast to Her Majesty. Above the roar of gongs and drums there soared the treble voices of the Padvinders outside:

> *Happily receive star*
> *Illustrious Prince.*

They paused. There was the sound of firecrackers. They began again, to intone the National Anthem.

Lunch was long and the conversation far from animated, possibly because the champagne was now followed by tepid beer, and although the *rijstafel* was certainly drab for so auspicious an occasion, we all as usual ate far too much.

As soon after lunch as it was politely possible, the guests began to leave. Only two or three of the regents remained, together with Walter, whom I had not seen in a month, and Goris, the Government archæologist from Buleléng, whom I found extremely sympathetic. From behind the thickest of glasses, mild blue eyes peered out myopically, but his devotion for the past was intense, and his conversation was delicately shaded with malice. We went outside together, to spend a peaceful afternoon watching the *gambuh* actors from Tabanan.

To the soft and hollow sound of great bamboo flutes, the actors slowly made their entrance, one after another. They moved with almost feminine grace, and their gestures and postures unfolded one out of the other in weary elegance. The play was an episode from the ancient legend of Prince Panji, but no one around me could say exactly which part, for the actors spoke in Kawi, and their lines were not translated.

The play had just begun. Some twenty characters, knights, ministers and buffoons, would have to appear before the plot, enfolded in this sequence like the seed within a flower, would finally come to life. Time stood still. The audience, composed of older people, sat watching in utter tranquillity, savouring the mood, the atmosphere evoked by the music and gesture, by the mere sound of legendary names, and caring very little when the moment for actual drama would arrive. Above the faint ring of tiny cymbals, the almost inaudible drums, the voices of the actors slowly rose to a high falsetto and dropped, in a declamation so strangely artificial, so altogether unreal that, what with the faint music, the gentle motion of actors no longer young, the faded costumes, the whole performance had the quality of an ancient tapestry, seemed to be something that was taking place in a dream.

When, in the late afternoon, I got up to leave, I passed a number of actors near the gates. They were still waiting for their first entrance.

On the way home we passed through Blahbatu. The sound of lively *kebyar* music grew suddenly loud as we approached a lighted pavilion, died once more in the distance. It was the club of Blahbatu rehearsing.

Waves of the Ocean! exclaimed Lebah. Everyone played it in 1931. I should think they would be ashamed!

For it was now the middle of 1934.

Not long after this I received another invitation. A boy sauntered in from Ubud one morning with a note in pencil from Chokorda Ngurah, the brother of Chokorda Rahi. I was asked to a feast the following week, when the Chokorda's first wife would adopt his daughter by his third.

It was Lebah who explained. She was childless. The third wife was of far inferior rank. In order to have a daughter whose nobility would be unquestioned, the Chokorda was raising her caste position by this ceremony. Then she would be a true Chokorda; she would be able to make a better marriage. It all seemed very logical and practical.

This time the feast dishes were memorable. The palace was famous for its cooks, and even the clowns commented favourably that night at the *arja* play outside the palace.

Little brother, what is the matter . . . are you ill?

Wah! Have I eaten just now! Am I full! What a feast . . . What elegant food! Turtle, duck, pig . . .all of the best! How can I *possibly* act? *Adoh! Ado-o-oh!* I have the cramps . . .

Here the clown bent double, writhed in agony.

Across the rectangle on a raised platform, I saw for the first time that day the women of the palace, seated crowded together. In ceremonial clothes, with golden headdresses, golden flowers, their tapering fingers covered with rings, they looked unbelievably aristocratic and fragile. Remote and beautiful, they sat apart from the crowd, like an exclusive party of goddesses that had just come down to earth to watch the play. . . .

With Labah I now travelled all over the island, for he knew musicians in many villages. I kept hoping I might discover some book, some ancient writing that had to do with the laws, the theory of music. But none existed, it seemed, which struck me as very curious, since there were books on everything else imaginable. As I talked with older men, hoping to gain a clearer insight into the form and construction of the music they had been playing, their answers were vague and hesitating. Laws existed in their minds, remembered instinctively rather than formulated, and I could learn more in a half-hour of observing than I could in an afternoon of conversation. I had, of course, the advantage of a complicated notation, and with this I could compare the music of a dozen different villages and draw my own conclusions.

I was now entirely absorbed in work. Everything seemed of greatest interest, from the detail of the "flower parts" in a far-off village by the sea, to the bare and simple melodies of the mountain *gamelans*. As the days passed, I found myself thinking less and less of composing. I began a work for orchestra, but I knew I should not finish it. I wrote a few short pieces and forgot about them a week later. The urge to write music had left, it seemed. I recognized this with indifference, with relief even, and I suddenly felt free and happy, liberated from some oppressive responsibility in which I no longer believed.

One day a package arrived from Java, containing reprints of a monograph I had written on the music of the shadow-play. It had been published, to my great satisfaction, by the Java-Instituut in Jokja, and I eagerly tore the package open.

Durus, Sampih and Lebah examined the books with respect, and exclaimed with delight as they recognized the rather glum *dalang* from Bangkasa among the photographs.

How much will you sell these books for? asked Durus practically.

But when I explained that these were for my friends they looked at each other in silence.

All that work, said Sampih. In vain!

They went out, to talk this over. I felt I had greatly disappointed them.

LOTRING

KUTA, WHERE I NOW WENT very often to pitch my tent for several days, was a small fishing village on the south coast, all sunshine and coral. Even the little temples were made of blocks of coral, and in the daytime, as the sunlight filtered through the palms, the village lay bathed in the tenderest gold and green.

The beach stretched in a wide crescent, and at low tide you

The garden at the house in Sayan

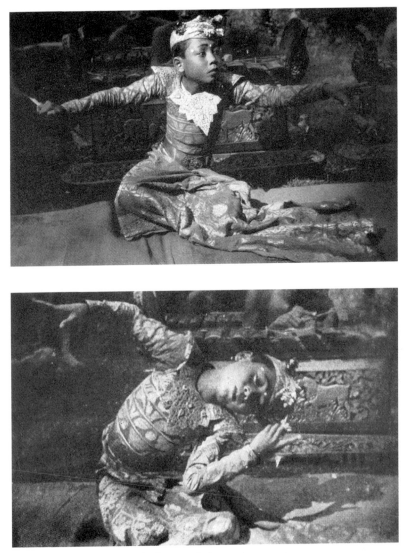

Sampih dancers *kebyar*: the opening

The dance comes to an end

Jew's harps

Arja musicians

Rantun, the cook

A fest delicacy—grilled sticks of turtle meat

The ancient and holy Selunding *gamelan* that came out of the sea

The soft-toned flutes of the ancient *gambuh* play

Gedé Manik, drummer, dancer, composer of *kebyar*

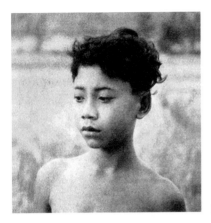

Sampih

Lotring, the composer, was also famous for his subtle spicing of feast dishes

Gusti Lanang Oka, a musician

Kuta fishermen

Durus

Prince and Princess in the *gambuh* play

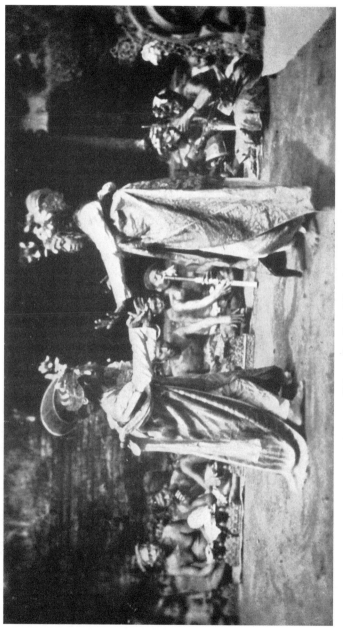

Prince Panji and Perebangsa

The new Stamboul Club near Den Pasar was encouraged by the Dutch

School Supervisor and visiting missionaries, who considered it a fine example

North Bali *gamelan*

could drive the car for miles along the wet sand. Here, in the later afternoon after a swim, I would stroll with Durus or Lebah, looking in the pools among the few scattered rocks for sea anemones, or picking up shells, tawny bishop's mitres, Venus' combs or shining porcelain olivas. Along the edge of the beach stood a row of tentlike shelters to shade the fishermen's *praus* from the sun, and for some months I had been thinking of building a hut in this fashion near by, where I could come from time to time as a change from the hills. For I was forced to admit that I found the skies of Sayan too often overcast, and the people a bit austere and stolid. It seemed to me that the people of the lowlands were very different from the people of the hills, more open, freer, sunnier, and I felt a lightness of spirit the moment I got out of the car at the market, all movement and luminosity beneath the shaded screens like an afternoon of Pissaro. Here, before turning down the road that led to the beach, I would sit for a while in the cool dark shop of my Chinese friend Nam Sing, a serene and gentle hedonist, and drink a cup of tea.

But the real reason for my frequent trips to Kuta was the fact that I could spend an afternoon with Lotring the composer, whose name was known from one end of Bali to the other.

I had first heard of him through Nyoman Kalér, soon after I came to Bali. I had been playing a few of my odd assortment of records for Nyoman and several musicians from the village—the soft hothouse *gamelans* from the courts of Java, the gay and brittle *gamelans* of Siam, primitive-sounding xylophones from Africa. They listened intently and were quick to recognize similarities with their own music. But soon they asked for my Balinese records, and now they relaxed, to listen in utter contentment. Among these were a few records made by the *légong gamelan* of Kuta. They had a radiance, an animation and perfection that far surpassed any *gamelan* I had yet heard on the island.

Béh! cried a listener admiringly. Lotring's *gamelan*! *That* was the foremost a few years back.

From Nyoman I learned that he and Lotring had led at one time parallel lives. They had both been trained as *nandir* dancers at the court of Blahbatu. As they grew older they both turned to music. Each had a preference for the light, swift music of the shadow-play and *légong*. When Nyoman began to train the dancers in Kedaton, Lotring had started the club in Kuta. His dancers and musicians had become so famous they had made records. They had also gone to Java to perform at the court of the Sultan of Surakarta.

We listened to the records. The music on one was exceedingly beautiful. Through a maze of intricate patterns a lovely melody was heard that slowly unfolded as the rest of the music rushed along at a breakneck speed. Suddenly the music changed. A short motif repeated over and over while the drums grew agitated. Tension increased like a spring being wound, but just at the moment when you felt it must surely snap the opening melody returned. Back and forth the two sections alternated until in a climax of syncopated drumming the music came to an end.

It was by Lotring himself. For Lotring was famed for his compositions even more than for his teaching. His music was played in all parts of the island. But this piece was so difficult that only his own musicians had ever learned it. Moreover, he would not teach it. He wished to keep it a secret.

What happened to the *gamelan* of Kuta? I asked.

It broke up. There was a quarrel. . . .

And Lotring?

It is hard! He has no *gamelan* now. He teaches *gandrung* now and then . . .

What does he do then, to live?

He is a fine goldsmith. His wives weave mats.

I was eager to meet him and said so. This was the first actual composer I had heard of in this strange island so passionately and yet so anonymously devoted to music. But perhaps there was too much enthusiasm in my voice as I spoke, for as Nyoman replied his own voice had all at once grown thin and distant.

But I waited in vain for Nyoman, and it was finally through Kesyur that I made his acquaintance one night after an *arja* play near Den Pasar. He had been playing the drum, and I was struck by his nervous and sensitive features, and the incredible lightness and speed of his drumming. As we spoke I had the impression of a shy and elusive personality, but he was obviously pleased when I said I had some records of the Kuta *gamelan*. I went to see him once or twice at his house in Kuta, but it was already near the time when I was leaving for Europe, and it was only after my return that our acquaintance developed into a friendship that was to last as long as I remained in Bali.

If Nyoman Kalér was the soul of the academic, Lotring seemed to me the spirit of all that was living and creative. He was everything that Nyoman was not. He was warm and gentle, naive, illiterate even, with a smile that went straight to your heart. Although, as I grew to know him, I found that he was vague and inconsistent about the theory of music, he was, when it came to practice, a keen critic and a superb craftsman, and the music I learned from him was, I think, the most beautiful of all I heard on the island.

For a Balinese the actual process of composing is something very different from our own. Music is not emotional self-revelation; it is before all, functional, an accompaniment to rite or drama. Composing is evolving rather than creating, and these days a new melody was rare. What marked a piece as new was style rather than content, and no one ever dreamed of criticizing it on the grounds that he had heard the tunes before.

But Lotring actually did create new tunes and new forms. He spoke of himself in the romantic terms of your true composer, and were it not for the modest, and rather worried tone of his voice, I should never have believed him.

Ké-wah! It is hard! to compose. Sometimes I cannot sleep for nights, thinking of a new piece. It turns round and round in my thoughts. I hear it in my dreams. My hair has grown thin thinking of music. But now, he sighed, I have no *gamelan*.

How do you get started on a new composition, Lotring?

Who can say? Sometimes a tune comes of its own accord, sometimes from something I've heard.

For example?

He laughed. I got the idea for one piece from a clock.

How was that?

A Chinese man here in Kuta had a little clock that played every hour. Really pretty. I often listened to it. I could not forget the tune. One day I made it into a piece for the Kuta *gamelan*. Soon everyone near Den Pasar wanted to learn it.

I was reminded suddenly of Prince Jojodipura as I listened to his *gamelan* one evening in Java. We have a new piece, he said, called Westminster. It was drawn from the chimes on one of my clocks.

And indeed, as the *gamelan* played, the familiar tones slowly floated in the air, perfumed and softly ringing, covered with dreamy arabesques that created a heavy atmosphere of langour and sensuous mysticism.

But this was a literal transcription, orchestrated in the elegant court manner. Lotring, on the other hand, had used the little tune from the clock merely as a point of departure for a creation of his own. (As I listened to it on the record I could not recognize anything that sounded in the least like a tune that might have come from a clock.) He had an unusual gift for continuity of line; his music built, and his melodies were full of surprise and charming irregularity. As for the compositions themselves, they were intended as interludes between dances.

He was clearly unhappy over the breaking-up of the club in Kuta. The quarrel, it seemed, had been bitter—a loud dispute over money. The big gong was now in the pawnshop, and although it was now five years since the altercation there were still hard feelings in the village. There seemed little chance of forming a new club. Now, at loose ends, his life completely lacking in direction, Lotring, indeed, seemed lost. He was no longer in demand as a teacher, for he had no interest in the style of *kebyar*, and his music had a far more subtle vitality. Even as a goldsmith he could no longer earn a living, for there was little money these days for the flowers and headdresses of thin beaten gold, the rings and bracelets, the silver bowls that not so long ago had kept craftsmen busy from morning till night. Instead, he now made a wooden tray from time to time on the turning-lathe.

It was perhaps as much for my own sake as Lotring's that I began to wonder if there were not some way to start a new club in Kuta. As I listened to the records I felt I would not rest until I had succeeded in bringing the *gamelan* back to life. It was not only the lovely sound and animation of the music. It was indeed, unlikely as it may seem, for the sake of one single piece, *the* one unfathomable and inspired piece of Lotring's, which no *gamelan* had ever learned, that I wished before all to bring this about. At one time Lotring had tried to teach it to me. But I never got past the melody. The rest was impossible to grasp except through a performance.

Bèh! That was the most stubborn piece I ever thought of! he would exclaim in pride. It took the club two months to learn. The Rajah of Solo was overcome!

Didn't his musicians wish to learn it? I asked.

He laughed. They thought it mad. It was too fast, too loud. They could make nothing of the flowers. But I was not surprised. The *gamelans* of Java sound as though the men were sound asleep. In their music nothing ever happens.

I had not seen Lotring for months, since the time he spent a month at the house in Sayan teaching me the music of the shadow-play. I had been preoccupied once more with Sampih's lessons, but now I began to think again of the Kuta *gamelan*. One afternoon I drove down to see Lotring.

I came into the little courtyard to find him playing to him-self on the *g'ndér*. He rose and gave me a smile of welcome. As I stepped up into the main pavilion I noticed a coloured print of the Virgin Mary and Child hanging on the wall. I was startled. Missionaries were now frequent visitors on the island, unoffi-cially making from time to time a quiet conversion.

What is this? I asked.

But to my relief he only replied, The Queen of Holland. I bought it in Buleléng. He chased a hen off the sewing-machine, drew out a chair and asked me to sit down.

I told him that my mind was set on bringing back to life the Kuta *gamelan*. I did not see why it could not be done. The in-struments were still complete. I myself would be responsible for redeeming the gong from the pawnshop in Den Pasar. We talk-ed for an hour. At first Lotring's face was bright, but he began to shake his head. It would be too difficult. A thousand obstacles stood in the way.

Let us call Limoh, I said. He will know, for he was secretary when the club broke up.

Lotring called out to a small child and said, Go fetch Limoh from the market. He called again to Renu, his younger wife, to make some coffee.

Limoh arrived at last, and for another hour we talked. He listened thoughtfully. He was an intelligent youth with an initia-tive that had made him head of the *banjar* before he was twenty. He agreed with Lotring that it would be difficult to form a new club. Some of the old members would follow; others would not, and these last would be sure to make trouble. He would call the *banjar* together that night and present my plan.

It was sunset by now, and Limoh and I walked down to the beach for a swim. We passed the fishermen dragging their boats down to the water's edge. There! I said, pointing to a plot of ground beneath the palms, where I often pitched my tent. I should like to build a hut there, where I could come and stay. I would be near the *gamelan*, and could know the people of Kuta better.

You are welcome to the land, said Limoh. It is my uncle's. I have only to ask for it. The *gamelan* club perhaps can build the hut. It will be easy.

It was only after a week of apparently discordant discussions that the *banjar* was ready to consider the matter at all. One night we talked the matter out.

The old members who would not return claimed a part interest in the instruments. They would have to be paid off. The *gamelan* must be repaired. The drums had been destroyed by rats; the gold on the instruments had been tarnished; the keys were out of tune. Moreover, a *gamelan* without dancers was not to be considered.

We now discussed these dancers. A theatrical troup, to give the Chalonarang play, was in the hearts of all. But this seemed too ambitious right now, and there was little money for costumes. It was decided to train *légong* once more. Lotring, and his younger wife Renu, who had been one of the famous dancers, would teach. We made up a list of expenses.

Goldleaf for gamelan	25 rupia (15 dollars)
Tuner from Karangasem	
(including bus fare)	10 rupia
Redeeming gong.	50　　"
Cloth for costumes.	25　　"
Gold leaf for same	30　　"
Buying off old members	100　　"

I stated that I would give the money for the gong and the silencing of the old members. This was my present to the new club. In return, they were to build me a well-constructed hut, one I could lock, on the beach. It was to be in the style of the lean-tos where the boats were kept. Agreed! Agreed! In a state of enthusiasm we sat talking and smoking for hours.

A week later the tuner arrived, and the men had begun to cut down the coconut palms for the pillars to my hut. For days the tuner filed away at the bronze keys of the instruments and adjusted new bamboo resonators below the keys. Until a bamboo "matched" with absolute precision the key above it, the tone of the key remained dead. Patiently the tuner cut, trimmed, listened for the echo in the tube. Suddenly the sympathetic relationship was found, and the key sang. He then proceeded to the next. At last his work was done, and that evening the club gathered to play for the first time. The tones of the *gamelan* rang with a new radiance, a softness and translucence impossible to describe. The tuner smiled.

No *gamelan* has ever had a more sweetly penetrating voice! he said. Shining! Like gold! He seemed very pleased with his work.

As for the hut, it was simplicity itself to build and was finished in three days. It stood at the edge of the beach, beneath the palms, and through the open door you looked straight out on the sea. It was long and narrow, and the palm thatch came down like a tent, touching the ground. The pillars were thick columns of coconut that had been planed smooth, and rested on heavy round blocks of coral. The floor was the white sand. A low bed of bamboo, a table and two or three deck chairs completed the furniture.

For three months I practically lived in Kuta, returning to Sayan only to see that all was well at the house. The finishing of the hut was, of course, celebrated by a feast to the club. Lotring and Nam Sing roasted a pig Chinese style, split flat, rubbed with soya, palm sugar and anis. Long after we had eaten we sat in the moonlight, keeping the fire alive and listening to one *arja* record after another on the phonograph. Disturbed by all this, the turtle-dove which Limoh had given me woke in its cage and uttered a few low notes.

This prompted one of the boys to begin a tale of birds who wished to become actors and musicians. Let us form a club, they said, and give a play. The turtle-dove was chosen for the part of gentle Prince Panju; the jungle-fowl seemed suited for the role the wild Prabangsa. The rice-bird would be princess. (And so on through the company the birds were cast according to their voices and appearances.) When the actors had been carefully chosen, they now considered the musicians. The lark, of course, would be the flute, the owl the gong. The seagull was assigned the two-stringed fiddle, the starling the cymbals, while the woodpecker would beat time on the *kajar*. All were delighted. Pleased with their success, the club thought they would play before the king, to show him they are as fine as the actors of the palace. But now a dispute arises among the birds over how much to charge. Five thousand copper cash, suggests one bird, ten thousand demands another. The birds take sides. . . .

Just like the *gamelan* of Kuta, I remarked.

They laughed. A club is like that, said Lotring. One day united, the next divided in thought. In the time when I was young it was different. Men were less restless in the old days. . . .

Often, as I sat on the floor of the clubhouse, listening to the men rehearse, I would ask a g'ndér player to move aside while I took his place for a while. I never was able to master the complicated technique of holding a *g'ndér* stick in each hand, silencing the keys just struck while at the same time striking the next. Instead, I used a single hammer, in the modern style. This was enough, however, for me to experience the sensation of being, at least for the moment, completely united, in close and absolute sympathy with the players, lost with them in the rhythm of the music. I knew the melodies by heart, and as I played I felt both peace and exhilaration in this nameless, tacit accord. Here there was no conductor's stick to beat time, no over-eloquent hands to urge or subdue. The drumming of Lotring was at times barely audible; you felt it rather than heard it, and the music seemed to rush ahead on its own impetus. You were swept along the stream, no longer knew what you were doing. It was something free and purely physical, like swimming or running.

The rehearsals were divided between training the new dancers and learning the music. A few new members had joined, boys of twelve or so for the most part, and they followed the older men, gave themselves up to the rehearsals with fierce devotion. In a few months the *gamelan* had regained its former brilliance, and to me it sounded even more enchanting than it did in the records that had been made eight years before.

Lotring had composed new music for the debut of the dancers. He was a different person these days, I thought. Word had already spread of this new activity in Kuta, and already he had been asked to train dancers for the Anak Agung of Kapal. The day of the consecration of the dancers and their first public appearance, people came for miles to see the performance.

The little girls were beautifully trained, in a style quite different from that in Gianyar. It was less classical. There were all sorts of little innovations. (Champlung would laugh, I thought, to see the raven jump down from a chair.) As I followed the dancers, watched the obvious delight of the audience in their smallness and swift agility, I was suddenly reminded of the puppets of the shadow-play and the little, sharply cut figures of the temple reliefs. There seemed to me a close relationship; a cycle presented itself. Through a series of transitions, stone became mobile; its hard contours had broken up and dissolved. Puppets brought the reliefs to life; men whose faces were still concealed behind masks gave fluidity to the stiff gestures of the puppets, and, discarding at last the shell that marked them as only half human, emerged from the chrysalis as humans, humans, however, whose faces were still frozen and masklike. Slowly the archaic yielded to a new sensuousness in the dancing of boys or girls, who gave to gesture the lyric grace of youth. But there was still a further stage of refinement, where adolescence gave way to childhood. Now the circle was closed, for in their sexless and doll-like performance the *légong* dancers had only to be petrified to become once more puppets or little carved figures of the gods.

The club flourished. The members seemed very happy, and they now played everywhere. They did not make any money to speak of, but this was not the objective. As for Lotring, he experienced a new popularity. He composed several new pieces, and was suddenly in great demand as a teacher. I too had benefited, for my hut in Kuta had become a second home. But perhaps my greatest pleasure lay in the knowledge that I at last had captured the secret of Lotring's music. There was the composition which had first caught my attention written down in full, intricate, ingenious, a miracle of rhythm. Yet it had not been too difficult to understand after all, for as the musicians practised it phrase by phrase the passages which I had once found impossible to grasp now became perfectly clear. I could only marvel at Lotring's imagination, for the ornamental flowers in this music were quite unlike any others I ever heard on the island. Lebah was quite as enchanted as I was, and when he had learned to play them (for he often sat in at rehearsals) he could hardly wait to return to Pliatan where he could teach them to the men in his own club.

THE CRICKET-FIGHT

ONE MORNING DURUS CAME into the room where I was writing to announce that an old man was out on the veranda with a set of cricket cages he wished to sell. If you bought them we could easily find crickets, he pled.

I went outside. The cages were beautifully made. Fitted into an elegant lacquered box were a dozen little cylinders of bamboo, neatly slit all around, and with a glass stopper at each end so that you could get a clear view of the cricket inside. There was also a set of tiny brushes with which to irritate the crickets and put them in a mood for battle. I was undecided, but Durus insisted, saying we could go that night to look for crickets in the fields. He and Sampih would look after them for me.

That night we hunted with our flashlights, and after we returned home we selected with much deliberation twelve that seemed the most spirited and shut each one in a cage.

Looking after them was like looking after a dozen royal children. Every morning each cricket was bathed, brushed, and examined for signs of a drooping spirit. They were fed on rice soaked in *arac* to make them strong, and spiced with red pepper to develop their tempers. Each must swim daily in a basin of water for ten minutes to exercise the leg muscles. The box was hung outside my bedroom door, and at night I could not sleep for the chirping.

Sometimes a boy from the village, or even Chokorda Rahi, accompanied by two or three followers, would come to the house, bringing their own crickets, and we would settle down on the floor of the veranda to an agreeable morning of diversion. Matches were arranged; bets made; little piles of money shoved forward. A little crowd soon gathered from nowhere to look on.

A fight was an exhibition of insect ferocity that drove the spectators quite wild with excitement. Two cages were placed end to end. The crickets were prodded to a state of frenzy; the ends of the boxes were then slipped out and the fight was on. We leaned forward, watching intently and exclaiming at each step of the battle as Durus or Chokorda Rahi urged his cricket on with the brush. It was usually a fight to the death, and you could hear tiny jaws click and snap as the insects rolled over each other. When a cricket gave up and ran to one end of the tube everyone cried out in disgust, and it was removed, to be impaled on a straw along with the vanquished and mutilated, and taken home and dried.

For a month or more my cages remained filled with crickets, but after a while we tired of them, and the cages were emptied and put away.

Sometimes I would amuse Sampih and old Rendah with tabloid versions of the people of Lilliput and how Gulliver walked off with the navy. They would listen for hours to tales of magic lamps, flying carpets, and tables set with food by invisible hands.

What was there to eat? Sampih would ask.

Oh, rice, perhaps; turtle, ice cream. . . .

The story of Cinderella reminded him of the *arja* play, of the princess who married Green Frog. Did I know that story?

I shook my head. Sampih began.

There was once a prince of Daha who was so filled with magic power that even his urine must be saved for six weeks. Only then, when it was no longer dangerous, might it be thrown away.

One day the prince was hunting in the forest. He came to a lake, where he made water. In this forest a young woman was gathering firewood. She was very thirsty; when she came to the pool she drank. At once she felt a burning sensation in her throat. She felt something slide up into her mouth, across her tongue, to appear between her lips. It was a small green frog, holding a pumpkin seed, and she took it home to care for it as her son.

The frog told the woman to plant the seed, and soon there was a vine with a handsome pumpkin. Green Frog now said, Take this pumpkin to the court of Daha and say to the prince that I wish to marry his daughter. But when the woman appeared at the palace she was killed, and her body thrown away in the forest. Green Frog found her and brought her to life. This happened three times, and the third time the prince consented.

All this time the princess was kept in the pigsty by her stepmother. Her stepsister beat her every day. She was very happy when they said she was to be married, but when she found her husband was only a small green frog she began to weep.

Green Frog was in despair. He went to the forest and prayed to Shiva. Suddenly a great voice was heard telling him his skin would peel off like a jacket. Green Frog removed his skin as he was told. There he stood, a youth of royal appearance.

He returned to the court and married the princess. She fell in love with him the moment she saw him.

One afternoon, as Lebah and I were driving home from Tabanan, we saw approaching a gleaming white car that drove along at top speed and passed us in a flash.

The dog ambulance! said Lebah.

It belonged to the little Australian veterinarian who lived with his wife and family in Den Pasar. He had been here a year, sent out on a mission of salvation by a tourist, an elderly woman with a great love for dogs. English or American—I had heard both rumours. She had seen only the dogs as she travelled about the island, and had found their plight apparently quite dreadful. The island was simply overrun with dogs, the doctor said, as I talked with him in the grocery shop of Nam Sing in town. The villages must be cleared, litters destroyed. Some dogs would be nursed to health, others shot. The programme was complicated. He spoke eagerly and earnestly.

He waited six months for his ambulance, when he could begin his work. At last it arrived, a beautiful modern van, complete with porcelain trays and shining instruments. Unfortunately, it was found to be too large to cross any of the bridges, and its activities were confined from the beginning.

Up and down the ridge that ran from Den Pasar to the mountains the doctor worked, shooting, curing, operating and chloroforming. Soon the villages were quiet, and much of the scavenging was now left to the pigs. The doctor felt he could take a holiday in the hills of Java.

He returned to find that a new generation of dogs were already growing up. In no time at all his ridge was noisy as ever. He started out once more, but when I met him in town he seemed a little depressed.

It's a handsome car, I said to Lebah, as we drove through its dust.

With that money, how many bottles of quinine could have been bought! he said. There are many sick people in the villages. If there are few dogs, he added, how will the villages remain clean? . . .

I said that in America many dogs wore coats when they went out in the rain, and shoes and knitted sweaters.

But this he refused to believe.

THE CREMATION IN SABA

I HAD NOT BEEN to the palace in Saba for over a year, and when I passed Gusti Bagus on the road his greetings were a mixture of reproach for having forgotten him and a haste to be gone about his own affairs. What was the news? we asked each other. Agung Biang was hurt because I no longer came to see her. His father, the old Anak Agung, was slowly dying. Only opium now kept him alive and out of pain. The expense was ruinous, said Gusti Bagus. They had sold more rice-fields. . . .

Sometimes a messenger would arrive on foot from Saba, having trudged twenty miles with a basket containing two or three fine durian fruit, if it happened to be the season, or perhaps an old mask or piece of stone sculpture, for the Anak Agung knew I collected these, although he could not possibly see why. When a thing was old you threw it out, and he could not understand my enthusiasm for a carving or ancient bronze green with age, any more than he could understand my love for the stiff, unadorned music of the mountain villages.

These little gifts were the most delicate reminders of his affection. Now and then, as though to put my own friendship to the test, he would send his messenger with a scribbled note saying he wished to borrow some ringgits. This was his favourite currency for the cockfights, and I was pretty sure that he was off to some contest, especially as he waited outside in his car, preferring not to come in and see me. Sometimes I obliged him, sometimes not. It depended on how much I felt indebted to *him* at the moment, for these little loans were never referred to, and it is a poor friendship where balance is not maintained.

One afternoon Kesyur arrived to invite me to his child's six-month birthday feast. He would kill a turtle, of course, and there would be a shadow-play at night. He also told me the latest news from Saba. Gusti Bagus had recently married the little *légong* dancer, whom he had "taken" last year. With the *kris,* that is, he added.

For as she was a commoner she had remained in the rank of a mere concubine. But when it was found she was to bear a child, the Anak Agung had had the marriage ceremony performed. She had gone home, but on the day of the ceremony, instead of going to fetch her himself, he had, since she was so much lower than he was, merely sent his kris.

Is the child born yet? I asked.

Yes, said Kesyur. It's too bad. . . . It's a girl.

But he already has a son.

A girl was always loss, replied Kesyur.

When, one morning, I finally drove to Saba to pay a visit, I found the Anak Agung before the palace gates, buried beneath his car. He emerged with caution. A gear wheel was broken, he announced dejectedly. But in a moment this was forgotten as he began to tell me of his new plans to restore the pool in the park.

This time I shall use concrete, he said. And run a concrete bridge out across the water. His eyes shone.

I nodded. We walked across the court to the main pavilion. On the table lay a large piece of cloth, covered with half-painted-in figures. He had been designing another picture. It was the Temptation of Arjuna, and in the centre Arjuna sat, hands clasped in the pose of an ascetic, his eyes focused on his nose in meditation. He would ask strength from Siva to overcome the demon Kala. On either side a smiling, teasing nymph (sent by the demon) attempted to distract him. Others danced seductively in transparent draperies, while below, old Tualén, the faithful attendant, made shameless, indecent love to still another nymph whose willingness was all too apparent. Fantastic trees with florid birds and widely indented foliage filled all spaces, and the picture was framed in a border of vines and flowers. It had the colours and artificial style of the shadow puppets, but the Anak Agung's lively personality seemed to shine through it all, for the lines were bold and exuberant, and the whole thing was done with sweep and flair.

He laughed at my admiration. It was nothing! There was only one scene. Later he would do a long and narrative picture about the abduction of the Princess Sita.

For a picture to be good, he said, it must have a little of everything in it—fighting, a little love, comedy and grief. Like a well-made dish there must be mingled sweet, salt, a taste of acid, a taste of bitter. . . .

And this? I asked, pointing to the incalescent love scene.

He laughed.

It gives the savour, he said. Like *sra*. Like shrimp-paste.

Where will you put the picture when it is finished?

At the head of my bed, above the pillows. . . .

At this moment Agung Biang appeared. She looked careworn, I thought, as our eyes met. But her smile had lost none of its welcome. She came up and put her arms around me. She stroked my cheek. Why have you not been to see your mother for so long? she asked.

I could not think why I had stayed away all this time. For in spite of its ruin, and the cares that now beset it more and more, the palace retained its atmosphere of unbroken peace and friendliness. The warmth of Agung Biang was so real, her voice so softly concerned, that she made you feel like a favourite child rather than an honoured guest. Our sympathy did not depend on words, for our conversations were of the simplest. Sometimes, as I spoke to her, I would use the wrong word by mistake, one you would use only when speaking to a commoner, and then she would draw herself up with sudden majesty and say, You may not use that word to me, for I am a princess. But then she would soften and laugh, and we would go on talking, for it was clear I knew no better.

It was perhaps six months later that a messenger arrived from Saba with the news that the old Anak Agung had died at last. Agung Biang was ill from grief. Preparations for the cremation had begun, and the day was fixed a month away. The Anak Agung invited me to the feast.

I arrived that day to find the square in front of the palace in a turmoil. Several lesser noble families of Saba had decided to take advantage of the auspicious day and cremate their dead at the same time, and along the road that led up to the palace stood rows of bright cremation towers. Coffins carved in the form of bulls, cows and winged lions; coloured red, orange, or black, and festooned with golden streamers, stood waiting at the doorways.

From within the palace came the sound of music which was played only for the rites of death. Above the dry, wooden sound of ancient xylophones that rattled a hollow accompaniment there rang the hard metallic tones of *gangsas* in a strange, anvil-like chorale, irresolute, uncertain, as though the players could barely recall the melody. On and on the music played, passionless, colourless, filling the air, with mournful sound that seemed curiously at variance with all the excitement and confusion. There were many guests, and the rich aroma of festive cooking floated over the walls from the kitchens, the smell of spice and freshly grated coconut, of roasting turtle and pig.

Before the palace gates the *wadah*, the tower which would bear the body of the old Anak Agung to the cremation ground, stood glistening like a Christmas tree. It rose high above our heads, a complicated structure of bamboo, and from the many little roofs that ascended pagoda-like above the platform high up where the body would rest there fluttered fringes of tinsel and gold, fringes of tissue-paper dyed every colour of the spectrum. A steep runway ran up to the little platform, like a gangplank to the sky, and the back of the tower was half hidden behind the enormous staring head and spreading wings of Bhoma, son of the earth. But even as I stood admiring this wonderful affair, the Anak Agung came up with the Brahman priest, a troubled look on his face. Something had gone wrong.

He had, it seemed, in his exuberant and characteristic love for the grand gesture, built a *wadah* with eleven roofs. This, however, was above his rank. He must have known it; for his family, in spite of their connection with the royal house of Karangasem, were *not* Déwas, but merely Anaks. The sarcophagus too had been built above his station. This the priest reluctantly agreed to overlook, since it was too late to change it, but he insisted with quiet firmness that two roofs be removed from the *wadah*. It was a bitter pill. Reluctantly, the Anak Agung gave the order, and three men climbed the tower, to disfigure it before the eyes of the world.

Do not take a picture of it, said the Anak Agung sombrely as we stood watching side by side. It is ruined. He stood looking a moment longer, then disappeared into the palace to take charge of other urgent matters.

It was late in the afternoon when there was a sudden sound of commotion within the palace, and all at once, through the high ceremonial gate a crowd of struggling, shouting men bore the body swathed in white down the steps, across the court and out to the tower, mounting the tottering runway to place it on the little platform high above our heads. A hundred men stood ready, waiting to lift the tower to their shoulders. The priest and musicians mounted the base, to accompany the dead prince to the cremation pile. To the sound of the soft, agitated music of the shadow-play the hands of the priest began to move, forming the holy gestures. Shouting, the bearers grasped the poles; the *wadah* quivered, began to lean.

It rose like a ship leaving port in a stormy sea. Slowly it got under way, and was born careening down the road. One by one the other towers began to rise, to follow to the sound of drums and gongs. As each *wadah* came to the dangerous crossroads it was turned around and around, to confuse the demons ever waiting to do harm. Once more, as the road turned south, the *wadahs* revolved and were lost to view.

Behind, in the square before the palace, the crowd was like the troubled wake of a ship. All were preparing to depart for the cremation grounds. I sent Lebah for my cameras, and decided I would take the short-cut through the fields, so that I might photograph the procession as it arrived.

But now, through the palace gates, at the top of the steps, a woman appeared, incredibly old and wasted, supported at either side by two young girls. Her hair was ashen-white, her face a worm-eaten mask; she wore a trailing *sarong* of black cloth, and from her waist her withered body shone pale ochre in the late afternoon sun that flooded her with a fading brilliance. It was the old, old princess, the mother of the dead Anak Agung. With unseeing eyes she looked down on the scene. Slowly, blindly, she descended the steps, to travel with difficulty to the outer gate. But there she paused, for she could go no farther, and as I left I saw her standing there, staring blindly out into nothing.

Scattered over the cremation ground the funeral pyres stood waiting. As the towers arrived a scene of wild excitement now took place. One by one the dead were lifted down and laid in the sarcophagi, which now stood in gaily decorated pavilions of bamboo above the piles of wood. Fires began to burn; smoke rose. Soon a wave of flames enveloped the great white bull which contained the remains of the old prince, and which stood there, stiff and staring.

I had not seen Agung Biang that day, but now I suddenly came across her in the crowd. There were no flowers in her hair, no bright scarf around her breast. Distracted, unhappy, she wandered aimlessly here and there, taking no part, talking to no one. I was shocked by the change in her since her illness. She was no longer the strong, protective mother, the regal princess. She was instead a child, an old woman wistful and lost, forgotten in the crowd, and her face was lonely and bewildered.

Darkness fell; the fires burned down. Little by little the confusion spent itself, and after the ashes of the dead had been gathered the crowd dispersed.

A month later I went down to the sea to wait for the *wadahs* to arrive from Saba with the ashes of the dead. It was midafternoon. High cumulus clouds lay piled along the horizon, and to the east the far-off mountains of Lombok reflected a golden green. I sat in the shade of a lean-to, while Durus, lying on the sand, began to tell of how, long ago, when men subsisted, like butterflies, solely on the juice of the sugar cane, a situation arose whereby, as though by accident, more nourishing plants began to grow in this world.

Batara Guru fell in love with the heavenly nymph, Ratna Dumilah. But she would have nothing to do with him before he had promised her three gifts—delicious food of which she would never tire, fine *sarongs* that would never wear out, and a *gamelan* that would play, without musicians, the sweetest of music. But while the demon Kala was sent in search of these she died. Suddenly, a month after her burial, from her grave different plants were seen to grow. From her head rose the coconut palm, from the pit of her stomach rice, corn, the sugar palm and the pendulous plants. From her feet came tubers—taro, yams, and the creeping plants whose fruits are cucumbers and the different melons.

That is the origin of the plants, said Durus. . . .

But now far off in the distance there was the sound of bright processional music, the melodious ringing of *g'ndérs* and little gongs above the rapid beat of drums and cymbals.

The music grew louder. Across the fields and down the road to the shore the procession of *wadahs* approached.

They were tall delicate spires of white, now decorated only with gold foil and a thousand little mirrors, and as they travelled along the road the gold and mirrors flashed in the sun as though the *wadahs* were lit with candles. In their fragility, their loftiness, their paper-white radiance, the slender towers celebrated this final and lovely rite when the ashes, the last earthly relics, would be dissolved completely in the sea. Now the soul was free at last, free to float away, join its forefathers, merge, said some, in the ancestral soul.

Along the sand the *wadahs* were set in a row. While men and women waded singing out into the water as far as they dared, to cast away the ashes, boys climbed the quivering towers to tear away the streamers, the gold, the precious little mirrors. Now the *wadahs* were set afire. One by one they fell with a crash. In the dusk the fires burned themselves out, and to the sound of music the procession returned to Saba.

A SECOND DEPARTURE

IT WAS MORE THAN TWO years since I had come to Sayan, and I began to make plans for going to America for some months, for I had business to attend to, and I also felt I needed to get away. It might be a year before I returned, perhaps longer, and it was decided after much discussion that while I was away, Sampih would go to school in Ubud.

He already knew how to read and write, for I had sent him three days a week, together with Luar, a friend his own age, to study with Madé Gria, the *dalang*. For a while the lessons were an excitement, and the two boys learned to write and read in both Malay and Balinese very rapidly. But after a month or so the novelty wore off, and one day I arrived unexpectedly at Made Gria's house to find both teacher and pupils stretched out, sound asleep. Soon Luar stopped going; he wished to go to school, he said, and though Sampih now wanted to go with him, I persuaded him not to with bribes.

For I dreaded the schools and the Indonesian teachers, with their hatred for the past and their determination to stamp out all traces of native culture. I had often looked in a doorway, drawn by the droning chant of lessons which were suddenly broken into from time to time by shrill cries of fury from the teacher. An art class was especially disheartening. No flower, bird or tree might now be drawn in the decorative, traditional style. Realism had become the aim, and the children learnt the laws of true perspective, in order to produce endless drawings in which a cat or motor car travelled down the straight road to infinity, a road invariably bordered by perfectly diminishing telegraph poles and vanishing in the exact centre of the page. Mood was given to the picture by flushing it with lavish sunrise or covering it with driving rain. The children also drew, from copies that hung about the room, countless pictures of wardrobes, tables, warships, planes and Dutch windmills. When a child drew without a ruler the teacher was beside him in a moment with his switch.

This physical punishment, this imported gesture, was something new for the pupils, for at home they were rarely chastised. They grew up in freedom, seldom giving any trouble, for at the age of four a boy was already a "small man," with a fine sense of his own responsibility in herding ducks or taking the great water buffaloes to the stream each day for their bath. At home the children of Rendah would mimic the teacher with that peculiar gift of the Balinese for cutting satire. They would have the family in fits of laughter as they reproduced the sharp, dry, perpetually furious voice, the quick raps of his ruler against the side of the desk, and the way he would descend like the wrath of Shiva, striking here and there and breathing hard in his excitement. This shameless exhibition of rage, this frantic exposure of the frantic inner self was, while terrifying enough at the moment, a subject for endless parody, once you were back in your own village, safe again within familiar walls, surrounded by familiar faces.

Neither Agung Mandra, the *perbekel* of Pliatan and the head of Sampih's club, nor I, however, felt that Sampih would now be the worse for a little restraint. He had become spoiled and quite unruly, practising and dancing one week with devotion, performing the next with utter indifference. He knew perfectly well when he was dancing badly, and I could not help smiling at the way in which he had already found out how to cover up a poor performance with some little trick—an exaggerated flourish, a quick manipulation of his train so that the gold brocade glittered magnificently, a sudden smile—the charm of which he was now well aware of—or the rapid veiling of his glance beneath long lashes. At present, said Agung Mandra, he was making absolutely no progress. He was both the delight and the despair of the club.

All this, however, I could sympathize with, for I secretly admired his quick resourcefulness, his already professional instinct for the camouflage of the artist, and I understood only too well his alternating moods of intense enthusiasm and utter boredom. But this sympathy I did not show, for it was clear he was in need of discipline.

Yet where to turn for the authority so badly needed to give his life direction? Not to me, alas! who must remain always the outsider. Nor to his family. Only recently his father had split his mother's head half open with a blow from his heavy knife, aimed suddenly as she passed in the yard for no other reason, apparently, than to silence her scolding tongue. We found her at nightfall, lying in the fields alone. I poured brandy down her throat, and then Lebah and I raised her to her feet and helped her stagger home. She recovered in a week, indestructible, and talkative as ever. But Sampih did not recover so easily from the terror of that dreadful moment.

I will surely *kill* him when I am older, he said in a low voice that was tense with ferocity, and I was startled to see how dark his face had become, how much it suddenly resembled his father's. . . .

All at once I remembered Ida Bagus Gedé. He never failed to remind me, when I went to visit him, that I had taken away a boy intended to enter later his household. What exactly the relationship was that existed between this old priest and Sampih's family I never knew, but it was something both ancient and feudal, for he always spoke possessively of Sampih, and made much to-do over the fact that I had robbed him of his rightful *budak*.

One afternoon I walked across the valley to Bangkasa to ask his help. I said that only he, it seemed, could guide and control the restless nature of this boy whom I had, perhaps, been wrong in taking from him. To his words only did Sampih seem to listen with attention. . . .

He smiled with great gentleness at the boy who sat before him with hands folded in a *sembah,* now docile and subdued, and touched him on the shoulder.

Let him return to me, he said.

We talked. It was decided that Sampih should live partly in the household of Ida Bagus, learning the ways of a well-brought-up *budak,* and partly at home. He would go to school in Ubud (Ida Bagus frowned) and rehearse each week in Pliatan.

Through the trees a shaft of light from the setting sun now fell on the priest as he sat there, turning the white folds of his robes translucent and luminous. I began the polite phrases of departure, but Ida Bagus wished first to give me his benediction, for I was leaving soon and would not see him again. Had I chosen an auspicious day? Would I remember to make offerings and take formal farewell of the gods at the altar of the Sun God in the cemetery? He prayed for my safety in travelling, cleansed me with flower-scented holy water. In the dusk, followed by Sampih, I walked through the fields and down the valley towards home, thinking of him sitting there, serene and so strangely reassuring, enveloped in his faith.

A few days later—it was the end of December in 1935—I left. Soon after my arrival in New York I had a letter from Lotring, written (I imagined) by Limoh, and giving me news from Kuta. Then there was a long silence, and at last a letter arrived from Limoh.

The club had broken up once more. The dancers were not sufficiently in demand. The gong was back in the pawnshop in Den Pasar. Where my hut once stood a "hotel" was now being built for tourists. Would I please send a cowboy belt from America.

I looked at the signature:

With all honour,

I Limoh.

PART THREE
TWO YEARS LATER

W HEN LEBAH MET ME IN Buleléng on my return to Bali two years later he was full of important news. The island was preparing to celebrate the restoration of self-government. By order of the Queen, the eight regents would be reinvested with a semblance of their earlier power; in a month's time each regent would, in his own district, swear a new oath of allegiance in the temple before the high priest and receive from the resident the new title of *Zelf-Bestuurder,* or self-ruler. For this event the Regent of Gianyar had already decided on a brilliant three-day feast, in which he hoped, as usual, to outshine the others. He had already sent out invitations. Lebah handed me mine as I got in the car.

A typewritten page outlined the events.

June 29: 6 a.m. Firecrackers to be set off before the palace. The *Gamelan* with the Great Gongs to begin to sound. 7 a.m. *Paduka Tuanku Zeifbestuurder,* followed by all officials of the land of Gianyar, to set out for the temple of Besakih on the slopes of the Gunung Agung. 1.30. Drill of the Padvinders before the palace; reception within. In the evening the *baris* or ancient warriors' dance; midnight till dawn—*alja* from Batuan. June 30: 6 a.m. Firecrackers. . . .

On the third day, I read, there would be a great contest of *gamelans.* I saw included the village of Pliatan. It was this that Lebah had been waiting for.

Béh! he exclaimed, his voice eager and excited. All the rajahs will come; all Bali will be there!

What is the prize to be?

He looked at me. Honour only! I knew as well as he that the Anak Agung was "not strong" on giving anything away. That did not matter. There would be renown, an increasing good name. . . .

The Pliatan club, he went on, had bought a new *kebyar* composition from Gedé Manik for seventy-five guilders. It was to belong to them alone; he might not teach it to anyone else. It was a dazzling piece, very difficult, lasting half an hour, and with a variety of flower parts that had never been heard before. Gedé Manik came twice. a week from Buleléng to teach them. They had already learned the first part; the rest was undecided. It would be composed and worked out in later rehearsals. *Modél!* exclaimed Lebah. Brand-new! We rehearse behind locked doors so that no one from another village may come in and learn our secrets.

Who, for instance?

The club of Blahbatu. They will compete, but they cannot afford so fine a teacher. They have long been jealous of Pliatan. Indeed they will try to find some way to make us lose.

We drove up the broad new road that cut through primeval forest over the mountains to the south shore. Monkeys leapt across the road at our approach and ran screaming up the banks, while through the trees that met and interlaced far above our heads there fell a soft subaqueous light. Lebah continued his news.

The son of the Regent of Karangasem would soon go to Holland to study medicine. The Anak Agung of Lukluk had sold his beautiful *gamelan* to pay his cockfight debts. He was ruined, they said. He now had a coffee-stall outside the gates of the palace and waited in it himself There had been several missionaries in my absence, but their converts had soon returned to Balinese religion after they left.

I held the wheel while Lebah lit a cigarette. He went on with his news. His brother had not been able to pay the taxes on his ricefields. For a while he had worked them off by joining the road-menders. But he was not strong, and after he had stopped working his fields had been seized and sold at auction.

And Sampih? I asked.

He had not gone to school very long. He refused to be struck, and had fought with his teacher. He was now rather tall, and had begun to study *baris*, the warrior dance. He *could* be very good, said Lebah. But he will not practice hard enough. He is too fond of pleasure. The club is very angry.

And his other dancing?

It is not like what it was. The freshness is gone. His gestures come too late. He dances often for tourists. . . .

The forest thinned and cleared. We had reached the summit, and a view of amazing beauty stretched far below. All at once we came upon an unexpected sight. A most surprising bed of zinnias sprang to view. At the angle where the road turned to descend, the ground had been levelled as though the top of the hill had been sliced off. Row after row of leafless plants bloomed dimly, their colours bleached by the sun. The little park was neat as a pin, and over the bench on which you might sit, a sign-board in Dutch stated the height of the mountain and the date of the completion of the new road. Far below, surrounded by jungle, gleamed the small and inaccessible lake where formerly I sometimes pitched the tent. But now the forest had been cleared at one end, where you could see the road run past the edge of the water.

Do you remember the time we found the tiger's footprints by the shore? I asked Lebah.

They've gone by now, he said. They do not like the sound of motors.

He started the car. The road ran down the mountainside and through the valley, to encircle now the sacred Bratan lake, once the scene of mighty sacrifices. Beyond the temple for the divinity of the lake the red-tiled roofs of summer cottages reflected in the water. It had begun to rain, and I told Lebah to stop at the resthouse where I could get a drink. It was dark when we turned into the gateway at Sayan.

All seemed very much as before. The lamps shone brightly; Pugig, Rantun and old Rendah stood waiting to greet me. Durus was already helping Lebah remove the trunks from the carrier. Later in the evening the *klian* and Daria the priest came in to welcome me back and give me the news of the village. In the morning I found that white ants had invaded the sleeping-house; the shrines of the house temple were covered with ferns and moss, and the garden had become a jungle. But I felt as though I had come home once more, and in a few days it was as though I had never left.

It was perhaps two weeks later that Lebah came in one morning with word that there was great trouble in Pliatan. The *gamelan* club was in an uproar, for it had just been discovered that Regog and his younger brother, two of the leading musicians, had been teaching the new piece to the club of Blahbatu. The secret was out; it was disaster! Regog, whom they could not spare, would only be heavily fined. His brother had been already expelled. But this would not make up for the fact that the music was now common property.

But who would have thought that Regog . . . I began.

The men of Blahbatu had made a vow to eat filth if they failed to learn our new music, said Lebah. They offered Regog a bicycle.

What happens now?

We must practice all the harder. Fortunately, they have not learned the music to the end. There is still some to compose.

Regog paid the fine. He also made the statement that he would gladly pay another if he were caught teaching in Blahbatu again. Was this a promise or a challenge? As time went on it was discovered that Regog was often seen returning from that direction. Spies followed, but the *gamelan* rehearsed within the palace, and as there were watchers at the doors, Regog could never actually be caught red-handed. There was only one thing to do. The Pliatan men must now perform the ceremony of "eating the curse" at the altar of the Sun God. Holy water specifically intended to "destroy the peace of the soul" of him who gave away so much as a note *from now on* would be drunk by every member, at noon, with the sun as witness.

But on the day of this solemnity, as the priest poured water into Regog's hands he refused to drink. There were bitter words, and the club expelled him on the spot. I looked at Regog. He was a handsome youth, quiet and withdrawn when you met him in the coffee-stall by the market, animated and full of ideas at rehearsals. Once he had taken great pride in the club, and I thought of the time when he had come with me to a *gamelan* contest in Buleléng, and how he had sat for hours listening with eager attention, in order to bring back to the club some of the newest tunes and flower passages. But now his face had a sullen, brooding expression I could not understand, and with a single word, a final Good! he turned and walked out the gate of the temple.

The great day of the contest arrived. In Gianyar the square before the palace was so crowded that I lost Durus and Rendah before I had been there five minutes. Banners waved; decorated bamboos curved high in the air; the pavilion for the *gamelans* was festooned with flowers. Youths swarmed greased poles for the roast pigs at the top, while through the mob vendors made their way with ices, balloons and trays of blacked smoked glasses, a new fad that seemed irresistible, especially to the young men from the mountains who wished to be in style. Lebah disappeared, but soon he was back, all smiles and triumph, with the news that the men of Blahbatu had lost their nerve, it seemed, for they would not compete. This left only two formidable rivals, the club from Selat, which would also produce a brand-new composition from Buleléng, and the famous club of Den Pasar.

All through the afternoon and late into the night the sound of gongs, drums and furious cymbals thundered and crashed in the air as one after the other the clubs attacked their prize pieces. It was a mighty battle of sound, and I wondered who would win, and for what reason. Endurance, energy it seemed, would sway the judges in the end. I thought of the savage contest of former times, when in a pit tiger was matched against water buffalo. The fury of such a contest was nothing to that of the competing clubs. I looked for Durus, for I was ready to go home after an hour. More and more the new *kebyars* seemed to resemble each other, seemed intended only to dazzle and bewilder. Moments of repose were now almost unknown, and though from time to time there were still snatches of charming melody, before you were aware of a tune it had disappeared, lost in the avalanche of sound.

There was, of course, no sign of the Regent himself at this event. Such contests did not interest him, arranged, moreover, for the sake of *ramé*, festive sound, and for the sake of the crowd that stood on all four sides of the pavilion, watching but hardly listening.

Late that night Lebah appeared at the house. He was completely happy. Pliatan had won. The judges had said so; the talk among the crowd later coincided. Selat had played longer, and perhaps with more fire, but the effects and flowers of Pliatan were considered more novel. In spite of the loss of Regog, they were still the leading club of the south.

THE *GAMELAN* OF SEMARA

I WAS GLAD WHEN ALL THIS excitement was over and Lebah could return to Sayan. At last I could settle down to my own work. I was eager to begin a study of the older music on the island, the ceremonial music of the temple and palace which now seemed to be on the verge of disappearing overnight.

For days Lebah and I had discussed a plan I had had in mind even before I left for America, which was to form a club in Sayan for the sole purpose of reviving the charming music of the *Gamelan* of Semara the Love God. This music was now rarest of all on the island, for its elegance and subtlety had no place in the village, and the palace *gamelans* had nearly all disbanded. It is true that the *gamelan* in the court of Gianyar still played from time to time, but I preferred to keep clear of obligations to the Anak Agung. There was the *gamelan* of the Regent of Karangasem, but that was too far away. There was also the *gamelan* that belonged to the Brahman priest in Den Pasar, Ida Bagus Anom. Here I sometimes spent a late afternoon listening to the musicians and exhausting Ida Bagus with my questions, for he could not see why I was not content to sit and listen to the music as he did, relaxed and meditative, delighting in the tranquil sound, instead of disturbing the musicians during a pause to ask them endless, unanswerable questions.

But even the lovely-sounding *gamelan* of the priest, with its unusual scale of seven tones and its music that modulated unaccountably into other keys, was on the verge of disintegration. The men were old; their memory failed. Already the young son of Ida Bagus was talking impatiently of recasting the gongs and metal keys, to form a *kebyar gamelan*.

But there is a *kebyar* club just down the road, I said.

But none in *our banjar,* he answered.

I had no idea of bringing about a belated renaissance in Sayan, for I did not expect much enthusiasm over my plan among the young men of the village. But for me there would be both pleasure and profit, for I was tired of going about the island with a notebook, asking questions like a government official. By forming a club not only would I have music near the house once more, but I could learn the forgotten court style of playing in the most natural way possible, by hearing it pass from teacher to pupils. I thought that the men of Sayan would rather have a new *gamelan*—no matter what they were called upon to learn—than not, and when, after a long discussion at the house, the boys and men whom Lebah had called together said they would be willing to play in the old style if I found them the *gamelan,* I put my heart and soul into bringing this about.

It was Lebah who suggested I borrow the set of instruments now used by the *légong* club of Tegas, but which actually belonged to Agung Mandra in Pliatan. Elegantly carved with phrenix birds, lacquered and gilt, with keys that gave the sweetest of sounds (for the bronze was old and contained silver), these instruments had once been part of the spoil of war between Pliatan and the land of Nagara to the south, taken from the palace of the defeated rajah before Agung Mandra was born. He had loaned them to Tegas some ten years ago, where they had remained.

The arrival of this splendid *gamelan* in Sayan caused much excitement among the members of the club. That night they gathered on the veranda to try the instruments and decide how they would organize. Only the older men had any experience. Some belonged to the old *gamelan* which played in the temple; others came from the *légong* club of the Chokorda. They would do, said Lebah, for the main body of the orchestra. But for the flower parts we would need. players whose minds were more alert, whose hands and fingers could move more quickly, and we now chose a dozen boys who, it is true, had never struck a note in their lives, but seemed very eager to belong to the club.

Lebah had been elected leader of the club as a matter of course, and the next night he began to train them on a simple piece. He started from the very beginning, teaching first the melody, and then beginning on the ornamental flowers. At first it went rather slowly, but in a couple of weeks wrists began to grow flexible, and the boys were learning to control their hammers. Soon the music began to flow, become alive, and Lebah started on another piece.

But as yet I had not succeeded in finding a teacher who remembered the ancient court music I was so anxious to have the club begin learning, and it was Chokorda Rahi who at last thought of I Lunyuh, an old man from the palace of Payangan, ten miles up the road to the mountains. He had been a musician of the court in the time of the old prince, when there was still the famous *Gamelan* of Semara, and he still played the drum when the ceremonial *gamelan* of Payangan was taken to the temple. His memory was phenomenal, said the Chokorda; he was a storehouse of melodies and music now long since forgotten. His style of playing the *trompong,* the row of melodious little gongs, was in the finest tradition.

When Lebah first rode up to Payangan on his bicycle to see Lunyuh he came back with the news that the old man refused to stir. For no reason, apparently, than that he did not wish to.

What is he like? I asked.

A hermit! An old bachelor! Like a very old turtle! He will hardly say a word. . . .

But Lebah returned again with Chokorda Rahi, and in the end they succeeded in persuading him to come to Sayan in a month's time, after the new instruments which I had ordered to add to the *gamelan* would be finished.

For although the twenty-odd instruments were complete enough for *légong,* there was no *trompong,* on which to play the melodies, and in this orchestra of the court the *trompong* was like the piano in a concerto, with the soloist doing all sorts of elegant flourishes as he performed. I also wished to add more *gangsas* to my orchestra, enlarging the group of flower instruments so that the music would have a still more shimmering and luminous sound. I needed new drums, and also a set of cymbals in the antique style, small and thin, with a delicate clash. As I talked this over with the boys and men of the club their enthusiasm began to rise.

We are a club of thirty, I said. We are going to learn the old music. Let us do it in the best of style. We will make this *gamelan* larger and even better than the one in the palace of the Regent at Gianyar. And later, I will call Lotring from Kuta, to compose new music, which will belong to you alone. . . .

The gongs and metal keys for the *gangsas* were being forged in one of the distant mountain villages to the east, long famed for their tuners, who carefully preserved old sets of metal keys, precious relics of the past to which they constantly referred when setting the pitch of the gongs they made to-day. These metalsmiths formed a guild of their own, were a proud caste by themselves, outside the Hindu caste system, a caste that was ancient and especially respected, with a right to the highest death ceremonies. A smith, said Lebah (he was of the smith caste himself), had a right to as many roofs to his cremation tower as a rajah.

There was something dark and secret about their ancient craft, for they had to do with metal, cold mysterious product of the underworld, charged with magic power. For centuries they manufactured from the same substance the instruments of both music and death, the resonant gongs, the spears and thin-edged *krises*. In their craft the elements of life and death were strangely united. For a gong when struck can (or once could) dispel the demons, bring rain, wind; or give, when bathed in, health and strength. And music, which is the most ecstatic voice of life, rang from the bronze keys even as they were hammered out in the forges, over fires that had burned from time immemorial.

How shall these gongs be tuned? asked Nang Mudi the smith, when I went to see him. With a deep voice, in the tuning called Brace Sea? Or shall I tune them shriller, in the pitch called Burnt Tamarind?

What is best for a *Gamelan* of Semara the Love God? asked Lebah.

A Field of Flowering Pandanus, said the smith after a moment's thought. *That* is the softest, the most perfumed. . . .

But I had in mind the rare and beautiful tuning I had sometimes heard down by the sea near Sanur. The actual change in the five tones was not great. Only a single tone—the second—had been altered in relation to the others. It had been raised, made sharp, and that was all. But this was enough to impart to the music a strange and subtle poignancy, a sweetly melancholy inflection quite impossible to describe. I had already heard this haunting scale at the Javanese court in Bandung. It was the scale of midnight, the scale in which singers sang before changing to the mode they would use till dawn. I had also heard it in Japan, in ancient flute melodies, and at the puppet theatre of Osaka. To find it echo here in Bali was a discovery, and to have my own *gamelan* tuned in this way would give the music, I thought, the final touch of antiquity and unreality. I returned to Nang Mudi a week later with a set of keys I had borrowed from Sanur, and said:

You have only to follow these in tuning the gongs. Then, when they are made, you can bring them to Sayan and tune the rest of my instruments to match.

He agreed rather doubtfully. But he admitted the keys gave a remarkably sweet sound. Like nothing he had heard before, he added. He wrapped the keys in a piece of cloth and put them away.

Some two weeks after this he arrived in Sayan one morning, to spend three days retuning the *gamelan*. At last he announced he was through. He gathered up his files, and after bidding me good day, got in the car for Lebah to drive him down the road to the place where he could get the bus for Karangasem.

That night, as I listened to the *gamelan* in all its fullness, and with its new tuning, it seemed to me the most beautiful sound I had ever heard on the island. I had invited Agung Mandra to come from Pliatan to hear what I had done with his instruments, and as we sat listening, together with Chokorda Rahi, who had been drawn, he said from the other end of the village by the new sounds, we all agreed that the *gamelan* was like nothing heard before. I could hardly wait for Lunyuh to arrive, when the club would at last begin to learn the music I was so eager to hear.

THE *GURU*

THE MONTH HAD MORE than passed, but still Lunyuh did not appear. We waited a week longer, and then Lebah went to Payangan once more to see him.

He says he is coming, reported Lebah. But he doesn't wish to be hurried. . . .

Finally, one morning he arrived.

Old, pock-marked, sturdy and moving with great deliberation, he seemed indeed a dusty tortoise as he approached the veranda to rest after his ten-mile walk. At first he would hardly utter a word (he was rather deaf, and we had to shout) and he sat there in somewhat forbidding dignity, very sure of himself. Lebah addressed him politely as *guru*, teacher, from the very beginning, but even this did not seem to soften him. He wore a faded *sarong* that was surely as ancient as himself, and he smelled rather like a dried fish. He had asked for a little *arac* to revive him after his walk, and he tossed down a couple of glasses with the sudden quickness of a lizard that has seen a fly. Slowly he began to thaw. We spent the morning talking, while Lebah and I explained my reasons for calling him to Sayan

Did he remember? I asked. The old music of the *Gamelan* of Semara? Lasem, Seduk Maru, The Sea of Honey, The Fire of Love?

Béh! It's a long time . . .

He gave a dry chuckle. He took a leaf of *sirih* from his wallet, folded it and put it in his mouth.

Yes! He thought he remembered. We would see. . . .

That night, after the club had gathered, the *guru* sat down before the *trompong* to try out the little gongs. He picked up the long sticks and tapped lightly on the knobs. Dreamily he began to improvise, rather stiffly at first and then with more fluidity. Soon his improvisation had taken the form of the love-music from the story of King Lasem. This the club already knew; there was a signal from Lebah, and the others joined in.

I listened in utter pleasure. The *guru's* melody was the missing thread in the weaving, the thread of gold in the design. Above the other instruments the *trompong* rang out like a chime of bells, penetrating and heavy with nostalgic echoes. The *guru* had begun very simply, but soon his playing began to take on life. Little flourishes and grace notes appeared; he began to go his own way, to play off the beat. Suddenly he had broken into the most surprising and alert syncopation. The music had become almost a dance, a dance that was light, agile, filled with sensuous grace. Yet he sat there, a stolid figure of apathy to the outside world, never moving, except to reach out for the farthest gongs.

The music came to an end. There was a silence. He finally spoke.

Like *that,* he said. *That* is how the music was played in the palace. . . .

It is very beautiful, I said.

What?

Beautiful, I shouted.

Ah, he answered. He looked for his purse of betel leaves and took one out.

Each week he spent three days in Sayan teaching. He directed his attention entirely on Lebah, who was to play the *trompong,* and on the drums, for the drumming to this formal music was intricate. He refused to consider the flowers. Let Lebah work them out the way he wanted. In his time they were very simple. They had only to follow the melody. But now . . . Words failed him.

It was decided to keep the flowers simple and plain for the *guru's* music. But this was far too unexciting for the club, and on the nights when Lunyuh was away they would practice other music which was more difficult, more involved, something they could really attack and master. One night I heard a new and charming melody begin, then stop, begin again, repeat, gaining in assurance. Little by little the *gangsas* joined in, and then the cymbals. There was a pause. The melody began once more.

What was the new music I heard the club practising last night? I asked Lebah the next morning.

He looked a little confused. It was nothing. It was merely a tune he had thought of. He thought he might try to make a piece. But he did not pretend to know how to compose. . . .

That night he added a new section. In a few days the piece was quite complete. It was only a brief interlude that lasted a few minutes, but I never seemed to tire of hearing it.

As the weeks passed, old Lunyuh began to feel very much at home, and our acquaintance slowly developed into an austere and pedantic friendship. I soon discovered that he remembered far more music than he would ever teach the club. As he sat on the veranda sipping *arac,* and playing as I wrote, one piece suggested another. He was extremely proud of his memory.

You'd never find another like me, he said, to give you all this music. Not in Badung, Gianyar or Bangli. . . .

I had known him six months before I learned that he had taught many of the ceremonial *gamelans* in the villages nearby the music to be played at feasts and temple anniversaries.

Where did you learn all this music? I asked.

At the court, he answered. From the old *guru* who had come from the court of Bangli. He had written down the *pokok,* the main tones, and kept them all these years.

I recognized it as a true mark of his favour when one day Lunyuh came in and handed me a palm-leaf book, saying:

Here are the tones to the old pieces, which I have written down for you. He read some of the titles. Madura; Dawn; The Sea; Falling Rock. . . . There were fifty pieces, in all the different metres, from the Beat of One to the Beat of Eight.

But do not lend this to the people of Bangli if they ask for it, he said. Or Sulaan. . . .

But why?

What?

Why not? I shouted.

He smiled craftily. They have not got music like this. . . . But if Lebah wishes to teach them in Pliatan, let him have them.

Sometimes, when I went to Payangan, I would find him at a temple feast, seated before the *trompong* of the *gamelan,* lost in the music. For me his long preludes, which prepared the musicians for the music which was to follow, were extremely beautiful. The melody seemed to be summoned out of nowhere, recalled from the subconscious, to grow tangible, definite, and be finally passed on to the musicians who waited. He would begin slowly, tentatively, improvising according to his fancy. But gradually two or three tones would become fixed; the germ of a melody came to life, expanded, became recognizable at last as the *closing* phrase of Lasem or Full Moonlight. The drummers picked up their sticks; gave a signal accent; and as the *guru* reached the final note of his prelude the music suddenly began with a crash, to move slowly at first, gradually become animat-

ed and gather momentum until, a half-hour later, it ended in a
thunder of drums.

Guru, I asked. As you sit there, waiting to begin, have you any
idea what music will come next?

He couldn't say. He thought. Sometimes, perhaps. But often
the melody came to him only after he had already started playing. . . .

THE CHILDREN'S MUSIC
ASSOCIATION

THE FIRST REHEARSALS OF the club had attracted the small
boys of Sayan as honey draws ants. They sat around watching the older boys in envy and begging to be allowed to try the
gangsas for a little while At odd times of the day, when there was
no one about, I began to hear sounds of drumming and the faint
ring of a *g'ndér* or *gangsa* coming from the pavilion where the
instruments were kept. The imitation was surprisingly good; the
group grew larger every day. Rather noisy cupids for the God of
Love, I thought as I passed by, pretending not to notice them.
I recognized the leader as Kayun, a serious child of seven, who
now came often to the house and polished spoons for Durus
with an air of great responsibility. Already he was imitating Lebah's motions and turn of the head as he sat at the *g'ndér*, leading
the others on. But soon I had to put a stop to these meetings,
for the parchment of the drum "got" split, no one knew how;
hammers broke, a cymbal disappeared. The *gamelan* was now
forbidden, and after a while the children stopped coming to rehearsals.

It was the time of the *galungan* holidays, when already for
two days strolling *barongs* had passed through the village; lions,
tigers and boars travelled down the road with their musicians,

to stop and perform at the market-place before going on to the next village. All at once I heard sounds of strange and lively music, uncertain drums, melody very out-of-tune, and the pathetic accents of a cracked gong. What procession, I wondered, had now stopped by the gates.

Rendah, who was working in the garden, looked up and laughed. It was the new players' club of Sayan, formed by the "small men" only. Did I wish to call them in?

Outside the gate I found a troupe of exceedingly juvenile but dignified actors and musicians surrounded by a ring of even more juvenile and serious spectators. The players were about to make their debut.

Kayun directed with the drum. Kantin, his friend, held the gong. There were also a *gangsa* and cymbals. The club had made its own *barong* out of straw; it stood there snapping, impatiently waiting for the actors to tie on their masks. There was a brief but spirited prelude from the musicians and the play began. It was the story of boastful Chupak and his gentle little brother Grantang. Chupak rescues the princess, carried off by the demon, but it is Grantang who kills the demon (enacted by the *barong*). Chupak pushes Grantang down a well and carries the princess back to the palace. Grantang kills the demon of the well and climbs out on a ladder he builds of his bones. He arrives in time to marry the princess. Chupak is thrown out in disgrace.

When played in the usual tempo, this drama lasted till dawn. The children had reduced the plot to its essence. We were given only the high spots of the1Jlay. Poor Grantang! Dreadful Chupak! The coquettish saleswoman and the lustful farmer. They performed the ribald moments with gusto. When suddenly an actor was overcome with shyness or forgot his lines, Kayun or some other boy called out, Go on! What ails you! *Ach*, you're simply *rotten*. . . .

Suddenly the play was over. It had lasted ten minutes. I gave the necessary engagement fee of thirty *képéngs*. Delighted with their first success they continued down the road, followed by their audience, to play at intervals until they reached the edge of the *banjar*. Beyond that they would not think of stepping.

Knowing the Balinese temper, the sudden enthusiasms and as quick reactions, I was not surprised to learn soon afterwards that the club had disbanded. They were, said Kayun, using a word I heard a hundred times a day, med—bored, fed-up and *through*.

Kayun and Kantin were in and out of the house all day long. They would sit for a little while and hammer away at one instrument or another lying about the veranda. They discovered that certain tunes could be played on the black keys of the piano, and improvised brief but astonishing duets. One day, when I happened to be visiting Nang Mudi the smith, he showed me a set of little four-note *g'ndérs* and gongs he had made for an *angklung gamelan*. It had been ordered, but never called for, and now the instruments stood gathering dust. They were so charming, so sweet-toned, so miniature in size, I could not resist buying them, for I thought I might take them back to America. I piled them into the car and brought them home, and when Kayun and Kantin saw them they were in raptures. They placed them in a pavilion near the kitchen; soon several children, hearing the news, had wandered in to try the gongs, the little *g'ndérs*, the tiny cymbals. The garden rang with music every morning.

One afternoon I said to Kayun, Call the members of the Chupak club to the house, for I have something to tell them. That evening fifteen small boys sat along the edge of the veranda, while I told them that if they wanted, I would give the new instruments I had brought home to them. We would form a club of small men, and I would call a teacher, Kayun would be leader; Kreteg, who had gone to school, could be treasurer. What did they think?

A *gamelan*? A real *gamelan* of their own! They talked excitedly. Yes, they would learn! No, they would not grow tired! They would practice every night. Only give them a teacher! I told them they could take the *gamelan* to Kayun's house, where they could try it out. Carefully they picked up the instruments and carried them off with shouts of joy. That evening I heard sounds of wild and confused music in the distance. This went on for a week. The club is *too* happy, said Kayun. When will you call a teacher?

I said to wait till I came back, for I was going to Java for ten days. It was actually a month before I returned to Sayan, for I spent a week visiting Goris in Buleléng, going to the "night fair" each evening to hear the newest *kebyar* music and see the newest dancers.

I came home to find the club had learned three pieces. It seemed they could not wait for my return, and had found a teacher for themselves, the father of a friend from a nearby village. That night they brought their instruments and set them in careful order on the veranda. After a little quarrelling over the distribution of hammers, there was a silence. They gravely caught each other's eye. An invisible signal was given and suddenly they began. I recognized Prancing Horse, an intricate composition of considerable length. It was quite admirable. Once or twice the rhythm faltered, and the drummer got out of time, but with complete assurance the children swept through the piece, to bring it to a nicely retarded end. They rested, began again. This time it was a short piece—Monkey Looks at Himself in the Water. After this came Golden Dragonfly.

Lebah produced cigarettes. Durus brought out bottles of orange crush. I complimented them and said it was indeed time for a teacher.

Kayun, representing the club, piped up. The club demands a *good* teacher, one who knows the *new* music. We do not wish to learn in the old style, with an old *guru*, like the men in your *Gamelan* of Love. Such music is out of date. It is too slow; too *simple*.

He is right, echoed the others. Give us a *younger* teacher! At this point Lebah and Durus could not keep from laughing, while I promised to call I Nengah, from Selat.

I had known him casually for a long time, for I often used to spend days in Selat in the house of Gusti Gedé Oka, the head of the *kebyar* club. Nengah was perhaps forty,. shy and gentle, but filled with an unsuspected energy when he sat with a drum. He was the head of the village *angklung* orchestra which played only for rituals, but played in the modern Buleléng style. Since this was what the children wanted, and because Nengah seemed to me a man of unusual sympathy and originality, I went to see him, to ask him if he would come to Sayan.

I had to plead with him for an hour before he could make up his mind to come.

It is far, he said, and I have never been to Java.

I explained that it was still in Bali, only fifty miles away, and that he had not to cross water, but he shook his head. Java was the great outside world, the unknown; even the offer of money failed to interest him. It was only when I said I would ask Gusti Gedé Oka to come along with him, to stay a day or so in Sayan, that he finally consented. To follow his prince into a strange land seemed not too hazardous. For a day or so he was ill-at-ease in my house, and when Gusti Gedé left he at first insisted he must leave too. But Lebah prevailed on him to stay; soon his shyness vanished, and he became a great favourite with the children.

The first rehearsal took place after sundown on the veranda, after the children had returned from the fields. Lebah, the *guru*, Gusti Gedé and I sat looking on as the lesson began.

Nengah's method was strange. He said nothing to the children, but began to play through the melody, gazing out into the dusk. He played it again. He then played the first phrase and told the children to begin. Kayun and Kantin commenced, following him and watching every movement of his hands. A third child now joined in, and then others. Seriously, patiently, they went from phrase to phrase, while Nengah said nothing at all and continued to stare into space. Bit by bit the children gained assurance. Phrase was added to phrase, until with a shout of delighted surprise they found they were able to play the long and winding melody from beginning to end. But it was now late. They were suddenly tired; in the back rows giggling and pinching had begun. I said it was time to stop, and the rehearsal was declared over.

A few nights later, when the melody had "entered," Nengah began to teach the flowers. Night after night the children practised, industriously, with utter concentration. They refused to be baffled by the intricate rhythms. Alas for the cymbal player if he got out of time, or if the big gong came in late. Nengah said nothing, but the children shouted in exasperation.

Dog and Bedil are too slow! They keep forgetting! reported Kayun one night. We must find new men.

But everyone in the *banjar* already belongs, I said.

He thought, frowning. There are small sons of Rendah, he said doubtfully.

What about Kinigan, his nephew?

Ach, Kinigan. . . . He always makes trouble. He won't play. That evening Ada, aged six, and Dapat, five, took their place in the front row of *g'ndérs*. They had come without their clothes, and the club insisted they first go home for their *sarongs*. They are quick, announced Kayun a few days later. We will keep them. Dog and Bedil can remain in the club, but only to help carry the *gamelan*.

Old Lunyuh would watch these lessons when he came to the house in blank wonder. A club of small men was quite unheard of. As for Nengah, he was delighted. Sharp as needles! he exclaimed. Quick as fieldmice! They keep asking for new pieces. Soon they will be able to play at the temple.

Are you happy here?

He smiled. I like to teach them, he said.

A hut was built for the children in one corner of the garden where they could rehearse by themselves and store their instruments. This was their own private clubhouse, and they came and went as they pleased. In a tree they hung their own *kulkul* or signal drum to call the club together. The members now numbered twenty-five.

When I met the children on the road as I walked through the village they were shy and gentle; unobserved they raced about full of malice and mischief. Like children everywhere, they scrawled on walls the latest and far from innocent news of some uncovered romance, and filled them with drawings of demons, shadow-play heroes and the universal diagrams of sex. They knew a thousand rhymes on the subject of the symptoms of desire and the phenomena of gratification. At one time I collected these at a penny apiece. Nengah laughed. I used to sing them too when I was small. He thought, began:

Bananas from Mas, mangoes from Bengil;
Jostled she yells—but laid she keeps still.

Here Kayun and Kantin, who had been listening, capped the verse with a second which I found even more astonishing.

One evening the *klian* and Daria the priest came in to see me. After the usual preliminaries the object of their visit was revealed. Did I think the children ready, would I *allow* them to play at the feast in the Temple of Ancestors, which would take place at next full moon? Nengah thought it possible. Night after night rehearsals went on. The club practised with a new determination, knowing they would soon make so important an appearance, and fines for lateness were raised from one to two *képéngs*. As I sat on the veranda of the sleeping-house at the other end of the garden reading, or playing dominoes with some visitor who had come from far off to tell me of a feast, the music rang out in the night, a joyful counterpoint above the graver, sweeter music of the other *gamelan* rehearsing out by the gates. I loved the confusion of sounds which sometimes jangled in dissonance, or merged every now and then to form surprising harmonies. At last the music would stop; voices and laughing died away as the children walked out to the gate. Soon the other *gamelan* stopped playing, and now there was no sound at all, except the faint roar of the river, or the hum of a deep gong far up the valley.

It is the day of the temple feast, and the children have gathered at the house to carry their instruments to the temple. I give them each a square of large black-and-white check cloth for a headdress, which will mark them as a club. They look for red hibiscus in the hedge and put them above their ears. They look very spruced up, and at the temple their appearance creates much excitement. The club of older boys has already arrived, and the two *gamelans* are set in opposite pavilions. The ceremony of blessing the instruments is gone through, and the priest tells the children to begin.

Enggéh! Tabuhin! he says. All right; strike up.

People crowd eagerly around; he asks them politely to stand back. It is the children's hour; they dominate the scene. The women pause in arranging the offerings, the older club looks on from the other pavilion, commenting in friendly irony. Kayun lifts his hammer, looks sternly about. Are they ready? He brings it down in a flash and the music has begun. It is Prancing Horse, their show piece. All listen in silence, smiling with pleasure and amused admiration. For once, the Balinese seem almost sentimental. But soon the music has ended, and the rituals must proceed. It is now time to go in procession to a distant sacred spring to bathe the gods. The children pick up their instruments, hook them to the poles for carrying them as though they had been

doing so all their lives. There is much shouting in getting started, but at last they go out the great gate, followed by the women
with the god figures on their heads. The larger *gamelan* follows
in the rear. Now the women have started to chant; the children
begin on Incense Smoke; from the rear is heard the thunder of
drums and heavy gongs in the stately Beat of Three. I see them
go across the fields, with gilded parasols and waving banners,
until they are lost from sight as they descend into a ravine.

It is dark when they return to the temple to the sound of firecrackers. The next morning I am told by Lebah and Durus that
the children, drunk with success, could not leave off playing,
but went through their programme several times, off and on, till
dawn put an end to the first day's ceremony and they suddenly
found they were very sleepy indeed.

THE LIGHTS IN THE VALLEY

ONE NIGHT AS LEBAH, the *guru* and I were returning from
Buleléng, we came to a village in the mountains bright
with lamps. Before the temple an *arja* play was in progress, and
we stopped to watch for a while. The clown attendants of the
Prime Minister of Koripan were on the stage, and the crowd
kept shouting at their lines in high delight.

Serog and Kakul, said Lebah. They are very funny. They are
telling about the month when they were Christians.

They had been converted last year, but after a month of nothing but trouble they had taken up their own religion again, after
the missionary had left. I could not understand their jokes, but I
imagined they were variations on a familiar tale.

X had been converted because he had been promised his
syphilis would be promptly cured. Y had been convinced that
it was cheaper to be a Christian, with no continual offerings
to make, or expensive cremation to save for. Z had been quite
terrified by the missionary's picture of Satan. But once they had

become Christians, all happiness seemed to have fled. They became quarrelsome and superior. They were no longer co-operative in the village, and since they would not pay the village or temple dues, they were left alone with their harvests. The village would not allow their dead to be buried in the graveyard. Yet, although they were now Christian, they were refused the little cemetery of the Christian Dutch. They felt bewildered and lost. The compensation was too vague, and life had become cold and empty. One by one they returned to their former faith, were purified by the priest, and took up once more their daily lives.

Why does he look so *unfriendly*? asked Lebah as we passed the Protestant missionary from Canada one day in Den Pasar. He does not look happy at all. . . .

It was certainly not compassion that one read in his joyless face. As he looked on unmoved at performances there was something sinister in his cold and provincial disapproval. All this must end, he said as he called on Goris at his office in Buleléng. This music and dancing—it was the work of evil. At present he was on the island to make a survey. But he would return, he said, when the controversy over conversion on the island had been settled once and for all. It looked now as though this might be very soon.

One day Houbolt, the impetuous little Dutch journalist who sent an acid column from time to time to the papers in Java, was riding on a bus that ran across the mountains, when he noticed several large packages addressed to the missionary. Some premonition caused him to tear open a corner; the packages were filled with Bibles! Had the torn wrapping revealed a nest of serpents Houbolt could not have been more startled, and he could hardly wait for the bus to reach Buleleng. He went straight to the house of Goris, and the two drove at once to call on the Resident. The missionary had been put on his honour to remain purely an observer, and this was the result! Houbolt's voice shook with anger. What happened to the Bibles I never found out, but the missionary left soon after.

A few months later I received a letter from America with a clipping from a Canadian paper that began with a headline:

BALINESE LAYING DOWN THEIR IDOLS
The people of the little island of Bali are rapidly turning to Christianity and throwing away their idols, reports Mr.
. . .

Why should I change my religion? asked Agung Mandra one evening as we sat talking together in Pliatan. Why should I want to change my way of life?

In the dusk a woman appeared in the doorway to the inner palace, bearing a tray of offerings. She walked slowly across the courtyard and disappeared through the gate to the palace temple. From somewhere near by there came the sound of a flute. Agung Mandra rose and lit the lamp.

But if I did, he continued, I should not like to become a Christian.

What would you do?

I should become a Moslem, he said.

For the past month I had been engaged in writing arrangements for two pianos of some of the music I had got from Lunyuh, Lebah and even the children. I had already given a little concert and performed a number of these with Walter, who played the piano very well, on board one of the ships from Java. There had been a "Bali Conference," a visit of Dutch archaeologists, officials and Javanese princes to the island, and two pianos had been sent especially for the event. I was now asked to repeat it in the little Harmony Club at Den Pasar, and this time I invited the Regents and a few musicians to come and hear what their music sounded like when arranged in this way. They were quite delighted. They had not believed it possible. The percussive sound of the pianos was at times surprisingly dose to the sound of the *gamelan,* and they wondered how only two musicians were able to play all the different parts, the melody, the flowers, the basic tones, the gongs. Only the drums were missing! When it was over the Regent of Tabanan made a quite charming little speech of compliments, in which he lamented only that the tuning of the piano did not always match.

Lotring was now often at the house. He would come up on the bus to stay for a week at a time, teaching the older club the music he had once composed for the disbanded club of Kuta. But this was old music by now, and he had decided they must learn something new. He now evolved some complicated pieces based on the music from the shadow-play, working out new sections each night as the men rehearsed. I could not understand how his mind worked. The pieces seemed to grow by themselves, imperceptibly, until suddenly, at the end of a couple of weeks, there was a brand-new composition, unwritten, yet firmly fixed in the memory of the men. His music was very much alive; his flower patterns like those of no one else on the island, and although his melodies were derived from earlier ones they were always a surprise, continually unfolding into something new.

The club now played with a perfection, a joyous impulse that seemed impossible to believe from so simple a village as Sayan. In the past year I had called musicians from widely scattered villages to teach the players—a boy from Sanur for some unusual flowers, an old man from Tabanan for forgotten *légong* melodies, and even Nyoman Kalér, who came to the house importantly, and at the same time innocently pleased that our friendship had been renewed. All this the club accepted with enthusiasm. The whole thing had become an adventure. They prided themselves on the number of pieces they knew, and never seemed to tire of rehearsals.

As night after night I listened to this music that by now had grown so familiar, its laws, its form, its design seemed clear at last. I thought back on how, through scraps of conversations, notes, expeditions and discoveries I had gradually put the puzzle together. There seemed nothing more to do. The parts fitted; the mystery was solved.

Or was it? I had, it is true, come into possession of a new set of rules and principles. Their logic, their freshness and ingenuity delighted me, and I thought with pleasure of the book I intended to write in which I would put in order my material and describe and analyse what I had discovered. But as I listened to the delicate, nervous drumming of Lebah or one of the radiant compositions of Lotring that seemed to burn with new creative life, the essence of music, its nature, its final meaning, seemed elusive and indefinable as ever.

In the past year my one great wish was to have this music on records as well as transcribed on paper, and I was now in correspondence with a young musicologist in Java. He had been making recordings among the islands, and we agreed that if I would supply the disks he would bring his machine to Bali. I planned to make as many records as possible, especially of the old ceremonial *gamelans* in the mountains, and I now went about with Lebah from village to village discussing with the musicians the best pieces to include in this programme. The days passed, and I waited impatiently for my visitor to come, for I was very eager to begin.

It was the month of August when he arrived, and although the rainy season was not till December, mist and mountain drizzle had enveloped Sayan for a week in a fog that showed no signs of lifting. Alas for my plans! From the beginning the machine unaccountably refused to run satisfactorily. I managed to get a few records of the children. They listened to themselves entranced as I played the first one back. But with the third record the machine began to run more slowly. It stopped dead for a day. Ran perfectly once more. Stopped again.

Was it the damp? The batteries? My visitor could not say. The sun came out, but still the machine was unpredictable. For a week we struggled with it without leaving the house, and I soon saw my plans for recording in the mountains fade. At last it was decided to take the machine to Java for repairs. We would resume work in a month.

It was about this time, shortly after I learned at the hotel in Den Pesar of the Munich crisis, that I received one morning an enigmatic visit from Sagami, the Japanese photographer in town. I was surprised, for I knew him only slightly, rarely having gone into his shop. He bowed politely, saying he had a friend with him from Java. He was showing him the island, and would I allow him to see my house, which was famous for its fine location? Sagami was full of smiles and self-effacement, but I thought his friend seemed to be counting even the coconuts in the trees around the house. I asked them if they would not have some tea, but no—they could not stay. They barely looked at the house, and walked quickly to the edge of the cliff to gaze intently up and down the great valley. Out came the camera of Sagami's friend. There was a rapid click-click as he turned in all directions, and they came back to the veranda, complimenting me on the view. I asked them to sit down, but thanking me elaborately, they bowed themselves down the steps and walked out to the car.

They say Japan will make more war, said old Rendah. With whom? Who will win?

Where did you hear that? I asked.

Lebah was speaking of it to Pugig.

It's not clear, I said. It's not yet certain. . . .

The end of September came, and I had a brief letter from Java, saying my friend had been delayed but would return in a few weeks. And then a letter followed in October. He had fallen ill with fever.

It was too late to do anything further, I realized with bitter disappointment. I had no money now for a more elaborate venture, the kind which I should have planned from the beginning. I was already thinking of departure. My work was finished. I had collected more material than I could ever use for the book which I now had in mind about the music of the island. The news from Europe made it clear that I must sooner or later make some decision, and already I was restless and unhappy. There seemed no point of prolonging this for the sake of a project that I now had so little confidence in; I wrote to Java for sailing lists, and finally chose a Dutch freighter that left Batavia on Christmas day, to sail around the Cape of Good Hope and reach New York by Halifax. The morning came at last when I forced myself to tell Durus and Lebah to take my trunks out and air them in the sun. Slowly, reluctantly, I began the disheartening business of packing.

The last weeks were spent in winding up affairs. The piano and the car were sold, the house placed in the hands of an agent. The older *gamelan* club was disbanded after an unhappy meeting, for the instruments must return to Pliatan.

As for the children's club, I could not decide what to do. If I gave them the instruments would they continue to use them, I wondered, or even keep them? One day I called the *klian* and Daria the priest, and appointed them guardians of the instruments, saying they might never be taken from the children, or sold. Or placed in the pawnshop, I added. I wrote on a sheet of paper, This *gamelan* I have given to the children of *banjar* Kutuh, December 2,1938, and signed it. Slowly, carefully the priest and old Rendah added their signatures as witnesses. When they had finished, the *klian* folded the paper and put it in his wallet. I will keep it until *tuan* returns, he said.

That night I told the children they must continue to practise, so that the village of Sayan would not lose its good name, and the gods would remain pleased at their temple feasts. Try to remember, I said, the gods feel dishonoured if the music is not worthy.

Enggéh! Enggéh! they called. Miring tuan; we follow, tuan!

They rose.

And do not leave your -drums in the sun, I added. Try to keep your instruments in tune. . . .

Enggéh!

They gathered them up and carried them away, to keep in the house of Kayun.

That night I awoke very suddenly, as though someone had called me, to find a bright light burning in the doorway of the bedroom. I spoke, but there was no answer, and as I reached for my flashlight under my pillow the light went out. It had been raining, and outside the grass was wet. But on the floor of the veranda there was no sign of a footprint.

It had happened so quickly, so silently that I thought I had been dreaming. I did not go to sleep again, for it was almost dawn, and already the cocks up and down the valley had begun to crow. When Durus came on to the veranda with my coffee I told him what I had seen. Or dreamed, perhaps, I added.

It was no dream, it seemed. The land was alive with *léyaks* once more. They had been seen several times in the past month by Lebah, Durus and even Rendah. In the graveyard, and in the trees, balls of fire glowed for a while and disappeared. An epidemic of fever had already broken out in the villages; there was illness in many homes.

But how is it I never see these lights? I asked. Not until last night have I ever seen anything unusual. . . .

They all agreed I had been lucky, for it was surely a sign of misfortune. But now, said Durus, once one has dared to come so near, you will surely see more.

It was perhaps a week later that I awoke again, late in the night, with the same strange feeling that someone had called. It was an unusually warm night, and I went outside on to the veranda. I could not believe my eyes.

Across the valley, halfway down the hillside, a row of lights glowed with soft pure brilliance. They seemed to move ever so slightly, floating up and down as though anchored. Suddenly they went out, as suddenly went on again, but now to shine in a perpendicular line, one above the other. They merged slowly, until only the central one remained, which now began to float slowly up the valley. All at once it vanished. But within a minute the lights were shining in a row once more, far to the north.

I went to rouse Durus and Sampih, who were sleeping in the next room. Look! I said. What lights can they possibly be? They are too pale for lamps, and besides, there are no paths where they are moving.

The *léyaks,* said Durus, softly, almost inaudibly. They must be from Bangkasa. . . .

Or from somewhere in the north, he added after a while.

We stood silently watching this magic display. The lights glowed and died, came close together, spread rapidly out in a long line. Slowly they floated back once more to where I had first seen them. One by one they went out, until only a single light remained. But all at once it was gone. The valley was in darkness.

All next day I was haunted by the weird beauty of the scene I had witnessed the night before. It was as if the stars had descended. If it had not been for Durus and Sampih I should have been unable to believe it had not been part of a dream. But when I mentioned it to Chokorda Rahi, and later to the *perbekel* in Pliatan, they were not surprised. Had I awoken out of an uneasy sleep? With a feeling of suffocation? There was only one explanation. Sorcery was in the air once more. It had only begun, and no one knew what was to follow.

Though I watched the following night, and the night after, the valley remained dark. Who could say when they might return? Perhaps that night, said Rendah, perhaps not for a week.

In a week I shall be gone, Rendah.

That's so, he answered. He stood there for a moment looking at me. I had told him to dig up the flowers in the garden and plant them at home, and now he knelt and began to turn up the ground with his knife.

You will not come back this time, said Durus. I see it on your eyes; I can tell it in your voice. You will never come back. He let the lid of the trunk fall and snapped the key. Then he carried the lamp across the room and set it on the table by the bed.

Look, he said. White ants have begun to bore through the floor.

I did not answer. I stood in the doorway looking over the valley. In the moonlight the mountains were now small and flat. The river had become a brilliant stream, and the ricefields shone as though covered with frost. From somewhere in the direction of the sea came the sound of drums. We stood listening. All at once the light dimmed. Clouds swept over the moon. A breeze rose. There was a stir among the leaves, and over the house the bamboos swayed and sighed.

But soon the breeze had fallen; once more the valley was flooded with light. Down by the river a lamp began to shine.

Someone is fishing, said Durus.

Come, I said, let us go down and bathe. We went down the hillside, to walk along the river's edge to the place where the water formed a pool among the rocks. Each blade of grass, each fern stood out in sharp relief in the moonlight. Each pebble reflected white from the bottom of the pool. For a while we swam in silence.

The lady in the moon, said Durus, looking up. Can you see her? There she sits spinning, spinning. She may not stop. . . .

Who is she? What is her name?

But he could not say. We dressed and slowly climbed the hill once more. At the top the house stood bathed in light, quiet, mysterious, as though it had already been deserted.

The night before I left I spent the evening with Lebah driving along my favourite roads. The rainy season was at hand, but although the day had been overcast, the sky was clear once more. I stopped at Marga to watch a shadow-play, in Mengwi to look for a while at an arja performance. Never did voices seem to carry such pathos, gestures seem so beautiful in their grace and fragility. At last I said to Lebah, We must turn back towards home. As we passed through Mengwi we came to a blaze of lights near the market. It was the new Stamboul company we had seen a month before, and which I had found so deplorable, but even now I felt I must stop to watch, if only for a moment.

The moonlight fell on a line of girls in short, flowered dresses, their faces powdered white as their cotton stockings and tennis shoes, and they stood in line, gesticulating aimlessly, dancing some strange step that seemed to have little to do with the music. Back and forth they moved, nodding their heads, waving their arms, singing the dreariest of tunes. They stopped; it was time for the hero. A boy stepped out in sports shirt, white pants, black smoked glasses. He was followed by a second in a coat of gold brocade and soldier's hat. A strident dialogue began. Back and forth the voices cried, harsh, furious, in fancied imitation of important colonial officials.

It's handsome, isn't it? I said to Lebah.

But at this point he drew me by the arm. Come, he said, very gently. It is time to go; it will soon be dawn.

That morning, as the car left Sayan, it began to rain. We drove straight to the western tip of the island, where I was to take the little steamer across the channel to Java. As we arrived the rain stopped, but the sky was black, and the gulls sailed through the air like bits of paper. Lebah carried the bags in silence to the boat. He arranged them in careful order beside the packages and little suitcases belonging to the Javanese and Chinese passengers. After we had said goodbye he stepped on to the dock and stood watching a moment as the boat drew away. Then I saw him turn and walk back to where the car was standing beneath the trees.

As the boat reached the middle of the channel the rain suddenly began once more. It fell in a heavy silver sheet, and in a moment it had blotted out the island completely from view.

GLOSSARY

General

anak	man
anak agung	title of a prince or regent
anak chenik	small man; child
banjar	village ward or subdivision
budak	feudal attendant
chokorda	a princely title
galungan	the great ten-day holiday which inevitably lasts a month, taking place each thirty weeks
guru	teacher
gusti	prince
jaba	commoner; peasant caste forming nine-tenths of the population
jero	sir; madame; polite form of address to a stranger
képéng	Chinese hole-money; "cash"
klian	Government-appointed village headman
léyak	a sorcerer in supernatural form
parakan	feudal attendant
pemangku	village priest and temple guardian
perbekel	Government-appointed head man of a small district
ringgit	silver coin worth one dollar, normal currency
sari	flower; essence
sembah	gesture of reverence
sirih	leaf of the sirih-vine, a species of pepper
tabé	salutation (Malay)
tuan	lord; sir; master; mister; (Malay)

Music

angklung	archaic musical instrument of bamboo
gamelan	orchestra of gongs, keyed instruments, drums and cymbals, developed in Java and spreading with Javanese culture
gangsa	lit. metal; keyed instrument which plays ornamental parts or basic melody
g'ndér	keyed instrument which plays the melody
jégogan	bass g'ndér which plays the pokok
kajar, kempli, klenang	small gongs
kantil	Javanese for the scented flower of the champaka, used in offerings
kantilan	"flower passages"; arabesque
karang	to assemble; compose (music, picture, poem, etc.)
karangan	house compound; a musical composition; painting; something composed or "put together"

kempur	medium gong
pokok	"stalk" or "trunk"; the basic tones of the melody
réyongan	ornamental parts played by four men on the réyong, a kind of trompong
trompong	row of little gongs on which solo melody is played, used either in ceremonial music or in the Gamelan of Semara

Dance

arya	modern operetta based on traditional theatre, with songs in old Javanese metres
bapang	music and dance of an official intro ducing a higher character
baris	lit. row; ancient warrior's drill-dance
barong	beast mask, in the form of lion, tiger, boar or cow
chondong	nurse or attendant of the heroine
dalang	puppet operator
gabor	women's ceremonial dance with offerings
gambuh	ancient court theatre
gandrung	lit. love; a popular public dance performed by a boy
jogéd	lit. dance; the same performed by a girl
légong	dance derived from nandir performed by little girls
nandir	ancient court dance performed by boys
rangda	the Widow; the witch Chalonarang
topéng	ancient play with masked actors
wayang	old Javanese for shadow: theatre, actor, puppet
wayang kulit	puppet play
wayang wong	play with humans

NOTES

THERE IF THE AUTHOR'S transcriptions for two pianos of Balinese *gamelan* music have been published by G. Schirmer of New York. Under the title "Balinese Ceremonial Music,"* the same firm has recorded an album of these transcriptions, which includes music from the shadow-play, *arja* flute melodies and the ceremonial music which opens a temple feast. A second album, which will include music from the *Gamelan* of Semar the Love God and music played only during death rites, is being planned.

*Chappell & Co. Ltd. are the London agents for these records.

ILLUSTRATIONS

Between page 80-81

Gateway to Besakih, Mother Temple of Bali.
Temple offerrings.
Cakes, fruits and sweetmeats for the gods.
Tropmpong player.
The deep-toned *jégogans* carry the bass.
The *gangsas* fill the air with ringing sound.
In the temple courtyard young girls perform the ceremonial *rejang*.
The little *lélong* dancers perform for the pleasure of both gods and mortals.
In the Temple of the Dead the women of Sayan dance before each shrine.
Each afternoon for a week the young girls from twenty villagers gathered to
 dance at a harvest feast in Tabanan.
G'ndérs play the melody for the *lélong* dance.
The children's orchestra.
The author's *Gamelan* of Semara, the Love God.
Cymbals and little bells add shimmer to the music of Sermara the Love God.
The *guru*, I Lunyuh.
The *dalang* opens his puppet-box.
We kill a pig for the *galungan* holiday.
Mask play.
The beloved but terrifyikng barong.
The witch Chalonarang.

Between page 192-193

The garden at the house in Sayan.
Sampih dances *kebyar*: the opening.
The dance comes to an end.
Jews' harps.
Arja musicians.
A feast delicacy-grilled sticks of turtle meat.
Rantun, the cook.
The ancient and holy Selunding *gamelan* that came out of the sea.
The soft-toned flutes of the ancient *gambuh* play.
Gede Manik, drummer, dancer, composer of *kebyar*.
Sampih.
Lotring, the composer, was also famous for his subtle spicing of feast dishes.
Gusti Lanang Oka, a musician.
Kuta fisherman.
Durus.
Prince and Princess in the gambuh play.
Prince Panji and Perebangsa.
The new Stamboul Club near Den Pasar was encourage by the Dutch School
 Supervisor and visiting missionaries, who considere it set a fine example.
North Bali *gamelan*.